Strong Words #2

Strong Words #2

The best of the Landfall Essay Competition

Selected by Emma Neale

OTAGO UNIVERSITY PRESS
Te Whare Tā o Te Wānanga o Ōtākou

Published by Otago University Press
Te Whare Tā o Te Wānanga o Ōtākou
533 Castle Street
Dunedin, New Zealand
university.press@otago.ac.nz
www.otago.ac.nz/press

First published 2021
Copyright © individual authors as listed on page 5

ISBN 978-1-99-004805-0

Published with the assistance of Creative New Zealand

Design/layout: Fiona Moffat
Editor: Imogen Coxhead
Selecting editor photograph: Caroline Davies

Cover: *FrenchBayDarkly … #3*, John Reynolds, 2017, oil paint marker on acrylic on canvas, 152cm x 217cm

Printed in China through Asia Pacific Offset

Contents

Introduction: Whorls Within Whorls Emma Neale   7

Tobias Buck Exit. Stage Left.   11

Nina Mingya Powles Tender Gardens   20

A.M. McKinnon Canterbury Gothic   31

Tan Tuck Ming My Grandmother Glitches the Machine   42

Sarah Harpur Ruigrok Dead Dads Club   52

Anna Kate Blair Notes Toward a Subjective History of Honey   62

Siobhan Harvey Living in the Haunted House of the Past   72

Joan Fleming Write First, Apologise Later?   83

Jillian Sullivan The Art and Adventure of Subsistence   91

Ingrid Horrocks Ordinary Animals   100

Sarah Jane Barnett Unladylike   111

Shelley Burne-Field If the words 'white' and 'sausage' in the same
    sentence make you uncomfortable, please read on   121

Anna Knox Ziusudra & the Black Holes: Rereading 'The First Essay'   131

Himali McInnes This Place   142

Derek Schulz Kiwi-Made   152

Una Cruickshank Waste   161

Mikaela Nyman Through a Glass Darkly   170

Matt Vance Lines of Desire   180

John Horrocks The Certainty of Others: Writing and climate change   188

Tim Grgec Drinking More Fruit Juice Won't Help   197

Emily Duncan Character-Building   206

Elese Dowden half-gallon quarter-acre pavlova pretext   216

Laura Surynt Feeling Around a Room in the Dark   224

Sarah Young The Space to Feel   233

Wendy Parkins Water Says Things So Clearly   245

About the Selecting Editor   255
Contributor Biographies   256

Whorls Within Whorls

After the announcement of the results of one *Landfall* essay competition, I received a scolding in the mail from a writer I've never met. He said that my choices of the highest-ranking essays disappointed him, as he felt they were 'somewhat solipsistic texts, and in my book solipsism doesn't make good essays'. (He also said the complaint had nothing to do with his essay not being placed.) This correspondent also sent me a second letter, concerned about the choices in an entirely separate poetry anthology, the selection process for which I had nothing to do with directly, but which the writer felt was an urgent enough national literary issue for *Landfall* to consider as a Letter to the Editor. (The complaint was similar to the disgruntlement about the essays: solipsism, and some points about craft.) It may seem as if by recounting this I have started my welcome to the reader with a bullet to my own foot, or as if I intend to settle scores and be unkind—but my correspondent raises some important points about versions of literary excellence. Even if they are, to my mind, self-evident, I want to reiterate my thoughts on selection criteria here.

As with other literary art forms, the essay genre doesn't insist on a single cookie cutter style: there are a number of different subgenres within the broad category 'essay': from the personal to the historical; from the poetic to the scientific. Perhaps the most vital thing to point out, however, is that any judge, and any editor, makes selections that are not only informed by their education, experience, an ear alert to pressing local and global social issues defining to the spirit of the age, but that are also inevitably coloured by personal taste. What one reader dismisses as solipsism can, in the best hands, actually demonstrate the ability to use intimate, vivid, sensory and specific detail that captures a personal experience *precisely in order* to illuminate something of greater significance. My stubborn (or let's call it staunch) opinion is that all of the more apparently intimate essays included in *Strong Words 2* lead the reader into a fuller and more compassionate understanding of situations or subjects that affect numerous people beyond the individual author of each piece.

As Anna Knox details here, in her excellent work on the essay form itself, several other critics have seen the potency and potential in a form that rides the impulse of a sense of discovery, of understanding as it unfolds. She quotes John D'Agata's description of 'a form that's not propelled by information, but one compelled instead by individual expression—by enquiry, by opinion, by wonder, by doubt'. Knox mulls over the essay as 'an art form of tendencies, straddling the storyteller's divide between recounting and creation'. Adroitly executed, this questing style, which fans and ripples out from the investigations of a particular sensibility, can expose everything from the turbulence of mourning to the psychological erosions of racism; the way misogyny, internalised or institutionalised, can impede both a fulsome sense of identity and falsely censor history; the relationship between physical or geographical space and psychic health; the compromises and challenges within care models for intellectually or physically disabled adults; the artist's responsibility to her sources; the links between a close contemplation of the natural world and the potential for social change.

Perhaps from that list alone you'll guess how sorely tempting it is to try to characterise and 'review' every single essay here, so that no writer misses out on the beams of praise, appreciation or discussion. Yet, on re-reading the collection, I'm forcibly struck by how, as with the best poetry or fiction, synopses are predestined to stumble short on at least one level, as so very often the *motion* of a work, as it accumulates its points and effects, is resonantly decisive in terms of the overall impression it creates. *Read these essays*, I want to say. *You just have to read them!*

I took a break from writing this and thinking over notions of literary value to refuel with coffee, a banana, and someone else's perspective—grabbing my copy of *The Best American Poetry 2020*, edited by Paisley Redkal, which had just arrived that morning—and *wham*, my eyes alighted on this, from none other than Harold Bloom, the 'Yale University Eminence', writing to series editor David Lehman: 'My dear [...] what matters in literature in the end is surely the idiosyncratic, the individual, the flavor of the colour of a particular human suffering.'[1] This felt like serendipitous grist to the mill—although my temperament also wants to add that at least some of the best, most memorable literature must also embody joy.

Several of the essays that I found most compelling carry sparks of euphoria in their descriptive gifts; several also have a nested effect of exploring whorls within whorls. For example, Sarah Jane Barnett's essay 'Unladylike' travels over memories of her stoic, no-nonsense grandmother, and spans out to gender norms, the performance aspect of gender and the 'ungendering' of menopause, which she calls a time of 'relearning … womanhood'. Or there is Sarah Young's moving essay both about how lockdown affected her ability to grieve major losses, or feel and release other intense emotions, and about how places mould our responses and identity; these ruminations were prompted by taking virtual walks through different cities on Google Maps with an old lover, as she also recalls family shocks and revelations.

Alongside such essays, which deal with the incremental leak of history into individual decisions and behaviour, we have here, too, work from Ingrid Horrocks and John Horrocks (daughter and father) whose essays—entered for the prize in separate years—look, from different perspectives, at both the immediate and long-term effects of climate change. John's essay focuses on the surge of local novels that deal with climate change fiction; Ingrid's on the effects that knowledge of climate crisis can have on parenting and major life decisions. As she writes: 'In myself I notice a dissonance in my own long-term thinking, so that discussions of ten-year plans at work can feel like make-believe games.'

Climate crisis is the biggest single issue facing humanity; how can an essay tackling its tentacular creep into our thinking at a personal level not also be a plea for governmental action? The personal (the solipsistic, from one angle) is, and always has been, political—and this is demonstrated ably, also, by the joint winners of the 2018 essay prize, which previously appeared in *Landfall*: Tobias Buck's 'Exit. Stage Left', which explores issues of prejudice and bias through the experience of someone 'the colour of cotton candy or pink marshmallows', and Nina Mingya Powles' work, 'Tender Gardens', exploring Chinese cultural and poetic heritage and how to maintain a sense of home in a foreign land, in an essay which also tackles the noxious reach of racism, from jarring microaggressions to the brutal, unconscionable murders at the Christchurch mosques in 2018.

This anthology gathers together a number of names whose sterling writing is well-known on the literary scene (Siobhan Harvey, Derek Schulz, Joan Fleming, Ingrid Horrocks, John Horrocks, Jillian Sullivan, Emily Duncan) as well as several brilliant and promising newcomers. The subject range is only equalled by the emotional range. We have Siobhan Harvey's dignified and distressing essay about memories of an abusive childhood stirred up by current house renovations; Sarah Harpur Ruigrok's irreverent, laugh-aloud essay about death, which springs from authentically sharp grief and anger; Emily Duncan's warm, dauntless memoir about acting classes in New York, conflict, challenge and inner character; Tan Tuck Ming's gentle, pensive essay about technology and how it mediates, enables and impacts intimate relationships; Matt Vance's essay about 'desire lines', the physical traces of our footwork that we leave in popular urban spaces; Anna Knox's work, already mentioned, which brings a sharp discussion of gender into the history of the essay form; Himali McInnes's love-song to an embattled suburb, which becomes a persuasive call for political action based on empathy and vision.

There are, here, essays that make persuasive, fascinating use of informative collations of facts (such as Una Cruickshank's 'Waste', and Anna Kate Blair's 'Notes Towards a Subjective History of Honey'), or thoughtful literary critical analysis (John Horrocks, as aforementioned, and also Wendy Parkins' piece, 'Water Says Things So Clearly', which brings together novels by Robin Hyde and Pip Adam). Yet if I had to cite some fibre that knits the anthology together, I would say it is the shared poetic skill and psychological insight—and one so often seems to carry the other. Selecting the best metaphor or simile isn't just about sound effects, or creating small 'neurological' pulses of sensory surprise for the sake of it. I think it's also about pressing as close to the experience or perception as possible, to help recreate it for the reader; taking tissue samples, we might say, with the image-assisted needles of language.

This anthology is a gift to readers, as it offers them the chance to immerse themselves in the invigoratingly high-quality work entered to the *Landfall* Essay Competition—without the agony of having to choose the winners. Of course, readers might on the other hand want to run their own private essay slam and decide which writers they would have awarded the top slots. You can always let us know what your choices would have been. Criticisms, after all, can be seen as a part of the larger cultural conversation—fuel to the lyre.

---

1   David Lehman (Series editor), *Best American Poetry 2020* (New York: Simon and Schuster, 2020), p. xix.

Exit. Stage Left.

I'm fair-skinned at best. And blond. But not the Aryan tanned-Adonis type. Most of my freckles have been too shy to join up. Got that Irish tan. That Kiwi tan. That sweet, sweet ruddy pallor. Chances are good I'm whiter than you.

Easily sunburnt, I could pass for Swiss or Swedish. I've been shouted at in Danish by people who think I'm ignoring them. But this isn't about that. At least, I think it's not. It's about being slightly, but definitely, pink.

Imagine being the colour of candyfloss or marshmallows. I appear strawberry-flavoured. It's a hard thing to complain about—I'm clearly delicious. People can tell when I'm getting worked up, angry or embarrassed. You can see my frustrations. You can see if I'm drunk. It's obvious when I blush.

'He's turning red! Look at him!'

Which used to make me further embarrassed, less prone to speaking out or being too vulnerable or emotional in public.

Both my parents are redheads. Dad was coppery-blond. Mum's hair was auburn red like an Irish setter. Dad still calls her Rust. Her great-grandmother Inez was born on Long Hope in the Orkney Islands, a way north of Scotland. She had such pale blue eyes they photographed as white. Startling. Ghostly. I read that it happens when generations live by the sea. There's a touch of something Viking or Celtic about it. Makes me think of distant islands, all in a chain … the cold sparkling shores of Oban. The windswept Shetlands. Uist, Benbecula, Barra, Rùm. The Outer Hebrides. The Northern Isles.

Inez had a cousin, Abraham, who one day was washed from the black rocks while fishing. Never to be seen again.

Dad's colouring is something else, something from Northern Ireland and tin miners in Cornwall. Along the Devon coast. Penzance. Fair-skinned, fair-haired, rosy-cheeked. There's a connection to Lille, to Île-de-France and Brittany. Perhaps a touch Norman.

In New Zealand I grew up mostly with white kids around me. Not as pink or pale as me, but still white. My blondness, my rosy shade—they work in your favour as a child. Growing up in the 1980s I looked angelic, apparently. Cherubic even. Blue-eyed. A Milkybar Kid. Heavy on the milk. Innocent. Cute. A golden boy.

'You could get away with anything with a face like that.'

When you're a poster child for some utopian dream you don't understand, you feel special. You feel 'good' somehow, but you haven't done anything to deserve it. Something from the communal psyche gets ascribed to you and you don't know why. It sits uneasily.

I've seen pictures of myself from back then. My chin tilted up, beaming. A bowl cut that reflects so much light it causes lens flares on the camera. I am the blondest, pinkest kid in every school photo, as if I've been picked out with a limelight. Overexposed.

Jeanette, who cuts my hair, says people would kill for the colour.

'Definitely platinum,' she says, measuring it with her fingers.

'It'll go dark one day. Dirty blond,' says another. 'That's what it does.'

In the summer of 1991 the Mongrel Mob had a New Year's Eve party in the public domain opposite my parents' bach. Short on bathrooms, they politely knocked on the door. For a few days they'd come over in two or threes. While waiting they'd sit on the couch with Dad and me and watch the Gulf War on TV.

It was the first televised war; cameras on Tomahawk cruise missiles showed black-and-white crosshairs flying down the streets of Kuwait. They zoomed down alleyways, around corners towards nondescript doors. Almost a video game, it was war by remote. Exotic. Across distant seas but, for the first time, brought close up, fed straight into homes. Unlike anything before, it made for a weird kind of reality show. The stakes couldn't have been higher.

I got so familiar with the gang being in and out of the bach that one hot day, seeing them riding along the beachfront, past the surf lifesaving tower—a mass of chromed bikes, tattoos and black leather—I pedalled my red BMX into the centre of the group. For a few minutes they let me ride among them. People laughed. I thought it was funny. It could have gone another way. A little blond anomaly amidst all that formidable metal gleaming in the summer sun. I was grinning ear to ear, proud as punch.

As I got older the way I looked got trickier. It seemed to pick up baggage as it rolled out into the world. My pink hue was less cute, its effect riskier and more complex.

At high school there's usually a nickname for the blond kid: Snowy, Bluey, Old Man. Old before your time. My brothers had theirs too. The oldest probably got the worst: Petit Cochon—Little Pig. The tradition at my school was to use the specific name of a real blond and pale kid from a decade earlier: I got John Boore. I never knew him but he hadn't been much liked; no doubt resentful at being singled out. That's the way it goes, though: the more you rail against a nickname the more it sticks. The urge to find a pigeonhole, to box up, name and categorise a person is universal. As with the mythical Bed of Procrustes, whatever there is about you that doesn't fit will just be abbreviated.

The names for pale kids had a pejorative element. You just knew, somehow, in terms of status on the social ladder that being this luminous shade was no advantage. Tanned skin speaks of health, holidays, pleasure. Too pale is the opposite. A Boo Radley. That kid in *Sixteen Candles*. Pale in comparison. It situates you on the edge of the crowd. Casper the Friendly Ghost. Reclusive. A milquetoast. Fauntleroy. Bookish. Effete. Cloistered.

The visibility made me self-conscious. You reflect more light. You attract attention and make an easy target. It's a peculiarity, like being very tall. People can pick you out in a crowd. You get called out for it.

'You're not an albino,' one girl says. Slowly. After some consideration. Before turning her attention to another boy.

I can tell you about the embarrassment. I didn't like mirrors. I wanted to fit in. When I was thirteen I emptied a bottle of tanning lotion all over my legs and headed out to town to show them off. Thought that was cool.

Plus, that choirboy look is a thing apparently. As a kid I'd been lured away once or twice while playing at a park, before Mum could locate me. As a teen I'd get the odd hand on the knee under a table. A breathy, hushed whisper. A friend's stepdad pushing porn and beer at you, asking when you'll come over by yourself. At university I'd be regularly propositioned if out late at night. Caught a bit off guard, I'd be stopped and furtively questioned.

'You alone? Where are you going?'

But, like I say, who am I to complain? People have much worse to contend with. Like the Pink Panther on Saturday morning cartoons, or Snagglepuss with his tuxedo collar and fancy cuffs, you learnt a certain footwork. You learn to make light of it, to make light of being light. With avoidance humour, almost theatrical, you dance around the subject. Head off script. Do your best to step around a subject that might leave you easily categorised or written off. Remove yourself as a target. Make it appear natural. Exit. Stage left.

Once, when I was fourteen, at a petrol station in the town where I grew up, I was standing on the forecourt waiting for a friend inside when a ute rolled up. Three, maybe four teenagers were on the back. Older than me. Bigger than me. While the driver filled up they nodded in my direction. I didn't know why. I looked at my feet and wished my friend would hurry.

One of the boys stood up, facing me. He extended his arm, just above shoulder height. Then they all stood and did the same. Arms out. Palms down.

They kept looking. Waiting for me to respond.

MTV was established and became a massive screen presence through the early 1990s. Breakdancing was the height of coolness. When a music video wanted to show it had credibility or flair, when the beat dropped and the chorus peaked, for a few seconds breakdancers would appear, flipping, spinning and worming across neon, graffiti-sprayed stage sets.

I immediately got out every available book on the subject from our very small-town library. I would cycle thirty minutes to get there, then return with my precious cargo to sit under the dining table and read. Large-format hardbacks had sequences of black-and-white photos showing how to do the robot. I would warm a cushion in front of the heater to practise my head spins on. In the living room I'd push back the couch and coffee table and break away. I had my own piece of cardboard. I would put on shows for family members.

At the wedding reception of an uncle who lived on the Kāpiti coast, a hired crew of breakdancers tapped me on the shoulder and brought me on stage. We did the wave. The robot. I wormed. I spun, briefly, on my back. Paraparaumu Town Hall rocked that night, unlikely to have ever beheld such questionably rad acrobatics. I'd worn shiny ski-pants in preparation. I had on a headband and fingerless gloves.

It felt good being the centre of attention but generally I had to fight my tendency to want to overcompensate and appear fancier than I was: fresher, smarter, worldlier, more interesting. I often wanted to reinforce or explain my uniqueness, to double down on a perception I thought already existed. Which made dating a bit weird. I sometimes wanted to adopt a louder, more intriguing persona. It took different forms. More cultured perhaps? Somehow removed from status games.

When social media became a thing I was shy of photos. On dates I'd want to stay away from beaches. Avoid the midday sun.

I could get paranoid. That Italian girlfriend who confides she has a thing for blonds and whose bookshelves are filled with the works of Oriana Fallaci, an impressive but also mildly fascistic journalist who once described Islam as a 'pool that never purifies'. The Iranian girl who calls you 'White Walker'. Half-jokingly. Half-resigned.

Twice I've been on dates where guys nearby have leaned in to chat to whomever I'm with.

'You with this guy?'

A slight guffaw.

For a moment that feeling of inadequacy passes through me. Timeless. Cold in my gut like ice-water. Like being told to go home or get back in your channel. Breathe. Relax. Laugh it off. Whoever really knows what it's about?

When I travelled, in the back of my mind I wondered whether how I looked would matter.

Visiting the Jewish Museum in Berlin, with its remembrances of the Holocaust, I look through the glass at photos of Hitler Youth. Apart from the uniform they just seem to be kids on camp. Everything I know about myself separates us. They're not me but they look like me. I notice someone looking in my direction. They turn to the photos then back to me again. They have an angry expression. I step away and head towards the exit.

Just by the door there's what looks like an old-school arcade machine with a single load screen. It asks whether Mel Gibson's *The Passion of the Christ* is anti-semitic. Without any irony I can discern, it indicates the joystick and says MOVE LEFT FOR YES OR RIGHT FOR NO. I wobble it uncertainly, thinking it can't be serious, trying to understand why it's there after all that impactful and complex record of human history and division.

THANK YOU FOR YOUR ANSWER it says.

There's a zoo in the centre of Berlin. It's near the houseboat I'm staying on that's run by Captain Edgar, a Kiwi. I take the U-Bahn with its canary-yellow trains. They have schnitzel sandwiches and vanilla milk available at each stop. From the window I see two people stuck in the revolving door of an office building. Frustrated, they're both trying to appear polite and apologetic but also both refusing to let go or stop pushing. At the zoo I see a kea. The first time for me. Bright green. Curious and aggressive.

Beautiful but caged. The enclosure seems too small.

I walk by and there are ducks wandering about on the grass. A lady shouts at me in German, waving her hands. She's telling me, I think, to pass one over to her. I chase one for a minute before wondering what I'm doing and stop. I really have no idea what she's saying. I'm speaking English but she won't acknowledge it. I don't understand and she just keeps on yelling. I back away.

I catch up with Kiwis living in the Prenzlauer District. They're loving Berlin's cheap rent and liberal arts scene. I tell them I'd like to visit somewhere a bit warmer.

'You want to go to Spain or France? Oh you'll be fine. They love people like you.'

I assume I'll move through customs easily but I don't. In transit, bearded, with a backpack and a bit dishevelled, I stand out. They want to talk to me.

'You're travelling light.'

'What are you up to?'

And when I catch sight of myself in the mirror I don't feel safe. I feel singled out. I know it will show and my cheeks will go red. I won't be able to control it. I'm like the Incredible Hulk, but for embarrassment.

In Brazil some people call out.

'Hey, Allemagne!'

You're a type locals know. More familiar than a gringo. It's said without malice, with recognition and warmth. Here the multitudinous shades of skin colour are discussed in depth and celebrated, almost fetishised. I meet a guy whose nickname is 'Seis da Tarde'. 6pm. Not quite light, not quite dark.

I rent a motorbike. As I walk through the blazing heat to the rental stand the business owner sees me coming from a long way off. He's black, but also dark, almost purple.

'Ha,' he says. One hand upwards indicating the sun. 'You're very white.'

Matter-of-factly. Smiling.

'You're very black,' I reply.

I shouldn't have said that, embarrassed for being simultaneously ungracious and foreign. Luckily he's caught the 'very' part and knows what I'm getting at. He pauses one second then laughs, shrugging his shoulders with some degree of shared acknowledgement.

Back in Wellington I bump into one friend then another, who both happen to be blond and pinkish like me. We haven't seen each other for a while and sit down at a café for coffee and a catch-up. Immediately the comments start.

'Ha! Look!'

'Like brothers!'

'Better watch out!'

Someone we don't know takes out a camera. It's an odd feeling. None of us like it so we pack up and leave.

The urge to locate yourself in relation to the world is natural. As a kid I used to get Santa Claus and God mixed up. I had the impression they were both bearded, magical Caucasian men who lived far away. I wasn't allowed to see them directly, they did good things for me, and I likely owed them something I'd never really understand. A bit like my uncle who got me to breakdance at his wedding.

I wrote a postcard to Santa asking him for a pet. I wanted a dog but I was prepared to negotiate. I remember signing it:

New Zealand
Pacific Ocean
Southern Hemisphere
Planet Earth
The Milky Way

There's a strong argument that my childhood and my ethnicity are both privileges. In terms of almost every opportunity I can't disagree. There's a continuous messaging about the superiority of whiteness just below the culture's waterline. To assuage ethnic anxieties we often attempt to drown out their complexity with the absolutism of nationalism or chauvinism. Maybe I just have some nervous response to the hierarchy of colour that floats through our culture. Also to the bullish type that unquestioningly embraces these unspoken tribal borderlines. Puffed up. Declarative. 'Big buffalo', my girlfriend's mum calls them.

It's dying out apparently. Blondness. It's a recessive gene. Which might not be a bad thing considering the prominent blond pinkness of a couple of recently elected world leaders. Are they tapping into some resurgent ideology? Is it intentional? Discourse and rhetoric that once seemed so distant and remote are now suddenly close-up. Ideology traverses oceans, overflows from screens into homes. Personal. Nearby. Full of consequence.

One of the funny things about ageing is that a thing like pinkness seems to matter less and less. The currents and eddies of external and internal identity get so intermingled it's hard to tell which came first. The solipsistic navel-gazing. The introspection. Over such a superficial thing. Who has time for it? What you do for others is more important. So, you look like a policeman. Try not to wear too much blue.

I straddle something. But I don't know what. Not hybridised. Bicultural? Not really. Pākehā? Sure. I guess. I think being a touch different has just made me suspicious. I suspect my own idea of being woke, or anyone else that puts energy into making sure others see them as having arrived. I say this not because my pale shade gives me any view outside of whiteness but because I'm double-dipped. A bit alien as a result. A little aware of the theatre of identity since, it seems, I have more skin in the game.

'Our family could do with a touch more melanin,' my mum says.

Aunt Sally tells me the family genealogy. I'm a restless footnote struggling to stay awake.

I'm thinking of Abraham, washed from the stones. The crystal waves colliding. Not parting for him, but closing in. Their ineffable weight. That diaphanous web of white crests on the surface, constantly shifting. The light aqua of oxygenated water rolls alongside emerald-black depths that frighten me. Thalassophobia. The sense of ice-cold water and of losing your energy to the ocean. Dissipating. Of having fought waves to stay afloat only to lack the power to swim to shore. Even though you can see it. The eerie calm of knowing that. Seeing coastline after coastline. Fetlar. Hoy. The Out Skerries. Zetland. New Zealand. Distance. Closeness. Geography. Opportunity. Repetition.

Ko Pacific tōku moana.
Ko Tukituki tōku awa.
Ko Taranaki tōku maunga.

I shuffle my feet saying my pepeha. Even though the words are meant and I'm proud of them. My tūrangawaewae.

Where you're born is like how you look. No one gets a choice about it. And I'm used to doing a bit of a strange dance, identity-wise. A step forward, a step back. Like Snagglepuss, I adjust my bow tie and fancy cuffs and try to appear confident and articulate. To speak up. To say where I'm coming from.

I choose my words carefully. I know I'm more than one thing, like everybody else.

Every potentiality doesn't have to be resolved. My emotions betray me now and then. I do go red when I get things wrong, when my blood rises, but no point being embarrassed about that now.

I'm glad it shows. At least that way you know I mean what I say.

NINA MINGYA POWLES

Tender Gardens

[seventh lunar month]
小暑 *light summer* ～ *season of scorched hydrangeas*

> 'The Chinese were in fact very friendly, very nice to each other. Not what you'd expect.'

In the white-gold kitchen, the lights above the table are glinting. Pink and purple sweetpeas in a vase on the table flutter in a breeze from the open window. I feel my body become tense. I look out the window, because I can't look at anyone else. The heads of blue hydrangeas are swelling and pulsing in the manicured garden. Lily pads and lotus flowers tremble on the surface of the hot, brown pond. Dusk is beginning to fall.

Over breakfast I had been asking her about the flowers in her garden: hydrangea, peony, nasturtium. There are flowers I recognise but don't know the names of; she points to each one and tells me its name, giving me the vocabulary to write about plants for the first time. Azalea, clematis, dahlia, allium. She notices trees and flowers wherever she goes. Two years ago she visited Hong Kong—her first time. The city was so much greener than expected. So much green.

Her words are partly meant with good intentions, but I don't know how to carry them within my body. Does she think of my mother as *a Chinese*? Does she think of me as half *a Chinese*? If yes, how did she think I would respond? If not, then what am I to her? I ponder what I am doing here in this unusually cold northern-hemisphere summer.

When I was last at my parents' house I borrowed a book of theirs called *A Field Guide to the Birds of China*. On page 18, the beginning of a chapter titled 'The Avian Year', the rhythms of certain lines leapt out at me:

China lies north of the equator …
And in the long days of the northern summer …
The birds are migrants descending in winter …

According to an ancient Chinese agricultural calendar, each lunar month can be divided into two 节气—'solar terms'—and every solar term can be divided into three micro-seasons, each one characterised by a single event in the life-cycle of plants and animals. This means there are 72 small seasons within one lunar year. Every five days a new season comes.

When I first learned about the 72 seasons I obsessively translated and wrote down the most poetic ones I could find. I discovered that I was born during the month of lined clothing, in the solar term of summer's arrival, in the season of the untangling of deers' antlers. My mum was born during the month of gathering winds, the solar term of rainwater, and the season of wild geese flying north.

[twelfth lunar month]
夏至 *southern summer solstice* ～ *season of pōhutukawa flowers*

'If you spend too much time there, you might end up looking like this.'

The woman places one finger at the outer corner of each of her eyes and pulls. Cold breath leaves my body. I feel the urge to run to my dog, who is waiting for us in the back of the car, to hold his soft ears and press him close to my face. I resist this urge.

We've just come back from a walk on the beach and my dry lips taste like salt. The skin around my ankles is rough with sand and the hem of my dress is wet, heavy. We are almost within swimming distance of the great island that guards the shore. The island is a witness to what has occurred, is still occurring. The island is my witness.

It's January, midsummer on the Kāpiti Coast. In the northern hemisphere it's midwinter, *the season of wild geese flying north*, almost my mum's birthday and almost lunar new year. It hasn't rained in more than a week and the edges of roses are beginning to scorch. Back in London, before we left, I planted spring bulbs (daffodil, iris, hyacinth) in plastic containers. I placed them in a line along the windowsill. I sent pictures of my not-yet-blooms to my mum, who replied to say she couldn't wait to grow some water hyacinths for this coming Chinese New Year.

[twelfth lunar month]
冬至 *deep winter* ~ *season of bulbs in the snow*

Is my otherness becoming more or less visible? Sometimes more—other mixed girls or women of colour approach me at work, kindly curious, wanting to know: 'You're mixed, aren't you?' Sometimes less—in a room full of white people they count me as one of their own, which makes me both invisible witness and invisible target.

Soon after moving to London, as the number of instances of casual racism I witnessed suddenly increased—both in London and when I went back to visit New Zealand—I began to realise the importance of keeping a record. I couldn't carry all the details in my body any longer; I needed somewhere to put them down, so I opened a new Google Doc and titled it 'INVISIBLE DOCUMENT'. I thought a spell of invisibility might help lessen the weight of it.

It was around this time that I also started to keep a garden diary. I became obsessed with gardens after seeing a kōwhai tree in a garden in north London. Its existence stunned me, all wrong at first, with no tūī diving towards its yellow bell-shaped blooms. Whenever I feel unsure of where I am and what on earth I'm doing so far from home, I think of the kōwhai tree. Where did it come from? Who planted it there? How many people, like me, have stopped in their tracks at the sight of it?

I found a purple crocus pressed between the pages of my copy of *A Cruelty Special to Our Species* by Emily Jungmin Yoon, a Canadian poet of Korean descent. I must have picked the flower in late winter and put it in the book for safekeeping. Its petals have turned translucent, rendering the poem 'Bell Theory' visible *through* the flower itself:

> *How to say azalea. How to say forsythia.*
> *Say instead golden bells. Say I'm in ESL. In French class*
> *a boy whose last name is Kring called me belle.*
> *Called me by my Korean name, pronouncing it wrong.*
> *Called it loudly, called attention to my alien.*

The speaker of the poem begins accumulating half-rhymes, small chiming bells: *lie, lie, library, azalea, library.* I'm reminded of a line from a poem by British poet Rachael Allen: 'Women's bodies collect materials the way metals accrue in organs.' I begin collecting the names of flora and fauna that sway in the background of my memories: azalea, magnolia, hydrangea, jasmine.

Since I am split between northern and summer hemispheres, my own seventy-two seasons are different. On my small sunlit balcony at the back of my flat in north London I begin planting a vegetable garden. I observe my little garden passing through various seasons: the season of sunflower seedlings, the season of wet jasmine, the season of cabbage butterflies alighting on broccoli leaves. But what does it mean to begin to put down roots in a country that forever finds you alien, an outsider, exotically mixed?

[first lunar month]
立春 *the beginning of spring* ～ *season of glasshouse orchids*

'On which side, your mother or your father?' He asks without preamble. The man, a friend of a friend I've met only once before, stands in the doorway of my blue kitchen. His body takes up the entire doorframe. He leans over me and I can see pores in the damp skin of his nose. He smiles down at me in a way that makes him look like he's baring his teeth.

Behind me, steam rises from the pot of boiling water where the jiaozi I made for our Chinese New Year dinner party are beginning to float to the surface, which means they're done. It's one of those cooking techniques I can't remember learning, only that my mum must have taught me at some point, just as she taught me how to put my forefinger in the pot of uncooked rice and pour in cold water up to the second knuckle. Steam coats the walls and my skin. I turn away from him to lift the jiaozi quickly from the pot and answer, 'On my mum's side.'

In late February we go to see the orchids at Kew. Up close they look more like animals than flowers. Pink mouths, violet tendrils, yellow tongues pressed up against the steamed-up glass. Their ancestors once grew wild in rainforests of Southeast Asia, like in Borneo, where my mum was born. There are curtains of climbing fluorescent blooms above a koi pond and a floating fibreglass Buddha surrounded by tea candles. I'm not sure if the display is meant to make me feel at home or if it's designed to make English people feel as if they've stepped into an exotic jungle. It can't be both.

When we exit the make-believe rainforest and re-enter wintry daylight, I see that the lake by the glasshouse is frozen over. Its fountain is encrusted in ice. In the giftshop I buy a dark purple orchid for £4 from the sale table, even though I know that means it's probably half dead.

9:57pm
do you have any orchid care tips?
what should I do once the flowers are drooping?

Mum 10:40pm
Prob means they are ready to drop!
Main thing is to resist repotting them.
Only a little water. Do not put in direct sunlight—
too hot; avoid windowsills. But still lots of light.

[first lunar month]
雨水 *rainwater* ∼ *season of cold mandarins*

Who was the first New Zealand-Chinese writer? If one like me existed before the mid-twentieth century, their name has not been remembered. 'We had no artistic or literary role models,' poet and novelist Alison Wong writes in her essay on being a Chinese New Zealander, titled 'Pure Brightness'. Instead of reaching far back into history, I need only look around me.

Alison Wong writes of the sinking of the SS *Ventnor* off the coast of Hokianga in 1902. It was carrying the exhumed bones of 499 Chinese people back to China for reburial in their ancestral villages. Wong recounts a gathering in April 2013 to commemorate the sinking:

We bow three times before apples, mandarins, almond biscuits, roast pork, baak jaam gai with feet and legs and head, red paper folded in the beak. We scatter rice tea wine; burn paper money gold; eat pork and baak jaam gai, an unwrapped sweet on the tongue. Electric fire crackers bang bang bang over the sand.

How many hungry ghosts can the sea hold? Like Wong, I have these long-ago sea voyages as part of my ancestry. From Wales to Aotearoa on one side; from China to Malaysia to Aotearoa New Zealand on the other. When I ask my mum what we know about my grandmother's early life, I get a series of tentative facts. She was (*likely*) born near Hong Kong and fled war as a young girl with her family by boat to the Malayan Peninsula. Her father, my great-grandfather (*probably*) didn't make the boat or (*possibly*) died on the journey. Po Po's ashes were scattered in the sea off the coast of Kota Kinabalu last year.

Wong's poem 'The River Bears Our Name' contains two places that are in my bones. It is the first time I have encountered them together in a single poem and, as a result, I can feel this poem unfurling somewhere deep inside me as if it has always been there.

As the sun eases red over Pauatahanui
You stand alone at the Huangpu River
Layers of dust catch in our throat
The water is brown with years of misuse

You stand alone at the Huangpu River
Your card lies still open on the table beside me
The water is brown with years of misuse
I write out your name stroke upon stroke

In moments of grief we offer up flowers, fruit, poems. Whenever we drove from the airport round the coast of Kota Kinabalu to my grandparents' house in Likas Bay, we would pass the great blue mosque and the Chinese cemeteries up in the hills, colourful gravestones cascading down the hillside. Some graves were draped in garlands of plastic chrysanthemums, with enamel bowls of mandarins, joss-sticks and folded paper money. Mum cleaned out Po Po's kitchen and gave me a box of her things: ivory chopsticks with 百年好合 engraved on the handles, melamine trays we bought for her from Daiso, enamel mixing bowls, and a dark blue enamel pot with a matching lid. I select the blue pot as a new home for my orchid from Kew Gardens.

[second lunar month]
惊蛰 *the awakening of insects ～ season of first magnolias*

'Lots of the Chinese girls at my school seem to be scared of dogs.'

'That's because they eat them.'

When the man seated across from me offers this response, a white-hot cloud of light billows up from the centre of the room, or from the centre of me. In the split-second after his words settle on my skin, I could choose to breathe or not breathe. I could speak or not speak. The plate on my lap holding a warm chocolate brownie tips forward. Melted vanilla ice cream dribbles over onto the dark blue fabric of my skirt.

'That was racist,' I say into the air, into the circle, my voice calm. For a moment my voice is present among the other voices and then it isn't any more. If anyone else in the room has heard, they don't make a sign. The room cannot hold on to the words for too long or else it might go up in flames. The room cannot hold on to me.

Over the course of the following day I feel sick and shaky. I have no appetite except for wanting to chew on something rich and soft, like a Cadbury caramel egg. I get up in the middle of the night and cut a blood orange, tearing the dark red flesh from the pith with my teeth. Outside, the wind stings my eyes and the first magnolia petals are starting to fly off the trees.

On my way home from work I buy a houseplant that opens its pink-veined leaves during the day and closes them at night, furling in on itself, making its limbs smaller in the dark. I learn that when plants do this it is called *nyctinasty*: a circadian rhythmic movement in response to the onset of darkness. The plant's light receptors in its skin, called phytochromes, cause the petals or foliage to curl inwards, asleep. Crocuses do this, as do lotuses, hibiscus, tulips and poppies. The exact reason for nyctinastic movement hasn't yet been determined, but it could be the plant's way of protecting itself from night-time predators, or to conserve energy, or both. I watch my plant closely. It is a *Calathea ornata*, native to Colombia and Venezuela, part of a family of plants called prayer plants because of the way the leaves and leaflets rise up at dusk.

My anger has nowhere to go, so it silently opens and closes inside me.

[second lunar month]
春分 *nearing the spring equinox* ～ *season of birds flying homewards*

To find a new poetic lineage I need to draw a line diagonally across the Pacific Ocean, connecting my two parts of the world. I begin with a slim book I checked out from the library, *Women of the Red Plain: An anthology of contemporary Chinese women's poetry*, translated by Julia C. Lin. I flick through the poems looking for traces of the familiar. Mei Shaojiang, a poet from Shaanxi province, measures time in things cultivated from the earth:

Days are garlic and wild scallions, still sprinkling loose dirt,
Days are newly rolled up hemp ropes, still damp with water

Days are a thirst-quenching blue plum, a paper-cut silhouette
Of farmers bent with grain under fierce sun on hills' plains.

In the days after the incident in the lamplit living room I became
increasingly attentive to the needs and rhythms of my balcony garden. I set
seedlings on my windowsill on a floral-patterned plastic tray, one that Mum
gave me when we cleared out my grandma's kitchen after she died, and watched
them obsessively. I measured time according to each centimetre of growth.
I watched the petals of daffodils turn papery and transparent, like discarded
butterfly chrysalises. I let them wilt and soften in their damp beds.

Flicking through *Women of the Red Plain*, I decide to create my own
translation of part of a poem by Bing Xin, titled 'Paper Boats' ('纸船'). Bing
Xin was born in 1900 in Fujian province, one region from which Hakka people
originally come. I created this translation in order to get closer to Bing Xin and
her distant dreamscape of mountains and sea. I also wanted to get closer to the
Chinese language, which I've always carried with me but lost pieces of over the
years. I wanted to make my own paper boat. I carefully unfold Bing Xin's paper
boat, add my own translation to the many already in existence, then re-fold it
and release it into the body of water that is closest to me now: the River Thames.

母亲，倘若你梦中看见一只很小的白船儿，
不要惊讶它无端入梦。
这是你至爱的女儿含着泪叠的 万水千山
求它载着她的爱和悲哀归去。

Mum, if you see a little white boat in your dream
don't be startled
It is full of your daughter's tears
It travels across ten thousand waves
to carry her heart home to you

[second lunar month]
春分 *spring equinox ～ season of white lilies*

On the day of the Christchurch terrorist attacks, because I'm so far away and
don't know what else to do, I cut the last two daffodils still alive and take them
with me to place in front of New Zealand House in central London, where piles
of flowers and cards and little flags have accumulated on either side of the glass
doorway—small mountains of grief.

On my way to the vigil that evening I see flowers everywhere. A man on the train has a white iris poking out of the pocket of his jeans. I'm holding a bunch of purple sweetpeas that I bought at the flower stall near Embankment Station. As I often do when I'm on the train at rush hour, I think about what it would be like if something happened just then. All the petals would fly up into the air and stay there, suspended. I step off the train at Hyde Park underground station and nearly collide with a girl on the platform carrying an enormous bouquet of white lilies in her arms. I understand that if I follow her she'll lead me to where I need to go.

London commuters stare at us and our armfuls of leaves and flowers as we carve a sweet-scented path through the crowded station entrance, walking against the current of the city to join the others. We find them all standing huddled on the grass around more valleys of flowers, arms around each other, singing softly, cheeks lit by electric candles flickering in the loud night.

[fourth lunar month]
清明 *pure brightness* ~ *season of koru ferns*

My mum's seaside garden in Wellington is made up of plants inherited from the house's previous owners and plants added by her over the years. It's beautiful in a haphazard, patchwork sort of way, the product of several people's hopes and dreams layered on top of each other. We inherited a giant aloe facing the sea, its red tentacles rising towards the sun; an old pōhutukawa that's been chopped back too far; dark purple hydrangeas; a slender apple tree; an unruly and abundant feijoa; and a yellow kōwhai. By the gate, one or two spring onions burst forth from the earth every spring—we don't know how long ago they were planted there but we snip them with scissors to put in our soup noodles. There was a withering wisteria above the deck that couldn't withstand the gale, now replaced by a bougainvillea that occasionally spits mouthfuls of magenta blooms. On weekends she is on her knees in the wet grass, composting and potting up new succulents, collecting up fallen feijoas and lemons. While my dad is out walking the dog on the beach, my mum collects bags of shells from the shore, whole ones and fragments, and spreads them between her plants, creating a bed of seashells resembling the bottom of the seafloor transported into our garden.

I begin to have recurring dreams of a garden that partly resembles my parents' by the sea but contains plants from various landscapes I've called home: a giant yulan magnolia with creamy basketball-sized blooms, a fig tree, fluorescent pink peonies. In the dream I am standing in the doorway of a high-ceilinged house looking up at the terraced garden, where a tall rosemary bush with bright violet flowers grows in the centre. There are furred peaches hanging from low trees and big orange and black butterflies hovering above lilac-coloured hydrangeas, some with parts of their wings missing, as if they would turn to dust when touched. There is a kōwhai, a lemon tree, and a red aloe.

Kiri Piahana-Wong is a New Zealand poet of Ngāti Ranginui, Chinese and Pākehā ancestry. Her poem 'Day by Day' tracks a series of solitary moments spent in the kitchen and in the garden:

> *(iii)*
> *At home, in the garden.*
> *My fingers cup the dirt,*
> *pull up weeds, weigh*
> *and scour. It is mid-*
> *afternoon.*
> *Early evening reading*
> *manuscripts. I reach*
> *through the pages,*
> *pluck out a koru fern.*
> *It needs water, it needs*
> *nurturing. That's why*
> *I am here.*

To garden is to care for, to feed, to *tend*: to offer up your own tenderness to the earth. Some days, in this other island country the furthest point from the island where I was born, this is why I am here.

REFERENCES
How to say azalea … Emily Jungmin Yoon, *A Cruelty Special to Our Species* (New York: HarperCollins, 2018).
Women's bodies collect materials … Rachael Allen, *Kingdomland* (London: Faber & Faber, 2019).
We bow three times before apples … Alison Wong, 'Pure Brightness', published in *The Griffith Review* : www.griffithreview.com/articles/pure-brightness/
As the sun eases red over Pauatahanui … Alison Wong, 'The River Bears Our Name', published in *Jacket2*: https://jacket2.org/commentary/alison-wong-comes

Days are garlic and wild scallions … *Women of the Red Plain: An anthology of contemporary Chinese women's poetry*, trans Julia C. Lin (London: Puffin, 1993).

At home, in the garden … *Tātai Whetū: Seven Māori women poets in translation*, eds Marea Rakuraku and Vana Manasiadis (Wellington: Seraph Press, 2017).

A.M. McKINNON

Canterbury Gothic

Great Auntie Beryl lived on a hill, dabbled with a lavender rinse and rarely went to bed before three in the morning. By the time I knew her she was stooped with age and widened by fruitcake. When I think of her, I see her dressed for cold weather: worsted skirts, thick tights, flat shoes, cream blouse and wool cardigans. She wore her hair in a permanent curl and a cross around her neck. She always remembered birthdays.

Beryl was a feature, and an emblem, of our visits to Christchurch, as much as the cathedral, the gardens, the sense of comfort. We'd stay with my grandparents where Beryl might call at any hour, though her nocturnality prejudiced her in favour of late afternoons. She would appear at the door with a blue leather handbag the size and weight of a small planet, knitting needles and bibles and bits of paper sticking out in all directions. She had round, rouged cheeks, fair skin and a voice as soft as a brook. Her greetings were full of God's blessings as she dispensed kisses and face powder to all. It felt like a visitation from a retired but still conscientious cherub.

When I was coming up for ten and Great Auntie Beryl was seventy-two, she decided to marry for the first time. Her husband-to-be was a widower of similar age called Peter, who was ex-RAF. After the war he'd left England for Christchurch and a career of religious devotion. This was how he and Beryl had met.

The wedding itself, I understood from snatched snippets, was to be in the cathedral. 'Of course she's having it there,' uncles and aunts laughed, not unkindly. And I agreed. Of course Beryl would marry in the cathedral. Someone said, 'It's what she's always wanted.' This latter was my first clue, unrecognised then, that lifelong spinsterhood hadn't always been Beryl's goal.

A fairy-tale ceremony was planned, driven by a pre-Raphaelite aesthetic. Beryl wore a high-necked and long-sleeved wedding dress with plenty of smocking. My older female cousins were maids of honour, my three-year-old sister a flower girl, and Beryl's three other great-nephews and I were pages. We wore blue corduroy knickerbockers with white hose, cream shirts with Fauntleroy collars and blue silk ribbon bowties.

During the service I sat at the front of the cathedral on the cold tiles and tried to keep my younger brother still. Across the chancel from us a beautifully dressed aunt governed my youngest cousin's mischief and my sister fell asleep across the altar steps.

*

I still have a copy of the service order, found years later amid Beryl's possessions. It reminds me that the final hymn was one of my favourites, 'Love Divine, All Loves Excelling'. I had it as the second hymn at my own wedding:

> *Changed from glory into glory,*
> *Till in Heav'n we take our place,*
> *Till we cast our crowns before Thee,*
> *Lost in wonder, love, and praise.*

As the final notes rose to the rafters we followed in Beryl's wake down the aisle. There were photographs first, of a vast and elderly wedding party gathered on the cathedral steps. Behind them, engraved into a limestone block inside the porch, was a small blue arrow pointing to the ground, and beneath it an inscription that read something like, 'This is the Christchurch benchmark; from this point all levels were taken.'

*

The earthquake-damaged cathedral that now stands in the centre of Christchurch was once the physical expression of the city's heritage as an Anglican colony and the aspirations of its English settlers.

Christchurch was the dream of the Canterbury Association, a colonising force in clerical robes that was founded on 27 March 1848 and, in quick succession, gained a Royal Charter and two-and-a-half million acres of Māori land for ten shillings an acre.

The first organised colonists arrived in December 1850. Shortly before their departure, at a farewell service at St Paul's Cathedral, the Archbishop of Canterbury himself, John Bird Sumner (known at Eton as 'Crumpety'), anointed them Pilgrims and bade them cross the earth and found an ideal

Anglican society in the south seas, away from the corruption of mid-Victorian London. They even had their own, eponymous, hymn:

Heaven speed you, brothers brave,
Waft you well by wind and wave,
Heaven shield you; Heaven save!
Canterbury Pilgrims!

Maybe it still rang in their ears as they were outward bound from Plymouth Sound a few days later on what came to be known as the First Four Ships—the *Cressy*, the *Sir George Seymour*, the *Charlotte Jane* and the *Randolph*. The aim was to transport a cross-section of society, from sturdy labourers to landed squires. The differentiation began at the ticket office. Those who booked cabins were colonists and served by a steward; those in steerage made their own meals and were known as emigrants. The Pilgrims brought cows, an organ, and even a bell to go in the first church, where it would ring on the hour as the colony's only timepiece.

The journey took a hundred days, with prayers each morning and a church service every Sunday. At last they rounded the daunting earth fortresses that we now call Godley Head, beyond which Lyttelton Harbour cuts deep into the land, a lapis harbour that used to be a volcano. Caldera walls form a steep and rocky barrier, and land suitable for settlement is limited. With summer starting, the Pilgrims moved over the hills via a precipitous bridle path to see their new world.

What they surveyed was the massive expanse of the Canterbury Plains stretching 60 miles to the mountains. It was known as Waitaha to its Māori residents, to whom it had been home for some 500 years. Roughly translated, the name means 'river margin', and the Pilgrims would have seen those wide blue gashes tumbling from the Southern Alps, and marshland at their feet.

The Pilgrims first built huts with flax roofs. These 'whares', as they called them, borrowed both name and architecture from Māori, who I imagine would have been as surprised as anyone to learn that they had sold several million hectares for a few hundred pounds to a London-based property developer (who on-sold it for six times the price). The spot where these new arrivals first settled on the plains is now known as Pilgrims' Corner. It's marked with a little cairn, well known by most boys I boarded with as a good shady place for drinking beer bought from the old Nancy's off-licence at the far side of the park.

There were long hot summers, and icy winters when snow capped the alps and blanketed the plains. The Pilgrims cleared woodland for farms and lined the banks of the Avon River with weeping willows. When the serious building began they chose local black volcanic stone, perfectly suited to the Gothic revival that was to become Christchurch's trademark.

The style's rise has been attributed to the French. Blood-soaked revolution and Napoleonic wars put an end to easy travel to the continent to absorb classical models. Instead, Englishmen looked to home for inspiration. Once barbarous Gothic castles and abbeys—the word Gothic was initially pejorative—were re-associated with chivalry, and the style was now seen as flexible and free, pastoral and democratic, wholesome and liberal. In contrast, the classical architecture of France and Italy was cast as rigid, unnatural, the style of absolutism and despots. Think Camelot versus Versailles.

In England the revival was led by the church, taken up by gentry, then immortalised by Augustus Pugin (the son of a French refugee) and Charles Barry at the Palace of Westminster. The timing was perfect for Christchurch, and the style's morality suited the colony's self-professed progressive goals.

In a world of high-rises and cheap glass it's easy to forget now that the original medieval Gothic architecture was all about letting in light. Norman or Romanesque buildings needed thick walls to support the weight of a stone roof. Windows had to be narrow and deep and admitted little sunshine. The development of load-bearing buttresses allowed for shallower walls and wider windows. Wealthy churches filled these with coloured glass, the better to communicate God's majesty. You can imagine the red- and blue-washed awe of labourers, soldiers, villeins, as they came to give thanks for whatever horror they had just avoided.

We now see the Gothic revival as gloomy: it's rain-soaked stone beneath grey skies; it's Edgar Allan Poe or the Addams family. Yet in its time it was anything but. Horace Walpole's mansion, Strawberry Hill, which started it all, was light, airy and picturesque. The style was approachable, romantic. It was flexible, practical. It let people see what a building did while speaking to supposedly ancient values. The Gothic revival was both ancient and modern, in Canterbury as in England. It looked backwards but was meant to speak forwards.

Thus the new city rose in spires and finials, turrets and towers and battlements. There were public schools, and provincial council chambers for the voices of the (European) citizens. The Canterbury Museum was opened in 1870, about a decade after the Oxford University Museum, which it in part resembles. The new university would have been England's fifth. There was even Sunnyside, a specialist asylum made to look like a French château. The mentally ill had previously been housed in gaols.

Here indeed was the perfect progressive Anglican city and, at the centre of it all, expressive of religion and community, the cathedral: great doors, rose window, asymmetrical single spire, slate and stone. Designed by one of the Gothic revival's protégés, George Gilbert Scott, it was then adapted and implemented by Benjamin Mountfort, a local architect, whose own later Gothic efforts gave old Christchurch much of its look. The dean of Westminster Abbey (whose brother had claimed the South Island for Britain) donated the font.

From the cathedral's doors radiate squares and avenues, laid in a grid to aid land sales and loosely based on Savannah. Christchurch's original plan is called the Black Map. It sits in the Canterbury Museum, and you could navigate with it even today. Its surveyors also christened the city's landmarks. With their feet up on a table in a ramshackle study at the end of the day, at the edge of the world, they bounced names off each other 'to hear if they sounded well'. The result was streets and avenues named for imperial Anglican sees (hence Barbadoes, Colombo, Montreal), the squares for martyrs, the marketplace for the Queen.

*

After Beryl's wedding we drove in cavalcade down Gloucester Street towards thousand-acre, oak-filled Hagley Park, tracing its boundary before turning into Fendalton Road. We turned in at a Gothic folly of a gatehouse, all steep roofs and fretwork beside high grey gates, and followed the gravel drive for half a mile. On one side were flower beds, on the other the Avon River. The driveway widened, the trees stood back and there in front of us was a large two-storey brick and stucco house with a high roof. The cars drew up, one by one, beneath a brick porte-cochère that enclosed the massive black front door like a fortress. We were escorted into a double-height hall with an enormous stone fireplace, bigger than me, in one corner. Ahead of us a dark staircase rose around two walls to an ornate gallery. The hall was dim, the day's dying light further muted by a large stained-glass window.

This was Mona Vale, and it had once been Beryl's home.

*

I have never found the house beautiful. The brick ground floor and white roughcast and timbered upper storey seem mismatched; the twin gables that face the river are a shade too high and give the house a top-heavy look, like a pair of thick eyebrows raised in surprise. And the roof really ought to be slate: the orange Marseille tiles clash with the red brick. But I can see in Mona Vale the echo of the Pilgrims' aspirations. Here is the ancient manor transplanted halfway round the world. But of course it's not. It was commissioned at the start of the twentieth century by a man who owned abbatoirs. Even its name is something of a forgery. Originally named Karewa, it was renamed by Annie Townend (then the country's wealthiest woman and the building's second owner) for her mother's home in Tasmania.

The occasion of Beryl's wedding was my first visit, even though Mona Vale had long been owned by the city and open to the public. Devonshire teas were sold to bridge groups and tour-bus parties on the ground floor, there was a rose garden to circle, and punt tours on the river left from a landing at the edge of the lawn below the drawing room.

As a ten-year-old I followed the elderly up the carved staircase. At the top was a large open space, painted white and brightly lit. Guests sat on metal chairs covered in red velour. The high table ran along the north side above the front door. One aunt pointed out that Beryl was sitting in what used to be her bedroom. How funny, I thought, to get married in your bedroom.

There's a verandah in the centre of the house on the first floor, set between those high gables. Behind the verandah had been the main bedroom, the room where Beryl's father had died in 1954. A rich man, his death duties amounted to 5 percent of all those collected by the state that year. My mother told me about the death only years later. She has a good ear for stories. Her own twenty-first had been a medieval revel, complete with faux-heraldic banners at a fake castle on the Cashmere Hills.

*

By 1859 Christchurch was a Bishop's see and Canterbury had been parcelled up into 200 vast landed estates. The leaseholders paid nominal rents and no one questioned the validity of their tenure or their profits. It was a system designed to attract people and hence revenue, so that John Robert Godley and other leaders of the Canterbury settlement could pay for their Gothic spires. There was a pastoral boom. This new gentry flourished.

With the estates came grand homes, sprouting from the land in the prevailing style of gables, dormers, towers, sometimes even battlements, an escutcheon carved above a doorway or a coat of arms on the side of a chimney. Their owners built similar residences in Christchurch and would come to town for the races or to meet at the club. Mansions appeared on the lower Port Hills, then in Papanui, Fendalton and Merivale. As much as the gardens and stone towers, they helped to define a certain selective public image of Christchurch.

In a city of grand homesteads, Mona Vale became one of the city's great estates, if perhaps a little showy. That's how it was known, as the 'showpiece of Christchurch', about the time Beryl's father bought it.

*

Beryl's father Tracy was no Pilgrim. He arrived as a thirteen-year-old boy with his parents in 1900, by which time the vision for the city was largely complete. The year 1900 was the fiftieth anniversary of Christchurch and Canterbury. The celebrations included a military parade, the singing of the ancient hymn 'Te Deum' and a speech from the governor. One historian has noted that, by this time, 'Edwardian Christchurch was an elegant colonial city.'

Mark Twain had visited in 1895 on his world tour, lecturing his way out of bankruptcy. He reported positively:

> It was Junior England all the way to Christchurch—in fact, just a garden. And Christchurch is an English town, with an English-park annex, and a winding English brook just like the Avon—and named the Avon … It is a settled old community, with all the serenities, the graces, the conveniences, and the comforts of the ideal home-life. If it had an established Church and social inequality it would be England over again with hardly a lack.

Tracy and his family would have landed in Lyttelton, uplifted their baggage, carried it to the station and taken the tram into town. Tracy's father, a cabinetmaker from Birmingham via Redfern in Sydney, opened a shoe shop on High Street. Tracy joined him. It wasn't the fashionable end of town, but over a dozen years it seems they were successful.

Tracy's father translated this success into a brick and stone home in Fendalton called Leeham. Tracy changed his profession from boot-seller to salesman and married a daughter of the First Four Ships. Decades later, her family name would be etched on one of the plaques cemented to the ground before the cathedral. For the marriage certificate Tracy used his father's address (though electoral records indicate he wasn't living there), and shot his hands into his trouser pockets for the photo.

The children started to arrive a year later: a girl first, called Alison, then Beryl (shunting Tracy well down the Reserves List just as conscription came in), and finally my grandfather in 1919. By the time they needed serious schooling Tracy could afford the best in town. The girls attended St Margaret's, at that time in Cranmer Square, and my grandfather went to Christ's College, a series of grey castles around a billiard-green lawn. The college was founded to serve the sons of the newly landed squirearchy, but a look at the school list shows that in 1934 many boys came from similar backgrounds to my grandfather: Christchurch mercantile and professional.

Tracy had had limited education, and sending children to these schools showed him joining that allegorical world of the Pilgrims. The migrant shoe salesman was a convert. A few years later he moved from shoes to tractors, selling large numbers to the government as it battled the Depression with make-work projects. On the eve of World War Two he went from Canterbury convert to Canterbury conquest by buying Mona Vale. It was his apotheosis.

The family worshipped up the road at stone-clad St Barnabas with its crenellated tower (where my own parents were later married). Beryl took up opera singing. They learned to ride at Mrs Southgate's in North Canterbury, took French lessons from a 'Viennese Jewess' who'd fled fascism. Tracy stalked deer, had his cutlery engraved with a claimed crest and filled the house with treasures: crystal, medieval furniture, silver, heavy oils.

Generations later, after the earthquakes that claimed so much of Gothic Canterbury, I stumbled across a small packet of snapshots no bigger than playing cards. They were in a box beneath a bed in my grandparents' damaged house, which I was now trying to clear out. There in black and white are Beryl, my grandfather and another girl, who I guessed to be their sister Alison. They're standing by the lily pond that Tracy installed at Mona Vale. There are dark hedges, giant urns. Beryl is blonde, aquiline, with a black spaniel at her feet. My grandfather is in a flannel suit with Oxford bags. Alison is very pretty. They're walking around the grounds and squinting into the morning sun.

Another photo: black tie in the drawing room, the young at the back, Tracy and the adults in front. It's New Year's Eve 1940, and they've become the perfect Canterbury family living in a Tudorbethan fantasia. They're happy and the war seems a long way away.

But it's not. Tracy has started adding armour plating to the tractors and calling them tanks. And within a few months two of the people are missing.

*

The Gothic revival's blend of ancient roots with modern outlook is neat but facilitates deception: brand new buildings that try to look ancient; a new settlement that claims antique links; a southern paradise made to look European; a city of stone built on flax and marsh; English estates on Māori land; a happy family that isn't.

My great-grandmother Julia died at fifty-four just a few months after that photo was taken. Sixteen days earlier my grandfather had received a letter from one of his sisters saying that the gardeners had been busy (they employed a dozen) and that Mummy was outside enjoying the sunshine.

Death at fifty-four wasn't unheard of, but was still premature. The death certificate listed three causes:

• Coma, 12 hours

• Acute Mania, 14 days

• Diabetes

Acute mania is an old-fashioned term meaning the opposite of depression. Here it could be a portmanteau for a woman written off as mad. The diabetes likely caused the coma via hypo- or hyperglycaemia. It's still odd though. Julia wasn't old, she could afford good care, and insulin had been in use for twenty years—unless she took too much, or too little.

Three days before her mother died Alison was removed from Mona Vale, first to Sumner, a seaside village where the family had once lived, and a few hours later back to town to the old Harley Chambers by the Avon. Both visits were to doctors, each of whom attested to her insanity. This was enough for the courts, who sectioned her under the Mental Defectives Act. Alison arrived at

Sunnyside Mental Asylum at 5pm on 27 May 1941. Her admission notes record bruising to her arms and torso.

Sunnyside was Mountfort's final masterpiece of the Canterbury Gothic: mansard roofs, gables, towers, chimneys and movement. It tries to say resort, not prison. But in the 1940s the death rate across the country's asylums was 8.5 percent per annum. The recovery rate was just over half that. Two died for every one who left. Janet Frame described admitting herself as a voluntary boarder in 1948: 'My life was thrown out of focus … I was terrified.' One 1946 pamphlet was entitled *Misery Mansion: Grim tales of New Zealand asylums.*

Alison's notes record her complaining loudly about 'that bloody woman'. She was treated for schizophrenia with a combination of sedatives and convulsants, the latter to jolt her back to her senses.

On 1 June 1942 Alison had been there a year and had just endured the anniversary of her mother's death. She was given the convulsant Cardiazol at 5pm and again at 3am the next morning. The following day, the anniversary of her mother's burial, Alison was given morphine at 11.50am. The next entry simply says 'Died 12.00'. The coroner ruled it was myocardial failure—a heart attack, most likely from the drugs. Alison was twenty-eight. She was buried two days later, the vicar of pretty St Barnabas presiding as he had for Julia.

*

Julia died on a Friday. There was a concert that night in town, and Beryl was carded to perform. Her choice was the 'Indian Bell Song' from the opera *Lakmé*, about tragic love between a Hindu girl and a British officer:

Where will the young Indian girl,
Daughter of the pariahs,
Go when the moon dances
In the large mimosa trees?
She runs on the moss
And does not remember
That she is pushed around
The child of outcasts …

*

Beryl ran away from Mona Vale after Alison's death. She went to Dunedin and trained as a volunteer nurse. She had no money and few marketable skills and her brother was in the air force. It couldn't last. Just before my grandfather was demobbed, in 1945, Beryl was checked into an offshoot of Sunnyside. Once in, she couldn't get out. She went through electro-convulsive therapy. After three years my grandfather secured Beryl's release: she was thirty-two, alone and immersed in religion.

*

Eleven days after Tracy buried his daughter Alison, he married his long-time secretary and the children's former nanny. They continued to live at Mona Vale with its little Gothic gatehouse, the Avon River as a moat.

REFERENCES

Edwardian Christchurch was an elegant colonial city … Geoffrey Rice, *Christchurch Changing: An illustrated history* (Christchurch: Canterbury University Press, 2007)

It was Junior England all the way to Christchurch … Mark Twain, *Following the Equator: A journey around the world* (New York: American Publishing Company, 1897)

My life was thrown out of focus … Janet Frame, *An Autobiography* (Auckland: Century Hutchinson, 1989)

One 1946 pamphlet … Arthur Sainsbury, *Misery Mansion: Grim tales of New Zealand asylums* (privately published in multiple editions 1946–48)

Where will the young Indian girl … *Lakmé*, an opera by Léo Delibes to a French libretto by Edmond Gondinet and Philippe Gille

Tan Tuck Ming

My Grandmother Glitches the Machine

A few years ago, I took part in a research study at an institute of parapsychology, an underground subfield of psychology that deals with psychic abilities. I was in my second year of university and did not think I was a psychic. The man who conducted the study led me into a windowless room with a hulking and unbranded pre-millennium computer. He said I would have twenty minutes to complete a series of tasks on the computer, for which I would receive $8 and a chocolate bar. He gave no other details.

The program started. I solved basic math equations, spotted animated foxes hiding behind animated trees and matched virtual shapes into virtual holes. The room seemed airless and I felt like I was being watched. Occasionally the screen would freeze, but would quickly unfreeze when I double-clicked the mouse. The whole thing took thirteen minutes.

I felt proud until the researcher told me that swift completion of the program was inversely related to my psychic ability. He explained. These psychic abilities were not conscious, he clarified, like whether my mind could enter the mainframe, but were the magnitude of my subliminal register: whether the wavelength of my anxiety, stress and frustration limit could disrupt the computer system, negative affect converted to appliance-level electrical interference. They had embedded some glitches in the program to amplify confusion, and were looking to see if my subconscious could glitch it more profoundly. He confirmed that I did not seem to have these abilities. But ever since then I've wondered—did I imagine the screen freezing? Was that a glitch, or some old silence in me finally making itself known?

There are other things I now pay attention to. My neck inheriting a persistent crick for many days in a row. The intermittent untraceable hum within the wall that I hear when lying down. An unnameable hunger for a rolled cucumber softened to semi liquid state. This morning I took stale bread to the river to feed some ducks, which flew away at my approach. One of the ducks stayed at a distance, solemn and strong-eyed. Instinct told me this was my grandmother. It was probably not all of her, the way a spirit once released is not coextensive with one thing, but was perhaps the swirling memory of her knee or her questions about the Apple store. I wanted to call out: 婆婆, *is that you? Why have you left your body?*

*

There is a word in Mandarin for 'glitch' but, as most translations go, it does not neatly correspond to the English meaning of the word. Google Translate says the Mandarin equivalent is 毛刺. Whenever we go back and forth, we get to a different place. Translated into English, 毛刺 means mechanical burr—the deformed edge of metal turned outward and askew after grinding or drilling has taken place. A glitch is similar in that it is a failure in a minor key, a moment of slippage when the code or the machine blunders and produces an unintended random output.

I believe almost everything today can be described as a machine. A machine is a family, is a city, is a nation-state, is a person, is a Toyota Camry. The structuralist account insists that language is the machine preceding all other machines, as it allows the phenomenal world to be abstracted and given a face—which is to say that language, on a cognitive level, is what makes possible the experience of phenomena. Paul de Man of the later school of deconstruction writes, 'If it were not for novels, no one would know for certain that he is in love.'

With language, we get the idea of *red* that enables a chromatic impression to strike our minds; *she* and *I* are pronouns that discover personhood from a set of cognitive functions. In this sense, to be alive and conscious is to enter a machine of consecutive hallucinations put forward by words.

In one machine is my grandmother and in another is me. My grandmother lived in a small room in my auntie's house in Singapore, and I left Singapore for New Zealand when I was five. Of the two languages she spoke, I never learned Hokkien and had only recently started to learn Mandarin. My grandmother's capacity for English extended only to the shrapnel phrases she had picked up before dropping out of primary school. In English, she was a happy woman. Back then I was nameless, referred to simply as 'Boy!' When she came to visit us in Wellington, a trip she made only once, I skirted around the edges of rooms and conversations, moving the only way possible for a gap-toothed insect of a boy who would otherwise not be spoken to.

It's true that when I speak of machines I also mean dimensions.

*

Because I cannot make it back to Singapore for her funeral, various family members recruit me to make a video about my grandmother for the church service. I choose Teresa Teng, the only Cantonese singer I know, for the backing track.

All day I have been receiving photos, spanning the last seven decades, from unknown numbers. One is of my grandmother as a teenager, holding a chicken. I linger on the avian connection between the chicken and the lone duck by the river. Three other people in the photo also hold chickens, fingers interlaced beneath the breasts and thumbs pressing down on the spines as if squeezing air out of a ball. There is a sepia note of joy on everyone's faces. What was the significance of the chicken?

My sister calls me the day after the funeral and tells me there has been a problem. After the funeral the casket holding my grandmother's body was taken to the crematorium. My family was directed down a series of corridors to the Ash Collection Centre where they entered a door with a sign, PLEASE COLLECT HERE. Once inside, a man appeared with a clear plastic bin about twice the size of a shoebox, which he set down on a piece of cloth.

There is an irregular assortment of white fragments in the box: bones, some ground to the size of rice grains but most of them larger, scaled approximately to cherry leaves, and the clacking of calcium gives the impression of building blocks. The man is nonchalant and produces a white jar. He tells my family to put my grandmother into the jar, piece by piece. Not the facial bones, he says, selecting a few delicate shards that are noticeably thinner than the rest. These are meant to go at the top of the pile in an order that follows the alignment of the body.

No one is prepared for this. A few bones are yellowed, and someone murmurs that it's the quantity of tea that she drank in her lifetime. My auntie puts her hand into the box, withdraws a piece of my grandmother's femur and places it in the jar. My sister picks a piece of the pelvis and places it in the jar. The man takes a long metal utensil and presses down heavily, because my fragmented grandmother, loosely arranged, is spilling out of the jar. Her cheekbone, or maybe her forehead, is pushed below the lip of the container, compacting the space between parts of her body that have never touched before.

There is dust on the cloth. Isn't that my grandmother? my sister asks. Yes, the man says, and shakes the dust into the jar.

I end up calling the crematorium, at midnight because of the time difference, and reach a customer service operator at the National Environmental Agency. He is surprisingly amiable when I mention the bone fragments, the plastic box, the non-pulverised remains. 'Oh, I see—you were expecting a powder? I'm sorry.' He transfers me to another switchboard where another guy tells me that the crematory machine can only break things down to minor parts. Any further processing needs to be done manually.

I think about this as an equation: what goes in and what comes out and the transfiguration between the two ends. A kind of release. But it bothers me: what happened to the smoke? I start the habit of leaving my window open at night.

*

When my grandmother was alive, most of the stories I heard about her were negative, tales of a woman alternatingly stubborn, severe, irrational and helpless. She was a single mother who beat her children, sometimes with a chain. To avoid the humiliation of a divorce she told everyone her husband had died. She washed vegetables on a seat next to the toilet. She hoarded everything—trinkets, newspapers, fabric—and stashed the bounty in broom closets in her daughters' houses. She carried plastic bags of groceries in the rain because no one offered help. She kept things to herself. She was alone a lot.

*

I saw my grandmother once every few years, and after I started learning Mandarin we called each other once every few weeks. I could sense a thin wire being established under an ocean. But the problem with learning from a textbook is that the discourses available to you are limited by subject chapters, which tend to be narrow, almost surgically specific. Chapter three was about an automobile accident where no one has insurance. Chapter nine was about the president having a scandalous affair. My Mandarin developed an uneven topography, ad-hoc glossaries from which I could express a crude ethical position. I learned to say things like, *Single-use cutlery is a cheaper option for street vendors but excessive usage will damage our global future.* Or, *I believe that people who illegally download music are essentially thieves.*

Then there are the words I learned only when my grandmother used them: sunlight, press, password, knee, appetite, pain, gushing, river carp. I can't remember the exact situation each word referred to or when it came up. That they are listed in my notebook means they have acquired a second skin. Even now, I'm surprised that I took so long to notice the clear and buoyant kinship between these objects and feelings.

The popular pedagogy for learning Mandarin is similar to most language classes––endless repetition, as if only by brute force can a new word be branded into the eye and the ear. I spent enough days copying out characters over and over again for this to become a ritual indistinguishable from knowing. Across the page, I've written: 阳光 阳光 阳光 阳光. Or: *sunlight, sunlight, sunlight, sunlight.*

*

If we believe Nietzsche then there is no truth, and we are just repeating worn-out figures of speech that are themselves cold and remote distillations of an impossible original. His suspicion of language comes from his suspicion of truth, which he suspects to be an illusion of language. Everything that is spoken and can be spoken consists of 'metaphors, metonymies, and anthropomorphisms', figurative terms we have used to nominate the unnameable, that we have mistaken for the real and fixed. All we have is language and we cannot get beyond it.

The problem with the machine as a metaphor is that it is claustrophobic: all that passes through and out of it is accounted for by a precise and unrelenting algebra. It will keep giving the same thing out, over and over again. It means that if I begin this way, I will always be out of time with something else.

It's true that I often find myself caught in the temptation to fix things into code, an insistent force that resides in me to form glottal noise into interpretable meaning. But I want more to linger on the ecstatic surface where my senses betray me astonishingly, to vanish into the skew of mishearing, misreading, doubled vision, the half-step.

Rosa Menkman, the inaugural glitch theorist, proposes an art form of corrupted images and aesthetic disturbance. 'The glitch,' she writes, 'is a wonderful experience of an interruption that shifts an object away from its ordinary form and discourse … But once I named it, the momentum—the glitch—is no more.' For Menkman, the glitch cannot be described because then it ceases to be what it claims: it is a lack, a break in the pattern of meaning that forces its own opening.

I've come to develop a certain tenderness for the glitch, the riddled dysfunctional thing that evades the conditions of what might be expected and what might be known, rupturing unfamiliar territories, or maybe offering a glimpse into a second reality you realise you have been living all along. I see the deer swallowed by thick black tarmac. I listen to the tap drip out a lament. I wake up in darkness to sounds, angular and weightless, like words sketched out of lost feeling coming out of myself. It's a bit like dreaming, which is always a bit like remembering.

*

My grandmother called her smartphone 'the small machine', the small machine that is inside all my memories of her. Even the older models outstripped her understanding of the technological world. To her, the phone was a sullen elusive thing, always withholding answers; the normal flow of the machine and its algorithms exceeded her analogue sensibilities. If she had problems with her phone she would call me, because everyone else had grown tired of her repetitive questions. Whenever we saw each other she insisted on convening in small cold rooms in order to study her phone—long soft afternoons spent trying to decipher her questions as she relayed between the bathroom and the television. *Is it sent? How to throw away? Done?*

Once when we met in Hong Kong she was locked out of all of her social media accounts because she had forgotten the passwords. I began to piece together an oblique organisation of profiles, a circle of mirrors bearing her English name, Shirley, created as each previous profile was sealed off by her faulty memory. One showed her gazing upwards at a multi-storey Christmas tree, a photo I had taken. Another was so zoomed-in her face took up most of the square. Online I was only connected with one of the Shirleys, the profile I created for her.

She peered into the screen and scribbled intently in her little blue notebook. I noticed she was not writing words but drawing miniature pictographs, sketching images of the buttons she should press. She said she was a poor student. When she practised and forgot which button to press she would frown, then laugh and look at me, her eyes querying.

I downloaded a translation app for her, which she treasured for the way it ingested her words and returned a script that she could not understand but others could. As she learned the combination of buttons to make this work, anything began to seem possible and everything communicable. She started using this as a second mouth, with a garbled joyful lyric. Glancing about furiously in the middle of the street, she would whisper into the phone, the small machine, then grip my arm tightly, her fingers making a bruise, and hold up the English translation for me to read: *Boy, do you eat yummy things and do you not swell? Do you know that we had eaten too much the other day and she spit and I now have to be careful but smiling? I don't remember much but I will remember for a long time. Everyone is happy and happy.*

*

We were walking along the waterfront with a family friend who spoke only English. Our friend asked my grandmother why, if not spurred by religious belief or vegetarianism, she chose not to eat beef. I had never thought to ask her a question so personal. My grandmother blinked, surprised. 'When I'm young, I see the cow work in the field every day,' she said. 'Working very hard, all the time. Still cow gets eaten.'

When my family is going through my grandmother's belongings they come across a stack of letters she received from her father, who was living in Malaysia. I want to read them but can't decipher the cursive script. Some friends try to help me translate them, but due to the antiquated syntax they can only make out some phrases: *Sometimes, I secretly cry for you.* In another letter: *Any other woman would have killed herself. I hope God takes pity on you.* At the end: *Life is just a dream.* No one finds any letters from her that prompted these responses from her father.

Grief can also feel relentless, like brutally efficient automation, something you cannot get out of until it is done with you and you are not what you were when you entered. At times I've tried to go in reverse: to take the thread and go backwards. Instead of thinking of the mouth as a machine, love as a machine, distance as a machine, loss as a machine, I think of the machine as a mouth, distance, love, loss—that is, all at once and the same thing. If you pass what you already know through the words you are learning, it may be possible to end up elsewhere.

*

Of dis-identification, poet and critic Fred Moten writes: 'The way you put yourself together every day is the way that you take yourself apart every day.' He is talking in an interview with artist Wu Tsang about the ritual of identity, where putting oneself together is synonymous with tearing oneself apart. There is a tendency to seek wholeness and continuity as conditions of a narrative, like a mountain only witnessed from a distance; but Moten is convinced of the value in small and wondrous acts of separation, how they may surface wayward objects and moments that do not connect, fugitive pieces that can be claimed into the self.

Wu Tsang replies: 'What limbs can we sever, or momentarily conjure, to constitute our place in this world?'

I am starting to see the sparseness as a condition of its largeness; that what appears as the limit, the approximations and the grasping quietness, was in fact its own tender opening. The last time I saw her she had three smartphones, someone's misguided ploy to solve her technological bewilderment with sheer volume. We were in a hotel that offered free Skittles, which she liked to heap on a plate and suck on one at a time. Outside I could see the sky heaving like a long white belly, a dismal overhang, a shimmer of umbrellas rippling upward, then rain.

She wanted to tidy up her shipwrecked contact list and asked me to go through them individually: Ah-Ching was dead, as was Cheng-Lo. Helen, He ren and HeLen T were the same person, also deceased. When she said they had died, it was like they were on holiday. She had forgotten how to use the translation app. I noticed she was sketching on the page opposite to her sketch of the same icon last year. She laughed when the mechanical voice translated the word for grandmother as old wife, like it did last time, and I laughed too, an infinite loop in which we were caught.

I told her I liked her chili sauce, a new word I had learned, and this made her happy. When I read the word now, I'm struck by a stray part of the rightmost character—又, a radical for which there is no direct translation but which, depending on context, can indicate the repeated continuation of an action or the coexistence of multiple situations and properties. Somehow, when stitched with other parts, this becomes the word for chili pepper.

*

Night, like a net, collected the calls I missed due to time difference. Each one brought with it a question or revelation. Other times, malfunctions. I'd wake up beached, my body stirring, sand tracking in me. My cousin told me how my grandmother had live-streamed by accident, warping around on one of her new phones. A fifteen-minute portrait of a frowning elderly woman scrolling down her newsfeed in still silence.

I called her back later in the morning, her night. She said yes, there was a lump in her neck, but because it was soft and not hard, she had heard it was not dangerous. She didn't want me to worry. Instead, she had called to talk to me about her phone, which she said was too big and defective. None of the drawings in her notebook matched any of the apps on her phone. She said her WhatsApp account had been deleted. After I hung up I noticed that in the past week she had called me three times on WhatsApp and left me several voice messages.

It occurred to me that maybe she understood more than she was letting on.

After she died I rebooted my old phone to look at the things I'd stored there. Once it was switched on, the old phone synchronised with the frequency of the present, a shell reanimated. Everything that had been sent to me in the past six months was regurgitated, an open drain turned inside-out onto the street, a bloated flotsam mass of photos, messages, missed calls.

Hnng, hnng, hnng the old phone vibrated for half a day, jerking suddenly every few minutes to re-enact the conversations of the recent past, struck thunderously by the return of another memory. My mother fighting with me on our holiday in Japan. Friends complimenting my new turtleneck. I had the feeling of being a ghost because of the way people appeared to be responding as if I was answering in real time, even though I was sitting in my bedroom in the future, motionless and silent. When your eyes are closed, the movement of the wind around an object can describe its shape.

Over and over again my dead grandmother messaged me about her new phone. *The machine's broken.* A week later, *I think the machine's broken*, and then, *Maybe machine's broken*. And I saw that, by some strange glitch, the old phone was showing my grandmother's status as active now. When I saw this, I stopped worrying.

REFERENCES

If not for novels … Paul de Man, 'Hypogram and Inscription: Michael Riffaterre's poetics of reading', *Diacritics*, vol. 11, no. 4, 1981, pp. 17–35 (33): www.jstor.org/stable/464972

metaphors, metonymies, and anthropomorphisms … Friedrich Nietzsche, *On Truth and Lies in a Nonmoral Sense*, 1873.

'The glitch,' she writes … Rosa Menkman, *Glitch Studies Manifesto*, 2010: http://amodern.net/wp-content/uploads/2016/05/2010_Original_Rosa-Menkman-Glitch-Studies-Manifesto.pdf, p. 5.

The way you put yourself together … Wu Tsang and Fred Moten, 'Interview with Wu Tsang and Fred Moten', 356 Mission, September 2016: https://356mission.tumblr.com/post/150698596000/interview-with-wu-tsang-and-fred-moten

Dead Dads Club

People can get a bit squeamish around the subject of dead dads. I can see where they're coming from but there's no need for alarm—dads have been dying since the 1960s.

Misfortune in life is not enjoyable but you learn from it. It makes you stronger, more resilient. No one became a decent person by getting everything they want. Cigarette burns taught me that Granddad needs space.

If you are reading this and your dad is not of the dead persuasion, please relax. I assure you that reading this will not jinx him. Your dad will be fine.

But maybe don't read it *to* him. Or print out a copy, frame it and send it to him. Dads don't like to consider their own deaths and they don't like their children to consider them either. It may impact on the quality of your next birthday present. But at least your dad can still buy you presents! Because he's not dead.

Our dad died in January 1998. Our favourite cousin lost her dad in September that same year. The Dead Dads Club is what happens when you combine four bereaved teenagers and come back two decades later.

Before I get too carried away it's worth pointing out three things:

We're Fine. Our dads died a long time ago—one of those classic things in life that are difficult at the time, funny in hindsight.

Seriously, we're Fine. Dads are like wisdom teeth. Losing them is painful, but you'll only have to go through it once.

We are so Fine that people don't believe we're Fine and they try to psychoanalyse us. 'How can a person be Fine with having a dead dad? Come on, you psychopath, cry!'

Grief is a long and crazy process. You have a short while to navigate this minefield before you are released back into the wild. Take a deep breath.

Everything is Fine.

Most of us will be familiar with the five stages of grief: Denial, Anger, Bargaining, Depression and Acceptance. These stages were identified in Elisabeth Kübler-Ross's 1969 book *On Death and Dying*. Perfect summer reading. Tuck it under your arm, spread out your towel, then devour it cover to cover on a white-sand beach while sipping a cocktail garnished with a cheerful novelty umbrella. Breathe deeply and know that death awaits us all. Anyone for tennis?

Figure 1. The Five Stages of Grief

The five stages of grief were ground-breaking, but are now seen as problematic. People have latched onto this concept, clung to it like a how-to manual ('Grieving for Dummies'). This has given rise to the concept of grief as a linear process, where we neatly move from one stage to the next until we graduate at the point of 'Acceptance'.

But in reality, grief is messy. The stages do exist, but you might experience all of them at once, or you might skip an entire stage altogether.

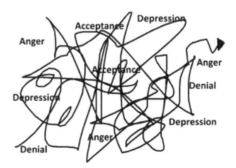

Figure 2. Reality

I have also identified additional stages of grief: KFC, Buying Dogs, Attempts at Humour, and Consulting Psychics.

My sisters and I have spent a long time in the Acceptance phase. I think it's because our dad was always going to die.

Our parents lived in Tokoroa, where I should've been born. Then Dad had a massive car crash and broke his pelvis in sixteen places. He spent a month in Waikato Hospital, so that's where I arrived—first-born, jaundiced, with a notorious appetite. I was born in Hamilton by accident.

It was never confirmed but I think we can safely say that Dad was not sober at the time of his accident. This was 1980s New Zealand, when drink-driving was less a crime, more a way of life.

An example. Mum and Dad were married in Dannevirke. After celebrating for twelve hours, Dad drove them back to their honeymoon suite in Woodville. Weaving along State Highway 2, Dad covered his eye with one hand.

'Mike! What are you doing?'

'It's for your safety,' slurred my father. 'Otherwise there are two roads. God, I love you.'

That man was always going to die.

After Dad's accident his left leg was five centimetres shorter than his right. His left knee could now bend sideways. Everything was a bit bung, like a cheap imitation Barbie doll.

He had to wear a special shoe with the sole built up. It's been theorised that his look sparked the Spice Girls platform sneaker trend, but this cannot be confirmed.

Dad survived that car crash but it didn't take long for us to realise he wasn't one of those immortal dads. The first heart attack happened when I was five. All I remember is the helicopter. Dad was delirious and asked if they could fly it upside down.

From then on his heart was essentially a faultline. It might rupture in a thousand years or … NOW! Kids would say, 'My dad could beat your dad in a fight!' We'd agree.

We kids lived in constant fear that we'd be the cause of The Big One. I'm sure he used that fear against us. We'd be minding our own business: doing a jigsaw, reading, watching cartoons—and Dad would stumble into the room clutching his chest. We'd leap up. 'Should we call an ambulance?'

Dad would look at me through scrunched-up eyes. 'Cuppa tea? Extra strong. One sugar.' I hated the day I was deemed old enough to make hot drinks.

Because my dad had a bung leg and a dodgy heart he wasn't allowed to work any more. It wasn't easy for a man like my father to be idle, so he found productive ways to fill his time. Like welding things that didn't need welding. And gambling on the horses.

As a kid I thought it was normal to sit in the car for two hours outside the TAB. This was a time when leaving your kids in the car while you gambled was less a crime, more an obvious childcare solution.

Usually, though, Dad would make bets over the phone and then we'd have to be QUIET as he listened to the race over his transistor radio. We hated that radio. It stood on top of the microwave, propping up unpaid bills, a monument of shhhhhhhh.

Horses raced through our childhood. Interrupted every conversation. Those horses, with their tiny riders and their stupid names. What is so wrong with naming a horse Simon?

Dad had multiple heart operations, but the successes didn't last. In 1998 he needed a new aortic valve. We knew our dad was mortal, but we never expected it would be suicide.*

*Disclaimer
Now that the 'S' word has been mentioned, it would be irresponsible—nay ILLEGAL—not to include a disclaimer.

Don't commit suicide. It's BAD. Have you thought of taking a lovely walk or joining a yoga class? Some people like to take deep breaths of fresh air. Have you been outside lately? Had a shower?

If you still feel like suiciding, here's a number: 0800 DONTDOIT. Call it! Reach out!

Suicide will make your family sad. They won't blame themselves—until someone asks, 'Do you blame yourself?' which will make them wonder if they should.

They will also be asked, 'Did they leave a note?' We're not in a note-leaving zeitgeist, but if you absolutely insist on committing suicide, it's only polite. This way, your family can make photocopies of the suicide note and a keep a copy in their wallet, just in case the subject comes up. And it will.

Every conversation is six degrees of separation from suicide. Your loved one might go to the supermarket for some Vogel's and a bag of onions and start talking about weather—which is a segue into family, which is a segue into 'What do they do for a living?', which is a segue into the fact they *aren't* living, which is a segue into 'How did they die?', which is a segue into suicide, which is a segue into 'Why did they do it?'—which is the ideal time to present the stranger with their very own copy of your suicide note so they can get back to contemplating which brand of milk is more likely to make them fat.

Don't kill yourself. Suicide is the least socially acceptable way to die. Other socially unacceptable ways of death include climbing into the Sumatran tiger's cage at your local zoo and autoerotic asphyxiation.

If you kill yourself, your loved ones will make inappropriate jokes. They'll find other people who understand and they'll laugh about it. Because grief is like Dannevirke—just because you have to drive through it sometimes, doesn't mean you have to buy a house there.

They'll joke about killing themselves if there is bad WiFi coverage or if they run out of coffee or if they step on a crack. This is NOT good. It devalues suicide, and we cannot have a society that doesn't FREAK OUT if we say the 'S' word. It must always be said gravely. It must always be the worst thing.

Your loved ones must never make peace with your suicide, because if they do, then they are accepting it as an option, which it must NEVER be.

We must rage and fight—celebrities must punch each other in the face to raise awareness—but we cannot joke or accept suicide because we need to maintain a CONSTANT STATE OF OUTRAGE if we are ever to fix this problem.

One day you'll be okay. You'll be glad you didn't kill yourself because there's a lot of great TV you haven't watched and a lot of weird novelty chocolate flavours that Whittaker's haven't yet released.

Patience is key. You'll die eventually, I promise.

It was our uncle who told us about Dad. As soon as I saw our uncle's face I knew it was bad news. It's like those times you enter a public toilet cubicle and the toilet lid is down. You approach cautiously. You hold your breath and hope for the best. But deep inside you know it's shit.

It's strange when your life changes forever in an instant, but the world carries on as normal. The radio was on and as we were trying to process the sudden and permanent loss of our father, live on air one of the presenters was getting his butt waxed. He yelled, 'Oh god! You bastard! It hurts!' That was the first time a radio jock said something I could relate to.

So our dad was dead and we were plunged into the role of bereaved teens. Apparently we didn't grieve appropriately. Kids at school heard about our dad's death and thought it was a rumour. How could it be true? Those girls are wearing colour and I've never seen them cry. Is that normal?

My youngest sister was ten. Her school books brimmed with poems devoted to Dad. They contained fragments of plagiarised lyrics from our parents' Time Life CD library, *The Emotions Collection*. This collection of twelve CDs was split in two when Mum and Dad separated, and reunited after he died.

Thanks to *The Emotions Collection*, my sister's poems for Dad spoke of a romantic love. She wanted to see 'deep into his blue eyes' and was 'hungry for his touch'. Her teacher insisted these poems were a healthy outlet. My other sister and I were horrified. Somehow those poems were lost. Such a pity.

When someone dies, you have to learn to speak in code, because no one will ever speak honestly about them again. All their flaws will be remembered as endearing character quirks:

Your dad …
- was such a character! (borderline criminal)
- was a real ladies' man! (a bit creepy)
- liked a drink! (alcoholic)
- was strong willed! (a nightmare)
- and I never really saw eye to eye (hated that guy).

No one joins the Dead Dads Club by choice, but there are pros as well as cons. On the one hand, it's a devastating loss. On the other, I got two weeks off school. The pros and cons continue:
- PRO: I don't have to be quiet during the rugby

- CON: My parents will never grow old together
- PRO: I'll never walk in on them having sex.

Burying a parent is tough. But it's better than the other way around. It's them or you.

The undisputed major benefit of having a dead dad is holding the sympathy card. Unfortunately, sympathy has an expiry date. It's highest before you're 47.5 years of age. Please see Figure 3, which charts the rise and decline in sympathy that one might receive upon admission into the Dead Dads Club:

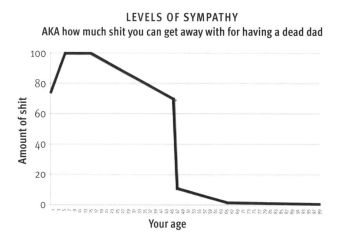

Figure 3. Rise and Decline of Sympathy

This graph illustrates how much you can get away with, according to how old you are when your dad dies. As you can see, babies get a decent amount of sympathy, but not at maximum levels. This is because of their lack of emotional investment in other humans. Babies are cold.

Sympathy peaks at age four, and stays high until age eighteen, when you reach adulthood. Then it starts to decline. However, you can still enjoy sympathy at about 80 percent capacity over the next two decades.

But something happens when you turn 47.5. There is a drastic decline in sympathy because at age 47.5 you hit Peak Dead Dad. This is the age when, statistically speaking, you are more likely to have a dead dad than not.

Peak Dead Dad is calculated by taking average male life expectancy, which is 79.5.[1] From this figure, we subtract the average age of fathers of new babies, which is 32. We are left with the age of 47.5 = Peak Dead Dad.

From this point onwards, if your dad dies, you'll get your three days' bereavement leave and society will expect you to be Fine.

Grief is a minefield. People say the wrong thing all the time. No one means to. They see their loved ones in pain and they want to fix it. And they want it fixed immediately, so they'll say anything to try and make it better:

'Your dad's an angel now.'

Yes, Aunty Barbara. My 47-year-old dad from Tokoroa is an angel. He's up in heaven, wearing a frilly white dress:

I'm not gay! I'm an angel. I love rugby. The way those strong athletic men relentlessly pound each other into the ground … I'm not gay. I'm an angel …'

Dad's angel dress has lasagne stains all over it, and he's not even embarrassed because in New Zealand in the 90s lasagne was very fancy. 'See that stain? That's lasagne. Have you tried it? It's Italian.'

My angel father spends his days up in heaven rubbing his wings together at speed, trying to create enough friction to light the sixteen Pall Mall menthols he's got wedged between the digits on his hands and feet. He smokes his cigarettes one by one, holding them between the ill-fitting false teeth he got when he was nineteen years old because he went to a dentist who told him he needed ONE tooth pulled out, and Dad said, 'Why don't you pull them all out?'

And the dentist said, 'Okay, I will.'

And Dad said, 'Do it then.'

And the dentist said, 'I bloody will.'

And Dad said, 'Do it with my blessing.'

And the dentist said, 'I don't need your blessing, I need you to sign this form.'

And Dad said, 'I don't have a pen.'

And the dentist said, 'Here's a pen!'

And Dad said, 'Good.'

And the dentist said 'Do you want anaesthetic?'

And Dad said, 'I'm not gay.'

So thank you, Aunty Barbara. Yes, my dad is an angel. What a comforting thought.

The most helpful words of comfort were bestowed upon Cousin Hayleigh at her father's funeral. We stood around Uncle Terry's grave and, as the coffin was lowered into the ground, Hayleigh began to cry—as you might at your father's funeral.

Kevin, a family friend, leaned in, held Hayleigh's shoulder and whispered, 'I used to cry because I didn't have shoes, and then I met a man who didn't have feet.'

Beautiful words.

First of all, Kevin. Crying because you don't have shoes? Ridiculous. This is New Zealand. We don't wear shoes. We call them foot oppressors. The soles of my feet are so thick I can dance on thumbtacks.

Second, Kevin. What if you're a man without feet, and you have a cry—as you might when you have no feet—and then you meet a man without any legs?

And then, Kevin, what if you're a man without any legs, and you have a cry—as you might when you can't do Zumba—and then you meet a man who's just a bellybutton? That's right, he's a semi-conscious piece of sinew, resting on a velvet pillow.

Kevin was making a valid point: There is always someone worse off than you, so stop crying, because it makes Kevin uncomfortable.

I say cry. It's good for you; it stops your eyeballs from drying out. Just don't cry in front of a man who is only a bellybutton.

Many club members get comfort from the concept of Heaven. I have no desire to debate its existence, but to me, Heaven sounds like hell.

You must believe whatever brings you comfort. I'm not comforted by the concept of Heaven but I do believe that my dad is still with us. He's still in our lives if we think about him, talk about him, laugh about him. My relationship with Dad is exactly like Patrick Swayze and Demi Moore's in *Ghost*. With less pottery.

In my mind, Dad spends his days protecting us from bad guys. He's in the scattering of autumn leaves, rolling around the ditch, batting our ankles. He's an invisible forcefield, he karate chops would-be attackers. He throws sand in their eyes and spits rain in their face. On a good day, he's in the try-scoring roar at Eden Park. On a bad day, he slaps the ref.

We still have a dad. He just happens to be dead.

Ultimately the Dead Dads Club is about solidarity. It's about connecting with others who won't judge you for rolling about in the awkwardness of grief like a pig in mud.

I made my dad a Facebook profile so he could thank my sister for posting how she missed him. Some of the family loved his social media presence. Others weren't fans of the concept. I would like to make it clear that I realise that making a Facebook profile as your dead father might not be the most mentally stable thing you could do. But I have to say my heart skipped a beat when he friend-requested me. It may be inappropriate, but how can there be an appropriate way to grieve? There's nothing appropriate about losing your dad.

Grief is different for everyone. But there will come a day when you're Fine.

I can't tell you when that will be. You might be Fine now. It might take months, years or even decades.

Being Fine might be a gradual realisation, or one day it might slap you around the side of the face like a dildo at a press conference. But when you realise you're Fine, that can be as scary and confronting as not being Fine. We're so conditioned to know the appropriate responses to loss. But what about the other ones?

Elisabeth Kübler-Ross apparently felt terrible about the way her five stages of grief were misinterpreted. In the last days of her life she said, 'I am more than these five stages. And so are you.'

I'd like to finish by suggesting one more stage: 'Making up for regrets.' I never spoke at Dad's funeral. And if you were to psychoanalyse me, it would seem I've spent the last twenty years making up for it. So, here's a belated eulogy:

My dad was a Bit of a Character. We didn't always see eye to eye. But I always knew that he loved me ferociously. I long for his touch.

We're Fine. Honestly.

---

1   When we look at life expectancy, it is important to let you know this is not a guarantee, according to a lengthy disclaimer on Statistics New Zealand's website. It seems that life expectancy is like avocados—not covered under the Consumer Guarantees Act.

Anna Kate Blair

Notes Toward a Subjective History of Honey

In ancient Greek the word for honeycomb is *kerion*; *ker* means 'fate' and 'death'. In ancient Greece, dripping honey was used as a means of divination. When I found a bag of honeycomb in a closet, fragments spilt out toward me like a prophecy, telling me that I was fated to (write about) death. I had not expected fragments of beeswax to lead me to sticky memories, to childhood and New Zealand.

This is honey, though: strange and unruly, hard to fix in place.

○

The first house in which I lived was wooden, the colour of honeysuckle, with a red roof. It was surrounded by trees, and beyond the trees was a fence covered with flowers. As I had been introduced to language only recently, my mother would lift me up to reach the flowers as I practised saying their name: *honeysuckle*.

○

It seemed, when I was a child, that my grandfather's sister and her partner were orchard astronauts, dressed in white and moving slowly against the gravity of their planted planet, each made indistinguishable from the other by the veils and shadows across their faces, dark gatherings of bees at the bends of their elbows and knees, around their ankles. They would leave the hives and remove their beekeeping suits when they saw our car roll up the driveway. I would be lifted onto the shoulders of somebody older, taller, so I could see the apple trees blossoming above me and the occasional bee collecting nectar. I was told to stay away from the hives clustered together in a corner, and after walking through the orchard we would return to the kitchen to drink apple juice and eat scones with the honey that the bees had created from those blossoms.

○

I think of honey as soft, pliable and yet resilient. I am wondering if honey might be a model for being, for an identity that does not become too solid, inflexible, afraid of uncertainty. How is it that hard things, difficulties, make some people stronger but turn others into quivers? I can say that honey is not a hard thing. It is easy on the body, on the mind; it has no centre. Is death a hard thing? It refuses to give, but it does not feel, in my mouth, like a nut. Death feels more like honey in the way it sticks and lingers, the way the memories are sweet like an aftertaste even as specific details hollow out and cave in on one another, making me feel as if something is rotting—just as honey, unchecked by toothpaste, might rot my teeth.

○

Whāngārei, where I was born, never felt easy. We had to cross the Brynderwyn Hills if we wished to travel south, and the two coasts glimpsed from the hilltops were forbidding. In the local park there was a waterfall, taller than any structure in the city. The tallest building was the hospital where I was born. It was once considered good luck to anoint a child with honey. I was, instead, the first baby in New Zealand to be immunised against Hepatitis B.

I spent most days loitering with my mother. She woke me up one day and said, *Today we are going to see Tāne Mahuta*. We drove for hours and walked through a forest. If I stretched toward the trees I had to check my skin for leeches. At the end of the path was Tāne Mahuta, large and old, wider than the path and tall, stretching up and out of sight. I knew, then, that everything was larger than me, that I couldn't do much more than live in wonder, gazing upward at trees.

After that we went to Opononi, where we sat in a shed by the pier and watched footage of a dolphin from the 1950s. I thought the town had been named after the dolphin, Opo, but the reverse was true.

My mother was always driving around, learning about Northland perhaps. I learnt a lot too, I realise now, but that was never the primary purpose. I was there because I was her child and could not be left alone—until she died and I was left entirely alone, with Tāne Mahuta and Opononi stuck in my head.

○

I am trying to write as if my words are like pollen stuck in honey. I am trying to avoid the deception of honey that's been strained, purified, made artificially consistent. I am trying to stay raw, unpasteurised, which always means the risk of the presence of pollen, of propolis, but the textured reality of this, too, retaining incomprehensible bumps and bubbles and some sort of connection, nutrition, which has not been edited away. I still want some smoothness, a polished yet sticky surface. It is true, though, that words are not honey, despite the ways in which I use them to preserve things. I am not sure about this experiment; I am trying to stay uncertain.

○

After my mother died the house was filled with flowers. We gathered them around and over the piano in the corner; nobody was playing it any more. Pollen from lilies fell onto the carpet. My grandparents, visiting for her death, for the funeral, for the aftermath, tried to get the pollen out with water but it dissolved and seeped further into the carpet, staining it.

How to remove pollen from carpet, I wonder into the internet, nineteen years later.

It is best to use masking tape, I learn.

I learn, also, that honey made from lilies is poisonous.

○

I wonder, sometimes, if New Zealand is a little like my mother; it is a home that I do not really know, a relationship constructed more by distance than intimacy. I can search for New Zealand on the internet and find results, but the same is not true of my mother. If asked about my country I can say that it is a land of honey, but I do not know what to say about my mother.

I wonder, sometimes, if I keep leaving because I cannot handle the proximity to my own youth, to the flora and fauna that compose the flavours. Honey is a preservative: the things that hurt stick in it, and it keeps them fresh.

○

My aunt's beehives are in the suburbs. It is quiet there, with palm trees and picket fences and my grandmother's car, parked on an angle, taking up space. My aunt's hives have not produced much honey. We drive away along the curve of the street and as we turn, I see pink and purple balloons tied to a tree.

'I wonder if someone's having a party?' says my grandmother.

Everything is still, as if we are panning across a diorama rather than sitting in a moving vehicle. There is a young child, maybe six or seven, perhaps a girl, hanging on a rope swing, her hair matted, her legs twisted around the brown hemp cord as if imitating its weave or the twist of the branches above her. She and I lock eyes and the car moves but she does not; she just hangs, suspended between clumps of balloons, indifferent, and there is no sign of anybody else. I wonder if the party is over, or if the party is invisible. I wonder if she is in the process of becoming a tree.

This is suburbia; only the trees chatter, make eyes. There isn't much wind this afternoon, so even the plants are muted, and the sky is bored blue.

The car keeps moving and the girl is stuck in my memory, preserved, as if I had taken a photograph.

At the end of the crescent where the street meets the main road, there is a stop sign on a white wooden post. We stop. Beside me a person, who might be a man, who might be elderly, stops jogging and does half push-ups against the post. He is wearing a cap, and a sweater that reads 'New York Marathon' as if it were a relic from a dream. I imagine him stuck here in this suburb where the only things that run are the engines of cars. I know that I am not writing the truth about this place, that it is empty only to me, everything muted by my own distance and disquiet.

This suburb is the only constant in my life, but I have never lived here. My relatives are transient, shifting away from the places that I know, moving out of reach through death or just a desire to start anew, to take a different job, to be further from or closer to whatever, whoever, whenever. I've done this, too, shifting away from myself, from others.

It is this knowledge that haunts me in this quiet suburb that is no more silent than any other, that is a place in which one might keep a hive. I wonder what it is that makes me old, makes me young; if it's exposure to the sun or the ways in which memories play in my mind, on my skin, on side streets, and how much nectar I must collect before I can make something of this.

o

I wonder if home is honey and water, if home is a relationship to time, an easiness with the idea of looking backward. My maternal grandmother, in

Devonport, tells me she feels sad because I don't have a home. I think of bees forgetting the way back to their hive. I think of other bees, wild, building new hives in fresh logs.

At five o'clock in winter the sky is on the glass table; in the guest bedroom the sun is tangled in the folds of the translucent curtain. I feel it resting in my fringe, on the edge of the spoon that stirs honey into my tea. The shadows behind me are like propolis, that darker resin that holds a hive together.

○

The Honey Centre, near Warkworth, is hexagonal in plan. It sits atop a hill, close to a satellite dish. This was the first satellite dish in New Zealand, accelerating communication with the outside world. It felt like an oracle, perhaps, in 1969. The dish was hidden behind a hill, the road to it announced by the sign for the Honey Centre; the bees led pilgrims toward the future.

I think of the sign for the Honey Centre as a marker for journeys. We saw it, when driving north on Highway 1, and knew we were almost at Warkworth, which meant 'almost there'. My paternal grandmother lived one block from the highway on the edge of the town, fifteen minutes' walk from the centre, and most of my father's other relatives lived across the surrounding farmland and orchards. I don't know anybody there, now, though Warkworth has become much larger.

When I asked my father about my mother's grave, he told me I should take the first road on the right after the Honey Centre, turn onto the last road before the town itself, drive up a hill. The local cemetery overlooks a construction site, a new housing development, a non-place for commuters who can't afford Auckland proper.

'This is Northland,' my grandmother always insisted, after they redrew the district boundaries twice. She is in the cemetery, too, alongside ancestors stretching back to the nineteenth century, when they came from Great Barrier Island to escape the memory of deaths at sea, of children lost in the Hauraki Gulf. It was easier to live in the Matakana, where the beaches were sheltered.

The government added a toll road, replaced twists with a tunnel, and made Warkworth the edge of Auckland about ten years ago. The old graves sit in a paddock beside a ditch and a dirt road, but the sign above, reading 'City of Auckland', is shining, unreasonably clean. My mother's mother, who drove me up from Devonport, had never thought to ask my father about her daughter's grave, had assumed it was elsewhere, across an ocean.

It is clear to me why my father's family are buried here, in the region where they spent most of their lives, but I do not know why my mother is here. It could be that my father's mother believed that something came after death, and my mother's mother did not and so did not think these choices mattered. I do not know if my mother was ever asked about her burial, about the bodies she wished to lie alongside. I wonder who she felt was her family. She struggled sometimes to speak to her mother and moved away from Rotorua, moved north. I think of kinship solidifying after death, of warmed beeswax taking form when it grows cold.

○

There was always somewhere further north where we did not go. I looked at maps and saw Cape Rēinga, the peninsula from which spirits depart, where the Pacific Ocean meets the Tasman Sea. I always asked to visit this place but was told I was too young; it was a long drive; the road was not sealed, was sometimes a river and sometimes a beach. I, nauseous in the Brynderwyn Hills, was not ready for the Far North.

○

For a long time, the temptation of sex was that it made me think of landscapes. I once asked somebody I was sleeping with to drive me to Cape Rēinga. The night before we went, as we moved across a bed in Kerikeri, I thought of the road that led north; this other person thought, probably, of our bodies. Back in Auckland I said I loved him, but what I meant was I loved that I could go now to places that I could not visit alone.

But the land isn't fertile at the tip of that peninsula: there is no agriculture that far north, and nobody has lived at Cape Rēinga since the lighthouse was automated in 1987. The last petrol station, in Waitiki, is also the last place in which to buy supplies. 'Rēinga' is the Māori word for underworld. If bees tried to forage on that northern shore they would be whipped out to sea by the wind, made messengers to the gods again.

○

In ancient Greece ambrosia was the drink of the gods, capable of conferring eternal youth upon those who consumed it. There was slippage, then, between mead and ambrosia, between intoxication and immortality. The gods were always drinking and making mistakes, blaming alcohol for everything.

It is the fault of honey that Love exists, conceived after the gods drank too much mead. Love, writes Plato, is neither god nor good, but exists in a state of ambiguity between the mortal and immortal, between the beautiful and the wretched. Honey, too, is uncertain, neither liquid nor solid, sometimes painfully sweet.

○

I am infuriated by Apollo, the sun god, misogynistic and afraid of the dark. Pierced by Cupid's arrow, he falls in love with Daphne, who Cupid shoots with another arrow, making her afraid of love and sex. Daphne, evading capture by Apollo, calls for help and is answered by a river god who transforms her into a laurel tree. Apollo, though, strokes Daphne's bark, pushes aside her branches and tells her that she will, forever, be his tree. He plucks her leaves and wears them as a crown.

But can one truly possess a tree? Long after I learn this story I discover that honey made with laurel nectar is bitter, astringent and deeply toxic. I see this as Daphne's revenge.

○

Until the seventeenth century, bees were thought to be sexless, without reproductive organs, and were a symbol of chastity, order and obedience. Honey's sweetness was a warning toward moderation. We live now in a world where a lack of desire threatens order, where voluntary chastity is suspect. It doesn't feel quite possible to forget the body, to avoid the questions. There is always the sting of a bee or the warmth of summer to cause the smarting of skin; there is the word *honey*, sounding dulcet, like an invitation or an allusion to the body beneath the clothes.

○

I remember a bonfire in Canada, built by somebody I barely knew, bouncing shades of honey and propolis across navy-blue waves. This girl made art and blueberry pies, gardened and pushed her hair behind her ears, expressed everything in the space between her eyebrows. I kept telling myself that I didn't know her, had only just met her, that I was constructing a fantasy, but the intensity softened only when she used the phrase *dream man*, and the sensations, the habit of isolating moments and lingering on them, did not disappear. We made sourdough and gnocchi, ran from the ocean to the sauna at midnight. Our two weeks together ended with that fire beside the lake. I look at photographs of her swimming through that warm light and I still think *dream girl*, which is reasonable; my feelings emerged as a haze of wishes, not something I could preserve. I think of the sun and the moon, secreting honey behind clouds. I feel like Daphne, sometimes, as if I've been shot by an arrow and made impervious to sex and love, or perhaps ambivalent, and part of this is that experiences never match ideas, that I always feel the sting alongside the sweetness. I feel the threat of those honeyed words, that *you will be my tree*.

o

I am reluctant to write that bees were symbols of fertility alongside chastity, to tell the stories about honey that are stories about flesh. There is a logic that links fertility to chastity easily; that suggests abstinence is a need, not a want, that springs from the procreative potential of bodies. This logic, which is not my own, presumes a certain kind of touching, a certain combination of bodies. I wonder if it is possible to write about honey without writing of euphemism and of the desires, acts and relationships with which the word has been associated. Must I write of licking and of swallowing? I wonder if it is enough to leave these actions unexplored, inexplicit; the word *honey*, after all, implies.

It's possible that I cannot access my own desires because I am afraid of my body, of the ways in which I do not understand it. *It*, I write, by which I mean myself; my torso; my nervous system; everything that I cannot see or name inside myself. I am afraid of the body's potential for disease, for death; I am afraid of the ways in which wishing does not undo decay. I don't know where desire is situated; I am trying to figure that out. I know, though, that sometimes honey smells like blood. In ancient Greece many believed that bees came not from the heavens but from the carcasses of dead animals; the best honey was that which had been wrenched from the body of a lion.

o

Apollo spoke through the Oracle of Delphi, offering prophecies for the future alongside three creatures who were sometimes women and sometimes bees. It was toxic honey that enabled these priestesses to divine the future; they spoke with the mantic madness of laurel, with the strange wisdom of metamorphosis. I wonder, now, if these women knew they were dying, that they lived in a liminal space.

○

I think of honey as a preservative, existing across time. I am obsessed with and troubled by memories; I feel untethered from my own past, unable to find my way back to myself, as if I am a bee made dizzy by the smoke I've encountered in the world outside the hive. I feel I am struggling against a layer of something that seems sweet but is sticky, dense, through which I cannot swim. I am trying to communicate, perhaps, that I am more fragmented than I appear, that organised paragraphs and numbered pages do not mirror my mind. I worry, though, about the kind of person who says *pull yourself together*. I would like to register the way it feels to pull apart, to pool, to rain, to drip and cloy.

○

At Sainsbury's in England the mānuka honey is locked to the shelf, 'security protected', and expensive. I am missing feeling free, feeling viscous, as if my edges are unguarded. Only the mānuka honey tells me the name of the plants from which the bees collected nectar. It is all the same brand, all pasteurised, and is advertised with a cartoon bee and a speech bubble that reads, without punctuation, *I love you honey*.

○

In ancient Greece many believed that honey came from the sky. Aristotle, a beekeeper, believed the creatures in his hive found rather than created the sticky fluid. It fell from the sky, he wrote. When the stars rose, those who were caught in this rain became gods, endowed with immortality.

○

In a burial mound in Georgia, in the Caucasus, archaeologists found fruit that, preserved in honey for 4000 years, still smelt fresh when they sliced into it. There were other things in the mound, too, including a wooden armchair and an arrow. I think of time capsules, sealed in various places, of the atomic age that preceded my coming to consciousness, that shaped my early schooldays. As a child I could never answer the question of what I wanted to place in a capsule, and I suppose I'm still not sure. I never keep honey; I consume it. I take too many photographs and I write too many notes; I have a desire to preserve paired with a confusion about what is worth preserving. I may have lost, or never found, the things worth keeping. I don't know if I would want them if they were in honey, sealed, fresh and untouchable.

Honey, as it ages, crystallises and loses its transparency. I wonder if the honey in Georgia was opaque. I wonder about my own opacity, about how much I reveal to myself and others. I have spent my life trying to edit myself out of the writing I produce, but I am learning, with honey, that I should not run away from my past indefinitely; that eventually time capsules must be opened and apples split; that preservation can't be the final phase; that sometimes the act of liquifying crystals requires admitting the possibility of change, of something underneath coming alive before rotting away.

○

In ancient Greece poetry was described as *star-fallen*, produced by the same alchemy as honey. It is an extraction, a gathering and processing of nectar, a slow transformation of the external world into something strong and particular, both nutritious and delicious. This analogy is supposed to pay literature a compliment, but I cannot help but think of honey that is so sweet that it becomes repulsive. I suppose the most interesting words are, like honey, rarely easy to enjoy; they stick to the fingers and the aftertaste lingers in the mouth, in the mind.

I read, again, of honey's mythology. If a dream shows honey falling from the sky onto a landscape, it is a sign that the blessings of gods will fall on this particular place. I wonder, if I dreamt of this golden rain, whether I would be tempted to move cities or countries again, if I would wish to stay fixed, or whether I would wake with no memory of the rain at all.

Siobhan Harvey

Living in the Haunted House of the Past: or Renovation, Writing and How to Construct a Living Room While Searching for a Home

One need not be a chamber to be haunted
—Emily Dickinson

This is a house, my first since settling in the city, an escape from my parents, my past: a narrow single-storey frame, a shell composed into existence in the 1930s by a man called Savage who saw in it, and its replication countrywide, space for the overlooked and struggling to enjoy a better life; its placement in the crook of a bay, which affords a panorama over fluctuating estuary and wide sky, dramatic in their transient performances, is a location many of my neighbours have paid millions of dollars for, even though the outlook doesn't belong to anyone; four tight rooms, all without doors, which I pass through as if a ghost; a floor that raises me above the solidity of the earth, floating me in space; a roof that masquerades as a tattered crown a functionary might wear to make themselves seem significant while they administer their temporary role; the whole thing held together, like my body, by heart and mind, those pieces of personal architecture I know have function and meaning but ultimately are fleeting tricksters, a moment from collapse.

*

This is also a house. Like smoke, memories of childhood drift through my mind. They seem as chimerical, as unanchored as the place where I now reside. From this distance, measured in decades as much as in kilometres, what endures most in my memory of the house I lived in until I was seventeen, is its skin.

The houses in the long, twisted street where I grew up were replicas of each other. Semi-detached boxes, four rooms upstairs, four rooms downstairs, dropped onto small squares of land. Colloquially, they were named after their builder, George Wimpey, who mass-produced them to house lower-working-class families across the industrial heart of England.

The peculiarity of the house where I lived lay in its placement. There was a dogleg in the street, and the dwelling that was built on the inside of the curve—ours—was different from the rest. The other houses, constructed to front the road, presented one face to the world, whereas our section bordered the curvature of the street and our house presented both front and side. It was, in a term that now seems apt, two-faced.

*

He appears, like recollections of my childhood house, at a time of inactivity.

The trouble is I'm not writing. An author is a tenant always at the mercy of a harsh landlord, their muse. It's a year since my last book was published. The days since have seen me try, but fail, to inhabit other projects, other ideas.

Into this fallow expanse my builder, Scott, fan of Coelho's *The Alchemist* after which he has named his business, arrives.

I need a new living room. I need a place that might possess the sea, mountain and air, that expensive panorama beholden to no one. So Scott starts to eviscerate my house.

*

Did I see, in the irregular position of that dwelling of my childhood, a mirror of my own difference? Before I could create a language—a poetry—to articulate my feelings of disconnection from home and family, did this house, frail in its uniform casing, slight as its glassy windows, replicate my unease?

Perhaps. Perhaps not.

The sanctuary a house can provide, whether it's formed in ill-symmetry or otherwise, is never composed exclusively of its shape or shell. That house, like every house, was substance physical and experiential. Within its higgledy-piggledy carapace it was—and lingers so in my recollection—the sum parts of so many things: everyday experiences and dysfunctions; relationships; emotions; memories. Interlaced, these meant that the house, through no fault of its own, could never provide safety enough to be called home.

*

A morning early in the construction: when alchemist Scott arrives with a worn-out copy of Pablo Neruda's *The Book of Questions* and his tools, I ask him, 'Where's home?'

Lyrically, he speaks of rural life in the Waikato, Elysium-like pastures and parents who love him.

Such a sheltered life, I think, dismissively; what does he know?

'But,' he adds, 'it's also elsewhere.' The Sun Gate at Machu Picchu; las casas in Cartagena where balconies flower with bougainvillea; Torres del Paine, Patagonia: he dwells on highlights of a South American OE. 'And, of course, Casa de Isla Negra, Valparaíso,' he exclaims, pointing to *The Book of Questions*, as if this says it all.

*

A memory of the residence of my youth displaces me: a time when summer's dry air and suffocating heat breach closed window, drawn drapes and locked door. It is 5pm, the room dazzling with light no nylon curtain can subdue. Sound spills in as children outside play chase and hopscotch; the screech, sweet as birdcall, of bike tires tearing along the asphalt; skipping games, girls singing, 'A sailor went to sea, sea, sea/ To see what he could see, see, see …'

They have knocked at our door, these children, to ask if I can play. But Mrs Y is having none of it. All morning and afternoon locked inside while a prolonged downpour refreshed thirsting grass, my endless noise and the sound of my toys clattering against floor and wall have roused Mrs Y into bitter admonishments and beatings.

Now the deluge has stopped and Mr Y has left for his night shift, a tired Tupperware box hiding cheese sandwiches, a weary flask of tea under his arm, another nocturnal crafting of mechanical parts ahead of him. Mrs Y is left alone with me. Without dinner, I'm hustled into bed, told to go to sleep or else, the door closed, so she can sit in my silence with a Vesta 'Boil in the Bag' chow mein meal and restful thoughts.

My seven-year-old body, feverish in its energy, aches to open the window and fly outside …

I imagine the sky, warm and delicately crimson in late summer heat, backdrop to me, my friend Karen and our games of make-believe houses, an old sheet framing our domain, dolls and a chipped toy tea set indulging us in our play …

This longing slips me through closed doors, scurries me into Mr and Mrs Y's bedroom, where I settle before a window open to free the oppressive heat. From there I watch young bodies dance in and out of a skipping rope as it spins in ripe air. There also I hear laughter and ongoing song, 'But all that he could see, see, see/ Was the bottom of the deep blue sea, sea, sea …'

From below, Mrs Y's growl rises like fire. Footsteps scorch the stairs.

I race back to my room, close the door, lie in fake slumber beneath heavy blankets. I feel my eyelids tighten as Mrs Y crashes in. Then there's the barking, 'I SAID, GO TO SLEEP!' My breath quickens as she pulls back covers, presses her left hand into my back, flattens me against the inflexible mattress while her right hand readies the belt. The lashes that rain down empty me, tears and blood spilling in silence until I'm hollow.

*

It takes a week for Scott to turn my laundry and hallway into a husk. That part of the house—facing the deep, the jagged ranges and the wild sky—once a dim washroom and cramped corridor, vanishes, enduring only in the mind. Instead, shadows remain upon the floor, tracing memories of where walls once rested.

Seeing them, I retire to the rear of the house where, because of the renovation, my bedroom idles as a transitory space in which to sleep, eat, read and contemplate. Against the symphony of Scott's saw and hammer, I sit before a ream of blank paper as, ghost-like, a few lines of something materialise.

'Momentarily, I look upon these frail outlines as if upon a vision: not the bones of something about to be born, but a fallen body, a crime scene …'

*

'I SAID, GO TO SLEEP!'

When I wake an hour or so later, these haunting words befriend sharp pain. The light has lowered. The sound of children outside is a dying refrain.

I wince as I creep downstairs, the prickle of my welted skin as keen as the realisation that I'm alone in the house, the back door open. I sneak to the step, spy Mrs Y cutting the sated front lawn with a hand mower, her face impassive as she refuses the glare of neighbouring parents who sweep yards and wash cars.

Karen is one of the few kids still outside. She sees me, waves but doesn't smile. It's enough to meet her eye, to be seen by her and to feel her warmth before I sneak a cup of water, satisfy an unbelievable thirst then make the slow climb, each step accompanied by invisible barbs to my body, back to the room with its drawn curtains and blood-stained bed.

*

While Scott labours, I continue to write. An anechoic chamber in my head banishes the grating of the Mitre saw and punch of the hammer as, half-memory, half-imagination, more lines emerge.

'There's a mystery here, where I hadn't seen one before, an arcane power to deliver evidence from invention …'

*

With its violence, spite, bickering and conditional love, Mr and Mrs Y's dwelling was an imitation—a simulacra—of the abodes constructed for them to reside in when they were young.

The ghosts of those places, houses haunted by inherited abuse, linger in me. They congregate, second selves, in my mind.

I can almost inhabit my parents' memories of them.

Here's the edifice of the house Mrs Y was raised in. Its rooms—naked floors, grey walls, slight furniture—are decorated with a poverty that exceeds the one I knew as a girl. Two bedrooms: five boys in one, four girls in the other; the departed soul of baby Patricia, lost to pneumonia, cowers in the corner. A third room, cramped by a single bed, accommodates the parents. Thirteen-year-old Mrs Y inherits the task of housekeeping this residence the day after she receives a letter informing her parents that she's one of only two students in her year to be offered a place at grammar school. I can almost see the spectre of her father, a callous grin to his maw as he shreds that invitation to academia, that escape from the destitution and constraint of this dwelling. He faces her down as he informs her that she won't be going back to school. Instead he constructs an alternative future in which her remaining youth is demolished by scrubbing floors, polishing cheap furniture, making tired beds, preparing all meals and cleaning all clothes, while her mother, thinned out by working four jobs, slowly succumbs to cancer, and he—that tiny, violent, chain-smoking, yellowed man—whiles away his mornings gardening before squandering his wife's wages in the betting shop on long shots and nags.

And here, separate yet somehow conjoined like a shadow to Mrs Y's childhood residence, is my mind's spectral delineation of the house Mr Y grew up in. A puzzling form. It seems almost normal, this place he shares with his mother, grandmother and grandfather, all of whom idolise him. Not this: the unspoken-of boarding home in Blitz-besieged Britain, circa 1941, to which my unwed grandmother might have been confined during her third trimester. No, not this: the foster home Mr Y might have been sequestered to, and there abandoned. Instead, Mr Y's childhood residence was a welcoming place, built so by his deeply pious grandparents, who refused the mores of a time that determined that an infant born out of wedlock, with no acknowledged father, should be rejected.

The problem with this almost idyllic depiction of Mr Y's childhood house is its invisibility. The address, the site of unconditional love and nurturing grandparents, was never spoken of, so stymied was Mr Y by his illegitimacy. It was my uncle, fathered by another man, who a few years ago let slip the existence of the property. In doing so he unwittingly and belatedly dismantled the last attachments I held to the house Mr Y colluded to compose for me, the one where walls were lined with conditional love, brutality and mutilations; where, even at the end, my suitcase at the door, the final words Mr Y delivered were callous and unimaginative: 'Good riddance to bad rubbish!'

*

Scott measures out the dimensions of my new living room and marks them in chalk upon dusty floorboards. Momentarily, I look upon these frail outlines as if upon a vision: not the bones of something about to be born, but a fallen body, a crime scene.

There's a mystery here, where I hadn't seen one before, an arcane power to deliver evidence from invention, to make inspiration concrete through the slogged-out realisation of something aesthetic, transformative and unique.

My eye returns to the lifeless chalk outline. Such erasure; such power to resurrect.

I slip back to my improvised workspace, where more words appear.

*

There's a point in the writing process that always feels most spectral to me: the mid-point, that liminal space between beginning and uncertain completion.

I'm writing an essay; as more sentences have emerged, I've come to realise this. Yet the cohesion of this extended work, all settled and fully mended, still eludes me, and this makes me feel exposed, unsettled.

I turn to the wise counsel of other writers, particularly poets who are also essayists, like Billy Collins and Mary Oliver.

I read a transcript of a discussion Collins gave about structure. It begins:

I am always aware that I'm writing something which is at least tidy, at least shaped in some way and that is both a box for the poem to live in and it's also the container that will embrace the reader when he or she is reading the poem …

I find room in my thinking for his advice on how to attain shape in the form of a finished piece. He calls on authors to use their eyes as much as their ears when writing. Here, he says, is a means for the work to attain an aesthetic symmetry on the page. In his opinion, lines of verse should provide horizontal support, their consistent lengths composing shape and solidity; stanzas should be arranged in patterns, their lines numerically similar.

I see an architecture in Collins' approach, a way to incorporate his advice into my essay and so give it a presence on the page. Thereafter, as I construct paragraphs into sections, I consider their careful placement in white space and, through adaptation, how their intersections with each other might complete a durable whole.

*

Once more my childhood house emerges like a reclamation, an act of recycling memory and self. Winter, the sky darkening as the evening news, in amplification, awakens me to factory closures and monstrous unemployment rates. Then the prime minister appears offering the phantom of hope: a Right to Buy scheme which, it's determined, will create a nation of homeowners.

It sounds like a disaster to me, millions of people burdened with debt—financial, experiential, memorial, ancestral—that will never be discharged.

But what do I know?

At that moment, burning like a fuse, Mrs Y returns from her minimum-wage shift in a wallpaper shop. Once settled to her seat in front of the fire she launches into a tirade about my failures: dinner not prepared on time or to her liking; my disappointing school grades …

I'm fourteen and, as captives often do, have normalised her abusive, depressive personality and Mr Y's reticent, largely absent disposition; their dysfunctions and the squalid site of their control. My coping strategies include pretending, along with the neighbours, that everything is a commonplace façade;

not answering back; passing out when punched, and hiding bruises and scars.

But tonight, whether through the attrition of living with all this, the decade-long suppression of something I can't name, or simply being a powerless teenager hungry for the possibility of adulthood elsewhere, I charge towards my bedroom at the top of the house where, in utter darkness, I scream. The sound and habitation of my voice surprises me. That such power and pain live inside me, have done so for so long, building, building … this is an occupancy, an agency I didn't know I owned.

Then the door breaks open like a wave. With nothing more than a fist and an energy born of a need to erase anything that might incite the neighbours to break rank and phone the police, Mrs Y knocks me to the floor, falls to her knees and continues the beating. Only when I'm reduced to a whimper no one but Mrs Y can hear does she stop.

The door closes.

Darkness complete.

*

At night when Scott lays down tools and vacates the reconstruction, I scour and cleanse. Always there's a film of grime like old skin (mine or another's?), which must be removed. At sink, floor and window, the growing darkness draws me to remove the stains I see, the stains I don't.

Later, as I lie in bed listening to the patient breathing of the house, I consider what ownership—of this place where I write, this place I'm rebuilding—confers upon me. Does it give me protection from the troubles of my upbringing? Does it sever my link to Mr and Mrs Y? Or—an act of ultimate irony—does it make me a mirror of my parents? Having escaped their tortuous abode, determined never to be like them, have I taken possession of something that to all intents and purposes is a replica of them?

*

The aftermath of any cruelty involving Mrs Y is usually the same: I steal downstairs, bruised and injured, to find her reclining on a rug before a brutal blaze. She seems lost to some kitchen-sink drama flickering on the television. I approach, kneel, kiss her on the cheek and whisper, just loud enough for her to hear, 'sorry'. Mrs Y says nothing, her gaze fixed elsewhere as if I don't exist.

But this time it's as if stains emerge, like contusions, upon the wallpaper of the house. After indulging Mrs Y in her ceremony I retreat to my room where, for the remaining two years of my existence in this dwelling, I eat my meals, complete my homework and spend my sleeping hours imprisoned in a nightmare about an isolated manor, derelict and possessed.

*

Weeks pass as I draft my essay. While Scott measures Gib, cuts holes for new power points, dry-fits sheeting then glues and nails it in place, I turn to Mary Oliver's 'Building the House': 'Whatever a house is to the heart and body of man—refuge, comfort, and luxury—surely it is as much and more to the spirit …'

Her prose poetic, Oliver carries me through the journey of building a writing cabin. Along the way she meditates upon the art of constructing edifice and creative work. In her measured, lyrical writing style the two become fused, mirrors of a desire, a need to craft.

'Building the House' is an extended poem as much as an essay, the author's supple language teasing out double meanings and evoking parallels.

Finishing it, I perceive a way to complete my own essay, to strengthen meaning by furnishing the work with poetry's limberness and lilt.

*

Another disturbance, a sleep-shard of a lost life, plagues me. In this haunting, the walls of an unfamiliar hideaway are lined with glass yet offer me no reflection, so that I'm unable to locate myself or determine where I belong.

This and other traumas become so frequent and fantastical while Scott renovates and I revise multifarious drafts of my essay, that I begin to believe there's purpose here: memory, dream, reconstruction and writing as remnants of some threadbare myth, oddities locked into make-believe space where something insignificant must be spun into something precious.

*

Piqued by remembrance of Mrs Y's father, I spend a morning on ancestry.com.

As Scott stops joints, applies compound and tape to near-finished walls and rough-sands them, I seek to locate the nature of my grandfather's birth. He who thwarted Mrs Y's dreams of learning. He of the ashen, tobacco-addicted form.

Scott is in the midst of his smoko, a cup of strong coffee close by, *The Book of Questions* replaced by Neruda's earlier *Extravagaria*, when my grandfather's birth certificate appears: 'Father—Unknown'.

*

Unknown, but not alone. Those great-grandparents I never met, who doted on their grandson, my father, and bravely rejected their era's abandonment of the illegitimate, preferring to hold their heads high in public even when hearing whispers in the pews and on neighbours' doorsteps. That devout, tender couple. What did they look like? More eludes me: the sounds of their voices, the smell of his newly ironed shirts fresh for Sunday service, or the taste of the roasts she laboured over.

Does writing live somewhere, a sanctuary, in the bodies and minds of my unknowable relatives? Somewhere within this misplaced whakapapa, is there an ancestor who was an author? Was the haven I find in words also found in their erased selves?

*

Eyes sharpened by scanning lines of Neruda's verse (*y así te espero como casa sola/ I wait for you like a lonely house*), Scott knows the pace of building isn't always even. The scope of the renovation, the tearing down of old walls and construction of a new area, requires new flooring. His work is nearing the end when he fetches me to inspect a flaw. It lies in a delivery of fifty bevel-backed radiata pine floorboards. The timber is threaded green with rot, the result of the wood not being covered adequately during a squall.

Justin, the timber supply representative, arrives to investigate the problem.

'I quite like the green, don't you?' he says, somewhat naively.

Scott and I do not. If left, the defect will spread, tainting all and compromising the integrity of the new space. The flawed timbers are replaced with fresh, faultless lengths of *Pinus radiata*, which Scott nails in place then varnishes golden.

*

I'm nearing the end of the essay when my builder knocks on the door to tell me the living room is complete.

There I take in the glistening floor, the walls a warm yellow called 'Bright Spark', the varnished skirting boards, the spectacular outlook—the one that stretches elsewhere. As I walk around the room, inhabit it, its emptiness reverberates with a longing for books, furniture, photographs and life.

There's something about the echo of my footsteps, though, that causes me to feel momentary doubt. I wonder if any building can ever be a shelter to me. If not, then what else is there? Is my body, that site built of blood, bone and brain, that site I liberated from Mr and Mrs Y's house, the only dwelling I possess?

Perhaps. Perhaps not.

As I survey my living room anew, I marvel at the undeniable artistry of Scott's work. The window frames, walls and floor: all hold a symmetry crisp as any song sheet. Like an image-cluster, they magnify the priceless view: settled water, expansive sky and nest of imposing cloud. I see now that this is more than a place to exist. This living room is a refuge where I can commune with word, form, metre, music and story, those elements of my being that—as unattainable as the origins of my need to write—predate the haunted house of my childhood. Yes, this living room is a window to sit at as I gaze into the changeable nature of my surroundings and discover inspiration for new work.

REFERENCES

I am always aware … *Billy Collins: On the road with the Poet Laureate*, Richard B. Woodward (director), 2003 (DVD).

Whatever a house is … 'Building the House', in *Upstream: Selected essays by Mary Oliver* (New York: Penguin, 2016), p. 160.

y así te espero … 'LXV', *100 Love Sonnets by Pablo Neruda* (Austin: University of Texas Press, 1999), p. 138.

Resene Bright Spark, Colour Code: 2BY45.

Joan Fleming

Write First, Apologise Later?

Yet I ride by the margin of that lake …
and have a small boy's notion of doing good
—Robert Creeley, 'The Way'

Once I took a trauma that wasn't mine and made a poem out of it. What's the name for that kind of power? How should I name that taking, and what is its relationship to love?

The tale of the trauma was shared with me in an art gallery during an installation for a show. She was up a ladder when she began to tell me the story, hanging photographs. She had a lot of dark lovely hair that seemed to me dangerously long. I remember wondering if she would put it up, or if it would catch on the work. She wore all black. Her photographs were as large as picture windows, their colours saturated to a degree too lush and too obscene to be called merely beautiful. They featured, always, figures. Never more than two. Also the sweet decaying skirts of crone roses, and mangoes and pomegranates, and farragoes of broken household objects exhumed from the tip. There was a cracked drama in the arrangements, a mystery that felt high and unforgiving.

I was hanging texts underneath the photographs. This was our conversation. My texts were quieter. I wrote down what I sensed going on in the under-stories of the photographs. We lived in different cities: the curator had put us in touch. In the months leading up to the show we spoke on the phone, traded images and pieces of writing. We circled around a central concept for the show—the idea of an Eden—but eventually this became less important to me than how the open texts of her photographs fed into the small, particular language squares that we decided should go underneath.

When I finally saw the photographs in the gallery space, it was both more and less intense than my experience of the A4 printouts I had been carrying round in a paper folder all winter. The printouts were grubby with handling and had become soft and dog-eared with all the thumbing I had done. I had found poems in them. They were, somehow, mine. The photographs for the show were huge, sharp, impenetrable: framed and perilously heavy behind their brand-new glass.

The story she told me, from up on the ladder, was a story about taboo. It was about the unrequited. You may have guessed, it was a story involving two figures. The gallery was like a blank space, a space in process, and during those days of the installation it felt like we could say anything.

Months later when I began to make a poem out of it, I wrote pages of imagined conversation in quick staccato lines. To me, they dazzled. I had thought that, as an artist, she would be moved by mere artistry, that she would be glad to see this storied version of herself dark and glittering on the page. Surely, she would gift me the rights to the poem I had written—but I would hardly need to ask. I would gift the poem to *her*.

The truth is, though, I didn't think much about all this. I didn't think much about her. I only thought of the poem.

It was over a year later when I saw her again. We were both passing through Wellington and met for a drink. I mentioned I'd written a long poem that had something to do with that painful story she'd told me. I lifted my fingers away from the frost of the beer glass, leaving hot prints behind. Her face didn't change. We kept talking, about sex, love, work, the future. Later she wrote to me, asking to read the poem. At that moment I had a feeling I'd done something not quite right. That evening, she rang me up. I remember exactly where I was sitting, even what I was wearing. It was spring in Melbourne. The window was open. I had a bandage on my face, holding my cheek together after a failed attempt at surfing. She began to speak, and her voice had cracks in it.

'You could have made me a dentist,' she said. 'You could have made me a third-grade teacher. You could have made me *anything* but what I am.' She said, 'You described my house, my photographs, my hair. People will recognise me.' She said, 'You put things into this poem I haven't told anyone else.' My heart was beating so fast, I couldn't quite breathe properly. I represent her here as reasonable, and she was. However, I can also count on one hand the times in my life I have been the recipient of such pure rage. By that time, every gesture in the poem was set in stone. The music was fixed. I couldn't change a single word without the whole thing falling apart. I had blended the story she told me with other moments of her pain, and I had done it without permission. I also wove in extravagant fictions alongside the 'truth', and she knew that people would read it all as fact, as biography. It was an intolerable mirror, and a warped one. It was not mine to hold up. It was an excellent poem, and I will never publish it. 'I'm so sorry'—I must have said it ten times or more. But what could it change?

In a later chapter of life I came to understand that not everyone dislikes having their experiences turned into content. When I met up with a man I had once been engaged to, almost a year to the day after I broke it off, he said the thing that upset him the most was that I hadn't written about it.

It was difficult for me to believe that this was the thing that upset him the most. I had left him for another man. I was in love, I was happy in my new relationship. He still had whiplash from how quickly I had ended things. A mere fortnight before I broke it off, I had printed our wedding invitations. The breakup was terrible timing for him, personally and professionally. I had known that, but it hadn't stopped me. After three years together and an engagement, I broke up with him on the phone.

The fact that I hadn't yet written poems about the breakup was proof to him that none of it mattered to me: not the relationship, and not how I'd broken his heart. On the one hand this man is a storyteller who would willingly throw himself under the bus for art. He has a blank courage of self-revelation that startles those who know him. He is willing to publicly broadcast the kinds of raw confessions that would make most people shudder. On the other hand, while he'd gladly be immortalised in art, he *had* asked me to change details of early love poems. He'd asked me to alter little flourishes of diction that, to a close reader, might suggest subterranean insecurities.

That night he had asked that we meet in a neutral hotel lobby bar, as if it were Chicago or New York on some rainy film set rather than Auckland, soft and average, on the cusp of another summer. He arrived in a suit. He never wore a suit. I sensed that he had rehearsed the meeting in his head a hundred times. Whenever he started to say something fierce, something that hadn't been in the script, he bit his tongue. Here was story bleeding into life, not the other way around.

In the year since I'd left him he had been hounding me, through a third party, to allow him to make a podcast: the 'true' story of our failed relationship. He wanted—needed—my consent. I didn't want to give it.

I remembered the first time he pulled out his phone. We were arguing in my bedroom. He was leaning against the bed with his legs sprawled, the bony knees I loved all akimbo. My back was against the door. I was trying to keep my voice low so our debate wouldn't permeate the entire 1970s apartment block with its fissured walls and its nervy flatmates.

'Speak up,' he said, fiddling with his phone. 'This is interesting.'

'What?' I said.

'This—this conversation. I want to record it.' He seemed to be enjoying his anger towards me, and I know I enjoyed the role of professor: calling him out on his blind spots, his hasty utterances, his questionable habits of perspective.

Soon the podcast project was between us like a noisy note-taker. More and more had to be recorded, and the ramping conflict between us was juice, fuel, fire. 'This is great tape,' he said.

Usually I went along with it, but sometimes I felt uncomfortable. 'I don't know,' I'd say. 'I don't think I want this recorded. Can we turn it off for a bit?' He reassured me that if anything ever came of the project we'd make it together. I would always have creative control. We just had to keep the tape rolling.

That night in Auckland, a year after the rupture, he was the one in the suit, though I had dressed carefully too. I wanted to look good but not desirable. This was not about being touched. This was about being heard. However, the thing about heartbreak is it makes it very difficult to hear the other's side of the story. My sense of myself as the villain made me savagely self-protective. His sense of himself as the wronged party gave him the aggressive ambition of the one who is *owed*. I *owed* him this project. Sometimes love can turn into such a dark entitlement. It can twist in on itself, and all the talk in the world can't untangle it.

A work of art is never the whole story. It is not even a story honestly told. In this essay I haven't told the truth about my artist friend. Nothing I've written is how it really was. I'm protecting her. I would even go further and say that every work of art is necessarily a fiction. So why do I mind what my storyteller ex makes? We had started the project together but now he wanted to continue it, from a place of grief and anger and pain. It was no longer a story about a couple trying to understand each other. It was now a story about how I had fallen in love with somebody else. At some point during the storm that preceded the end he stopped telling me when he was recording. Unbeknown to me he had even taped the phone call where I broke it off. I remember thinking at the time that there was something oddly performative about his reaction, but I was too deep inside my guilt and nauseous determination to challenge it. 'I'm so sorry,' I said, over and over again, 'but I can't do this any more.'

We go to poetry, to story, to art, to hear our lives echoed. It matters that story is paying attention to life. This is what art is for. However, it's not just attention that matters to me any more. It's attention and care. If someone is making work about a moment in my life when I was my most foolish, my hastiest and most vulnerable, I want to be convinced that they have thought deeply about how the story might affect me. I didn't think through any of that with my artist friend. Not only that, but her story had nothing to do with me. I had no blood in it, no skin in the game. Nothing to claim. They say that when you write about those you are close to, you should be hardest on yourself. But with her I couldn't even throw myself under the bus. She was a subject, and the knowledge I held was radioactive.

The cord that binds a story and its subject can be so hot it scorches. Somehow, the cord must be loosened or cut so that it is *the story* that can burn, not the person. Sometimes fictionalisation loosens the cord. Sometimes a kind of complication or obfuscation does it—Dickinson's 'tell all the truth but tell it slant'. Sometimes it is trust alone that does it, mere goodwill, a sense that the storyteller has properly grappled.

Because I was not satisfied that my storyteller ex-fiancé had really grappled, and because he could not promise to make 'a good and right story' that I would not be scorched by, and because I had asked to be kept out of it but instead was cornered into signing a legal release form, his third party offered me a sum for the rights to the story. I asked that they quadruple it. In the end it was my inability to bear being hated that forced my hand, and I gave him the consent he wanted. Whatever the story he's telling now, it is both true and false. The lens is skewed. Apologies have floated down the dirty river.

He will tell of his own trauma, and an actress will fill in my side of the conversation. My string of bad behaviours will be reanimated into a sanctioned piece of theatre. Money has a strange and dirty power. It stands in for energy but something is always lost in the translation. If I was to be scorched, I suppose I wanted him and his team to feel a little scorch too. That sum has both bought me time and muddied my moral position, my clean distrust of the project. For the sake of the man I once loved, and still care for, I hope the project will be good. Still, I wish I had never confessed to him all that I did within the bounds of the trust of our relationship, and I wish that he hadn't recorded it.

I wonder if friends and ex-lovers feel that about me? Do they regret their confessions? I think there is some near-pathological openness in me that draws out revelations from those I'm close to. Perhaps I, perhaps all artists, should make a practice of warning the world that we are not good secret-keepers. Story flows in, and it seeps out. Vulnerability and confession can be a high. It strips back the masks, and good art should do that too.

My practice of drawing out secrets started early. I remember being fifteen and looking out the window of my mother's car at a landscape made flat with my boredom. My mother was speaking to me but my mind was tethered to the mobile phone I had begged as a present the previous Christmas. I had a consuming crush on my best friend Jeremy, a kid with a white-blonde gelled quiff and a black Honda Acura with automatic seatbelts. However, he was dating my other best friend, a waifish depressive named Shannon, and because I couldn't admit my feelings to anyone, least of all myself, I had made myself over into the model female friend. Breezy, sexless, endlessly available. The kind of friend to whom you can tell anything. My mother watched me jump at the ringing phone, and watched me bend myself out of my shape to meet the caprice of the voice on the other end. With the sometimes-prescience of the parents of teenagers, she said, once I'd hung up, 'What is it about you, Joanie, that you always need to be needed?' Everything Jeremy told me I shared with Shannon, and I never won. She dropped him, he found someone else, and I stayed on as confessor, receptive to the dirty details as a way of gaining some level of power when I was the undesired one.

Half a lifetime later a brief experiment in open relationships taught me a little more about my capacity for betrayal. I started a relationship with a woman

I liked, and without really thinking about it I told my partner everything. Then one day she asked me, 'What do you tell your partner about us?' and I said, 'Umm … everything.' She was alarmed, angry, even a little sickened. She had known from the beginning that I had a partner, but she hadn't guessed that I would kiss and tell. We talked it through. An open relationship means endlessly talking it through. Finally, we came to an agreement where certain things could be shared and not others. We spent the next few months together but I could feel us falling, and I knew I couldn't do it. I knew I couldn't keep both relationships. She was pale and strong and smart with glossy black hair. She dressed in expensive patchworks. She doubted herself in a way I found difficult because it was familiar. One night when we were trying to cut the cords that were binding us together with a pair of wet scissors, talking and crying together in her bed, she turned and said to me, 'I don't have anyone else to say all these sorts of things to.' It was painful to me that she wasn't the first person I would call in a moment of crisis. She wasn't even my primary love. I had the lion's share of the power; it didn't oscillate back and forth the way it should in a healthy relationship. And maybe that's the thing about someone you're close to making a work about your unshielded self: it's not like sharing a story in a conversation, where the balance of power is fluid. In a piece of writing, the story is set. The writer has the last word, the power of representation. Once we parted ways I tried to be less of a capricious arsehole. I don't know how well I managed it. I burned her in life, and I have tried not to make anything that would burn her in writing.

Like 'consensual non-monogamy', perhaps what I'm talking about in this essay is a peculiarly millennial thing. We want to write all the grit and burn of love and its failures, yet we want to do it ethically, cleanly, without arseholery and without betrayal. I have a brilliant novelist friend who seems to care slightly less about showing her claws. She said to me once that anything which can't be honestly discussed between two people is fair game to write about. At the time I think I interpreted this as the big family secrets that can't be broached. It's the savage thing you think but never say aloud. It's your mother's unacknowledged addictions. It's the massive blind spot you know your brother won't see. There is a part of me that admires those who can be mercenary in their writing. Those who write first and apologise later. Those who have the courage to be cruel.

'Fair game' is a hunting metaphor. It evokes targets, trophies, display and consumption. Where is love in this equation? Should we use the legal metaphor of 'fair use' instead? There are no laws here but I have tried to find my own code. When you are listening so closely to someone that you become a hold for their pain, perhaps there is no time to understand your own reactions. Is *this* the thing that can be written about? Surely some writing should call people out, even those you love. Some writing should be the articulation of how you call yourself out. I would like to say that I have found a way of making art from life that falls just a crucial few beats shy of betrayal, or at least that I have sufficiently thickened my skin to deal with any consequences. But I don't know. I keep eating the apple and risking the sins of knowledge. Love and writing and their close relationships are too multiple to believe oneself prepared for. Sorry is a hinge, and the door keeps swinging.

The Art and Adventure of Subsistence

1.

I came from a neighbourhood where the violence was as underground as the potatoes in the vegetable gardens behind our houses. We didn't speak of it to our friends. We didn't display it in public. But what do I know about how it was for others? I like how Joy Cowley writes in her memoir, *Navigation*, of the weary policeman who would arrive on his bike when her parents were fighting. I like how she looks back with compassion, rather than shame.

When my own mother called the police on my father, the cop car pulled up in our drive and neighbours clustered on the footpath.

'I should have hit her years ago,' my father told the policeman, who seemed to concur with him, my mother told me later. It was the 1960s.

I wonder how much frustration boiled over into violence, then: my father rubbed narrow into a life he didn't want, pulled out of school and made to work in his father's plaster factory; my mother forbidden to play the piano when what she wanted was to write songs. And secretly did, winning Studio One, a national song-writing competition, under a fake man's name. She didn't think a judge would let a woman win.

How does this need, and drive, for meaningful work affect us? I think of that childhood cacophony of despair and mismatchedness, the underground rivers of desire and the 'weary policeman'.

In a quest to understand the deep needs of people, Chilean economist Manfred Max-Neef and his colleagues at the Center for Development Alternatives in Santiago developed a detailed set of nine authentic human needs, which he proposed are common to all, regardless of nationality, education or social or financial status. Emma Kidd, in her book *First Steps to Seeing*, discusses Max-Neef's work and lists these needs:

Subsistence Protection Affection
Understanding Participation Creation
Idleness Identity Freedom

'[I]t is not just an inability to meet our need for subsistence that leads to poverty,' Max-Neef's team asserted, 'but that if any need is left unmet, "poverty" is created.'

2.

When I teach writing on a week-long course, I allow a day for the study of nature—a slow, sense-filled study, some of it in silence, to give students an opportunity to change the way in which they look at the world. I first began sending students into the garden ten years ago. They were to isolate their senses and spend time really seeing, smelling, touching, listening. They ran their hands over bark, leaves, ferns; inhaled tree trunk, thistle flower, grass blade; listened to birdsong and wind (and traffic) and watched light shine on the ripple of green.

Emma Kidd studied the art of seeing with scientist Henri Bortoft (a co-worker at one time with Max-Neef). Bortoft, a British lecturer and writer on the philosophy of science, was a scholar of the work of eighteenth-century philosopher and scientist Johann Wolfgang von Goethe. From the study of Bortoft and Goethe's work, I deepened the way classes spent time with nature. Students studied a plant in a process Goethe called 'exact sense perception', until the wonder of design and uniqueness revealed itself. Goethe believed if we look respectfully and clearly at the phenomena around us—that is, at all that makes up our living, natural world—then we have the chance to understand that we are but one part of an interconnected society. This way of perceiving would lead to social transformation, he hoped, and would possibly protect our natural world and humankind from extinction.

3.

In a small garden at Rosemont College, where I teach in summer, you walk down stone steps past a stone statue of a child angel under a maple tree to a grassy opening and planted borders, where wild raspberries thrive along with milkweed, comfrey and ivy among the hostas, coprosmas and ferns. How easily the world gives new life; how plants, given sun and soil, will fill a place with their exuberance: the low-growing, spreading plant with its leaves splayed in rosettes, the ivy clambering over the top, the comfrey's coarse leaves softly bending, and the thistle, that wild imposter with its tufted purple flowers, surging through them. The thistle's perfume adds to that of the wild raspberry. Their sweetness is for the bees, their minerals for the soil. In that garden plants find a way to live abundantly together and to contribute. How vulnerable we are if we do not have even the basics of connection.

The oak's trunk is so old and cracked that an ivy weaves through its apertures. I press my nose to an insect hole in the worn bark, my skin against the tree's rough skin, while birds cheep and chime. And there it is, a smell as far off as the days when I polished my mother's oak dresser with a cloth: the sweet oil fragrance of tree.

4.

My mother told me it is always good to have two strings to your bow.

'I'm a teacher,' she said, 'and a pianist.' And a songwriter, though that wasn't an earner. When I told her I'd earned eleven dollars in royalties from APRA for a song, she said that was more than she'd ever earned on account of her winning song being stolen and released overseas.

The second string to my writing/teaching bow came about from research for a young adult novel. *Shreve's Promise* featured a teenage girl and a woman in her eighties. To gain a broader view of older people, I joined Age Concern as a volunteer visitor and completed a one-year certificate in care of the elderly. That job has helped me out over the years, when, as now, I live hours from a city, writing income is sporadic and teaching workshops far flung.

In my new life in Central Otago I applied for a job as a nurse aide in the rural hospital. There were so many applicants that five of us were given one permanent day each. To supplement my income I received a top-up from the jobseeker benefit from Work and Income NZ (WINZ). When I returned from a two-week job teaching writing in America and still couldn't increase my hours at the hospital, I found my benefit had been cancelled. I applied to have it reinstated.

'You'll have to come in for a video appointment,' I was told. The next week I drove forty-five minutes to Alexandra, walked in past the black-clad security guards to a small room where there was one other applicant, a young man who had been released from jail the day before. We sat together and watched a video that encouraged us not to take drugs, especially in the workplace, and told us of the benefits of making an effort to be employed.

'How are you getting on?' I asked him, when it finished. 'Have you got somewhere to stay?' He was tall, lean, dark-haired like my own sons.

'I'm at the campground. They put me up in a cabin.'

'Are you warm enough? Do you have enough blankets?'

'I have a sleeping bag, but it's cold.'

'You can go to the hospice shop, or the Salvation Army shop in town,' I told him. 'They have lots of cheap duvets.'

'Through the eyes of [Max-Neef's] Human Scale Development,' Emma Kidd writes,

> most of the social 'problems' we identify today, such as depression, alcoholism, eating disorders, unemployment, racial conflicts and dissatisfied youths, can be seen as pathologies. This means that, if we look carefully, each 'problem' can be traced back to an array of fundamental human needs which are not being met.

A woman came into the room to tell us we didn't qualify for any support today but must come back in a week and fill in forms.

A week later I again made the forty-five-minute trip to the office, walked in past the security guards, took the clipboard and forms I was handed and sat down next to a young man who turned out to be my friend from the week before.

'How are you doing?' I asked him. 'Did you manage to get a duvet?'

'The shop people were good to me. They gave me two duvets. They even gave me a radio.'

'That's great.'

'I never want to go back to prison again,' he said.

5.

It's quarter to seven in the morning and I'm making toast for two corridors of people. They lie in their beds in their darkened rooms, the sun about to rise over the Kakanuis. Their weary eyes are shut and the night is behind us all – the bells ringing for the toilet and the commode, for pain relief and a cup of tea and for the toilet again, which means they can't sleep. The wake up calls are done for the midnight pills, the damp beds changed, the laundry folded, the dark corridors mopped, the handrails dusted, the toilets scrubbed and bathrooms cleaned. Now the radio is on, tuned to the local station – The Burn. Toast pops and I know what each person wants: marmalade or jam or Marmite, just butter or no butter.

There's something about the bright clattery kitchen with the tinny radio playing the Bee Gees and the smell of warm bread, about knowing what each tray needs, that as I turn to push down the lever on the toaster, bopping to the music, I realise with some surprise that this ease and sureness I feel in my work, in making breakfast for those who can no longer make breakfast, is joyous. How to describe it? It's not the job I wanted or yearned for; it does not compensate me well for the long nights with the alone, the dying, those who want to die, those who are afraid to die, those who will live a lot longer than they imagined or care to, and those who have stoically settled to life here, who will turn to me with a smile when I wake them for their porridge.

What is this happiness? It's brief, it lasts no longer than it takes to turn it over in my mind, than it takes to name it, this cocoon of music and light and simple tasks. A job that is needed.

The other aide walks in, ready for the morning shift. 'Oh good, it's you,' she says. It could easily have been another, who would rightly think the opposite. But we grin at each other and finish off the trays. I hold the door while she pushes the breakfast trolley through and up the long corridor, the teapot lids rattling over the bumps.

6.

I'm writing an application for a writing residency when the phone rings. It's my case worker at WINZ.

'Something needs to be done about you,' she says. 'You can't just shift here and sit on a benefit.'

I remind her that I have a permanent job one day a week at the hospital, and other shifts and teaching jobs as they arise. 'And right now, as it happens, I'm in the middle of a long application for a fellowship. It's about six hours' work to get one in.'

'You're always applying for something and it comes to nothing,' she says. 'You need to accept your writing is a hobby, because you don't make any money. We don't pay you to write.'

'And that is true,' I wrote to the manager at WINZ in Alexandra. 'WINZ pays me to survive until I am able to earn enough income by other means, with enough money to help pay for food and the mortgage, for which I am deeply grateful. The fact that I work at my writing at the same time as all the other jobs I do, paid and unpaid, and while looking for other employment, is a bonus. Having someone tell you that what you do comes to nothing is distressing.'

It was hard to be in this world and not desired, my mother told me. Not desired by her mother, her first husband, even her children sometimes, especially when we were teenagers.

'I'm fat, and a crabby old woman at times,' she said. 'But I always told you that you could do anything, and I believe it is still possible. I gave up on my art. I had too many hard things. My weight. I didn't have a voice for my music, and my song was stolen. One more thing taken from me. If I'd made it as a songwriter, where would I be now? Not in this old people's home.'

'You were a beautiful songwriter, and a talented pianist,' I tell her.

'Not now,' she says. 'I forget the music now. But I was.'

'Mum, just burn your bridges,' my oldest daughter said. 'You're trapping yourself by having an income from WINZ. Just stop it. Work will flow towards you.'

'Why did you even come to this district?' my case manager said at the next meeting. 'You should go back.'

Because my marriage ended, and my home was gone … Because I had to go somewhere … Because I wanted to be near my grandchildren … And back to where?

'The trouble with you,' she said, 'is you're too bright.'

After my appointment I walked out past the security guards, climbed into my car and cried.

I rang WINZ and asked to cancel my jobseeker benefit. 'I'm not walking through those doors one more time,' I said.

'You don't earn enough to go off the benefit,' the woman on the end of the phone said. 'You only have work one day a week. You won't get by.'

'No, but I …'

I tried again the following week. 'I'd like to cancel my jobseeker benefit.' This time I did it.

In his book *Theory of Prose* Viktor Shklovsky wrote that art exists that one may recover the sensation of life. It exists to make one feel things, to make the stone stony.

David Shields wrote in *Reality Hunger*: 'There is something heroic in the essayist's gesture of striking out towards the unknown, not only without a map but without certainty that there is anything worthy to be found.'

7.

Due to staff illness I now have three shifts a week. On the morning shift after the breakfast run and the showers and dressing, cleaning begins. I enter the room of a man felled by illness in the night. His wife sits in the chair beside him. I greet them both and proceed to clean the basin and taps, first with a wet ribbed cloth, then polishing with a dry cloth until the enamel and taps shine.

'Everything has changed,' the man on the bed says. I turn with my cleaning cloths, the bag of rubbish.

'I know,' I say.

Later I bring them both a cup of tea and hold the cup to his lips. I lay his head back on the pillow.

'Everything has changed,' he says again. 'When you walked in the door, all my pain left.'

'It's true,' his wife says. 'He told me.'

'Oh,' I say, remembering. 'In my car, before I came into work, I said a prayer asking that all patients would be free of pain.'

Hopes, intentions, the energy you put out into the world, all mean something. I walked into a room to clean the basin, and the prayer I'd uttered came in the door after me, rolling up its sleeves. I'd forgotten the prayer. All I was thinking about was my cloths and hot water, but there it was anyway.

What does that mean for the thoughts, intentions, wishes we set loose in the world? Perhaps to be conscious of asking. Perhaps to trust in what we receive.

8.

Sometimes our whole world is comprised of meeting subsistence—as if subsistence is our main reason for living and not the springboard into joy and connection. Into understanding and participation. If what we do is not examined with a close eye, it becomes the dark well we draw on unintentionally; becomes the hard hand, the tears in cars, becomes the prison walls.

That desire to endure. Sometimes we need to unpick that and ask why, and why, and then how? Even if we don't know what our needs are, we know what they are not: exhaustion, frustration, sadness, despair. It is to sing we were made, not to endure.

9.

The time came to leave my hospital job. To trust that giving up night shifts, early morning shifts and the desirability of the fortnightly pay would open the time for writing. For idleness and artistry. To trust that I could rent out my room, teach enough workshops and sell enough stories to keep paying for my shelter. An unknown future. The Romantic poet John Keats described the ability to be in a state of unknowingness as negative capability. He thought it urgent for the poet's craft. Negative capability—capable of living with '*uncertainties, Mystery, doubts*'.

And then there is that wonderful essayist Edward Abbey, who, in the introduction to *The Best of Edward Abbey*, wrote: 'Each of my books … has been met with a sublime, monumental, crashing silence.'

What did I want to say? Not how hard this is, but how necessary.

What matters is to take responsibility for the source of joy. Not joy bestowed, but joy up-willed, like a thistle from the damp of earth. The sap constructing its own container. The white down lifting the seeds to air.

REFERENCES

Subsistence Protection Affection … Emma Kidd, *First Steps to Seeing* (Edinburgh: Floris Books, 2015), p. 145.

[I]t is not just an inability … Ibid., p. 150.

Through the eyes … Ibid., p. 151.

There is something heroic … David Shields, *Reality Hunger: A manifesto* (London: Hamish Hamilton, Penguin, 2010), p. 136.

uncertainties, Mystery, doubts … Stephen Hebron, 'John Keats and "negative capability"': www.bl.uk/romantics-and-victorians/articles/john-keats-and-negative-capability

Each of my books … has been met … Edward Abbey, *The Best of Edward Abbey* (New York: Sierra Club Books, 1984), p. xi.

Ingrid Horrocks

Ordinary Animals

In Wellington the last week of the school holidays was hot—really hot. Tuesday broke records. Australia was also hot. Australia was having the hottest summer on record again, with back-to-back heatwaves and temperatures in the high 40s. There were uncontrollable fires, mass fish deaths, health warnings about going outside, and fruit cooking on trees. Much of North America was in the grip of a polar vortex that brought life-threatening windchill. A friend emailed me from a plane grounded by snowstorms.

But things were fine here in Wellington, where summer being a bit warmer is a good thing. There was something uncanny about it. When we exchanged pleasantries with friends—Great summer!—it was often with a provisional laugh, as though we thought this couldn't last but didn't really believe that it wouldn't.

The world is burning. And yet, here we are in it.

*

On the most blistering day Tim texted me at work mid-afternoon, and an hour later I was on my bike. It was even hotter out of the office, where I'd spent the day with emails and online video meetings. There was a soupy thickness to the air.

I took the still vigorously opposed cycleway to the South Coast. It was pure pleasure to careen down the road by bike, warm air pulsing past, hills rising on either side, right through to the sea road and along to where we swim at Princess Bay on the Taputeranga Marine Reserve.

I spotted Tim and the kids among crowds of children and adults—the parents released from work and glad of this gasp of sea air. The holiday extended.

'It's like a European beach today,' Tim said, offering me a towel to stand on while I changed.

It was. It felt like the Mediterranean—warm and still with groups of people standing around waist-deep in the sea, talking. We were more used to watching a few kids running in and out of the cold water screaming.

Our daughters waved to us from the rocks, then pulled their goggles on and plunged into the water, swimming out to what they'd been calling Jacuzzi Island, a rock with a warm dish of a pool. Not that they really knew what a jacuzzi was. We watched a whole group of kids pile into the pool like small animals wallowing in the heat.

There had been rumours all month of a pod of dolphins off the coast, and from time to time we gazed out to sea, searching the still water beyond. I lay back and felt the heat prickling down the length of my skin; I was content. This is happiness, I thought. And also, this is home.

We got in the water twice and stayed until evening. Finally, we loaded my bike on the back of the car and drove over the steep hill towards our house. We kept having to slow right down to edge past carloads of people on their way to the water. Windows down, tanned arms, sunglasses and flowery shirts. In New Zealand swimming is *what people do*. As Annette Lees writes in *Swim*, it's like sleeping or eating. On that day it felt as though the sea was all any human being could ever want or need.

*

We didn't get to the beach for the rest of the week. On Saturday we had a friend of our daughters' around who had an injury and so couldn't swim. I got grumpy, as I do when I can't get out. The kids couldn't decide what to do. I went to the garden to dig up some agapanthus, and when I came back in, my hands sticky with clinging residue, the kids were still niggling at each other.

Tim eventually came inside to help our daughter Natasha get going on some sewing project, and we were up and running again—until the sewing machine jammed.

I texted the parents, some of my best friends, asking where they were. It was a short-tempered message.

We pulled up YouTube videos on bobbin threading, and I pushed my way into the sewing seat while Tim held up his phone and the girls continued scrapping in the background.

'I'll do it,' I said. 'Clockwise. Like that. Hold the phone closer.'

It still didn't work. The listless hot children left us, and the mess they'd made, and headed out to climb the pūriri tree.

In the quiet I looked up across our living space. It was cluttered with the leftover detritus of a Harry Potter dormitory and a cascade of Lego among half-built and abandoned buildings, and the floor around our feet was awash with scraps of dyed material. We were swamped, our world channelled into this small dysfunctional machine on which all our (exhausted, furious) attention was focused. I was gripped by a sense of panic, ready to shout at just about anyone.

*

Only after five did we manage to get organised to go to the beach. Tim stayed to keep working on the sewing machine and cook dinner. I imagine he needed a break from me. I did.

As the girls and I tipped the hill before the descent, we could feel the wind shaking the car. Our house was sheltered and we hadn't registered the southerly whipping in off the sea. Today Princess Bay looked like what it was—a thin line of sand and rock between steep hillsides and the ocean. A place deserving of a different name.

The carpark was almost empty. There was no one in the water and just a few buffeted people on a beach. One group had a wind shelter. The water looked choppy and uninviting.

But I found I was glad. The rugged beach had returned. I'd been reading David Wallace-Wells' *The Uninhabitable Earth* and kept thinking about his observation that water is not a 'beachside attraction for land animals'; it makes up 70 percent of the Earth's surface, our Earth's predominant environment. The ocean was the subject, the main character here; we were but transitory figures dipping in. We'd been returned to our true size.

The water was cold. I needed a few countdowns from the girls, and I missed the first two in my reluctance to leap. But then I dived through the skein of a low wave and stayed under long enough for the water to take and float my body, and there was that familiar wash of life, of pleasure, the tingle of skin, the rush of blood to organs as my body literally pumped itself alive.

I left the girls in the shallows and went further out, doing my clumsy version of breaststroke through the breakers. I kept going until I was really in among the waves with no view of the hills, just blue-green water. The beach itself washed in and out of sight. I let myself drop under, forcing my eyes open against the salt, the churned-up water. I was alone.

The sea could have me, I thought. There was a definite tug, a pull towards the ocean and away.

When I came up for breath the girls were calling and gesturing.

'Too far, Mum!' Natasha shouted.

As a wave passed I saw her standing, planted firmly in the water in her new spotty cheetah swimsuit, beckoning me in.

'Mama!'

Her voice was insistent, almost strict; I felt its throatiness across the waves.

As I began to push in I felt a hint of fear at the pull of the wave going out. I made it in some of the way on the incoming waves, which would pull at me as they sucked back. But gently. It was just the insinuation of a tug from the depths. And all that water between us.

Then I was back and could stand again.

Lena and Natasha joined me as I headed in to shore. They were like fish, like eels, like seals, diving and slipping through the water, brushing their slick bodies against mine. I would have liked to carry them on my back, as whales do.

'It's wonderful,' Natasha said, her teeth chattering. Shivering is good; it helps your body keep itself warm.

*

The next day was Sunday, the last day of the school holidays. We walked through the town belt, along the spines of the hills, past the girls' school, to the coast. We went up through the eucalypts with their naked grey trunks and past blackberry bushes where the girls stretched their arms to get the last plump berries missed by dog-walkers. I tried to remember lines from a poem I teach by Galway Kinnell about the 'the silent, startled, icy, black language/of blackberry-eating' at the end of summer.

From the peak we could see the Kaikōura Ranges to the southwest across the strait and the bare sculpted hills to the west. At the new water reservoir we stood among plantings of flax and grasses in reds and browns and greens.

'Mum,' Natasha said, taking my hand, 'how high will the sea be in fifty years?'

I felt her exact height beside me. She was the right height for me to stand

and hold her hand, as if to say—you're nine, don't worry, the adults have got this one. There's an order to these things.

Except, of course, I didn't say that. I looked where she was looking, down over the Rongotai isthmus with its houses, schools and airport, all built on land raised not so long ago by geological upheaval, decisively pushed up from the sea in the earthquake of 1855. This is the place where the taniwha Whātaitai tried to force its way out of the harbour to the ocean.

Tim and I glanced at each other.

'I don't know, love,' I said. 'Higher.'

After the 2016 Kaikōura earthquake, whenever I walked the girls to school I would look out and imagine how a tsunami could roll in across the isthmus, right through to the harbour.

But I know it's a different kind of fear, this imagining of a sudden rush of water. I've been reading climate change fiction lately, and I hate it when they do this—going for the sudden excitement of the apocalypse, of flooding water like in *The Day After*—rather than evoking the slow, complicated process it seems more likely to be. Or imagining what we could do to stop it or survive it. 'Apocalypse comes swiftly and charismatically … climate change occurs discreetly and incrementally, and as such, it presents the literary imagination with a series of difficulties: how to dramatise aggregating detail, how to plot slow change.' I'd read Robert Macfarlane quoted on this in several online pieces recently. His essay, written back in 2005, was called 'The Burning Question'. On New Year's Eve of 2019, as we watched news of fire sweeping across Australia, it seemed change might, in fact, be swifter than we'd thought.

But perhaps thinking about earthquakes and tidal waves really was like thinking about climate change. After the Kaikōura earthquake it was easier to imagine an altered Earth, the shifting of the ground on which we stood. Now we knew how the very hills could shudder, how the beds in which we woke could sway like small boats. I'd stood in the doorway in the dark with one daughter I'd managed to pull from her bed, shouting at the other to stay where she was in her rocking bunk. Later, the thing she would remember about the night was that I grabbed her sister but not her.

'Mum?' Natasha was pulling at my hand.

We were moving on, Natasha darting to catch up with the others. But now I was preoccupied by thoughts of how my daughters imagine.

*

The scale is impossible to understand, even as an adult. The stretch of a human life has been put in a new relation to the changes of the Earth, which we'd imagined previously as incomprehensibly slow. I'd read writers' meditations on deep time too, including Macfarlane writing on the vastness of Earth time as compared to the human instant; when I saw the Grand Canyon it felt like the Earth's cross-cut diagram, an evocation of the geological sublime. Macfarlane also writes of the 'ethical lotus-eating' comfort this intimation can seem to offer, when instead it should be a 'radical perspective, provoking us to action not apathy', making the Earth eerily alive. He writes of a 'web of gift, inheritance and legacy'. I think of kaitiakitanga, of which I still have so little understanding.

But then, as Wallace-Wells writes, 'the perspective changes when history accelerates'. Instead, there is something like 'a feeling of history happening all at once': 'You will find it already by watching footage of an iceberg collapsing into the sea.' Or by your children asking not about the past but about the future of their adulthood. Timothy Morton calls climate change a 'hyper-object', a conceptual fact too large and complex to comprehend. Wallace-Wells writes that 'the facts are hysterical'. The facts are exponential. In 2020 we would all begin truly to learn what 'exponential' meant.

It was scorching hot on the hilltops we were walking now, the harbour below to the north, to the south the whole blue-green ocean.

I'd read in my newsfeed that morning about the Waiwhetū Aquifer, the reserve beneath the harbour that supplies 40 percent of Wellington's water supply. I'm not sure I'd known it existed or even thought about where our drinking water comes from. That cross-cut diagram, which I still only half understood, deposited layers of greywacke, gravel, marine beds, salt- and freshwater beneath my shallow imaginings of the harbour.

I caught up with the others and tried to tell Tim about the undersea vents I had read about, but everyone was singing on, literally.

The aquifer releases pressure via the vents through the hard clay of the harbour bottom. Beneath, the gravels of the aquifer itself were laid down by the Hutt River, Te Awa Kairangi, nearly half a million years ago. But the vents. If the aquifer is drawn on too heavily, as it regularly comes close to being in dry summers, or if sea levels rise, then the vents will be in danger of allowing seawater *into* the aquifer. In 2018 the equivalent of 9300 Olympic swimming pools were sucked out, and demand is predicted to rise by 60 percent by the end of the century. By then, if we continue with our business-as-usual approach, global sea levels are predicted to have risen by as much as a metre. Some studies suggest much, much more. It was unclear what the plan was. My throat was dry.

We were still on the exposed path and my actual children, rather than imagined future ones, were pulling at my attention.

Lena was pink in the heat. 'But you promised it would be shady!'

Always, the promise. Kids remember these things.

Tim laughed. 'It will be, look, just down there.'

Her shoulders drooped; she was an early expert at parental culpability for how things turned out. In time, there would be plenty of ammunition for it.

But Tim was laughing at her; he's better at making both girls laugh their way out of things than I am. And at making me laugh too, pulling me out of my tendency to cataclysmic thinking. Knowledge inhabits him differently.

There is certainly something boring about the incessant predictions of doom. Something off-putting, too, about the excitement that I sensed some commentators felt in terrifying us all with visions of 'cascading violence, waterfalls and avalanches of devastation, the planet pummelled again and again'—a projected spectacle in which everything is a drama of different forces doing battle, the sea a killer. It doesn't help much with the question of what to do.

'You're having such a good chance to complain,' Tim said to Lena now, and she almost laughed.

Her shirt was gloriously stained with blackberry juice. I could have licked her then—and Tim too.

*

I'd had conversations recently with younger colleagues at work about whether they should have children. 'Fuck climate change,' I said at the end of the last one, unable to imagine we were really there. But there was a genuine ache to it when coming from a woman in her mid-thirties.

I would keep thinking about these conversations over the coming months, in particular when I went with my daughters and parents to the first of the children's School Strike 4 Climate marches. We walked beside girls in blue school uniforms with neat ponytails and masks covering their mouths. Written across the masks were the words 'Exit Generation'. Another girl stumbled along in a box up to her waist painted in the colours of the ocean, emblazoned in black lettering: 'This is what two feet sea rise looks like.' Behind us two gangly boys sounded out chants in deep voices, new instruments even they seemed surprised to hear resonating from their chests. 'What do we want? Climate justice!' But it was 'Two, four, six, eight, save the world, it's not too late!' sung by my daughters and thousands of other young people that really got me.

I wanted to say to them, you're the best thing that's happened for a long time. I remembered being at similar marches when I was the age my children are now. I stood beside my own mother and father in the crowd outside Parliament and cried as a sixteen-year-old girl gave a speech. And I wondered what I'd done in between—and what I hadn't. My parents' environmentalism had seemed both admirable and optional.

What are the effects of inhabiting this sense of doom? In myself I notice a dissonance in my own long-term thinking, so that discussions of ten-year plans at work can feel like make-believe games. How did those young people feel when released from the embrace of a march, when they were alone in the vast mental space of their bed at night, trying to imagine careers and sex and families and a world of unknowable futures?

The possibilities for climate grief, environmental depression and eco-anxiety felt all too real, too pressing, too present. Perhaps it was closer to climate paralysis.

Instead, I wanted to add volume to those newly resonant voices.

*

We were on the bus home from the School Strike 4 Climate when news of the Christchurch mosque shootings began to pulse in on the phones everyone was suddenly holding. It was a spray of hatred, puncturing the lungful of hope the march had gathered.

I'm still unsure whether I shielded my own children too much, or not enough, from the full understanding of what happened, and from all the grief and conversation that followed about what it could mean. How, on that afternoon of 15 March 2019, a white supremacist man walked into places of worship in Christchurch and shot and killed fifty-one Muslim men, women and children and injured forty-nine.

Among so many other things, it was a violent reminder that we were not all in this together. People carry different losses and different hatreds. At times in recent years I've felt that Princess Bay and the hinterland valley behind it in which we live are too safe, too homely, too sequestered. The mosque shootings shook that certainty, at least for a time, altering my sense of how quickly things can change. I wasn't sure anyone would ever again be able to pretend that here in Aotearoa New Zealand people are safe, as if we are removed and insulated from the world in some special way. A myriad of underheard voices came forward in grief and rage to try to explain how, given this country's history of colonialism and racism, this shouldn't have been new knowledge. The shooting was only a shock to some of us.

It became impossible to look at these hillside gullies, seas and sweeping skies and not see the need for an adjustment in vision. As though the scenery didn't fit together any more. For a fraction of time the majority seemed to be listening to those who were trying to explain. The majority where, in this sense at least, I lived. For that moment, we were all shaken.

Some people, of course, had been shot and killed. Others lost mothers, fathers, daughters, sons.

Our children will carry this. I hope they can understand it better than we try to.

I thought again of those teenagers from every school in the city, home from their hopeful march, videos streaming out at them from their phones.

*

We were starting to walk down off the hilltops. The sense of dread receded again into the background.

We entered temporary shade as we dropped down further, a coolness smelling of earth and fallen leaves. Lena and Natasha ran ahead singing a song about a school of killifish: 'Who are the teachers here, and which ones are the kids?'

We followed them down through the ngaio and scrappy mānuka, the path criss-crossing an empty streambed before spilling us onto the tinder-dry grass by the playground.

Finally, we reached the crashing water. It was rising in enormous waves this time, great steady blue walls of it. We crossed the road at the giant bronze propeller, a relic from a decommissioned naval vessel sunk in 2005 somewhere out there for divers to explore, a tiny premonition of a drowned world. The propeller's gorgeous petal-shaped blades, even in their hefty stillness, give the impression of motion. I tried not to think about the fact the ocean now has dead zones the size of Europe; the sea itself is suffocating, as well as rising to pull the land back in.

At Houghton Bay, to which the girls' school is working hard to restore its Māori name, Haewai, signs warn against swimming: 'Strong undertow'. There was a great rolling surf, the sets huge, regular and steady, breaking white and alive with surfers. The waves curled in and we could see a figure inside one, her white tail plume disappearing and reappearing as she came out on top. Two teenage boys, their bodies slick and dark in wetsuits, tumbled onto the beach then plunged back into the sea.

The four of us leapt across small chasms of churned-up water between rocks to reach Princess Bay. It was almost a party scene there, as many people as on Tuesday, but today the beach was shrunken as the tide pulled up. The waves were huge in a way we weren't used to. Usually a precise curve of rock protected us but this time a storm was close—though not yet close enough to feel, still happening under a blue sky.

We found a group of friends and set up towels behind the driftwood. Lena and Natasha went straight for the water but even they paused at its edge. When Tim and I joined them the girls let themselves be knocked over in the shallows. In moments like this they seemed to have no fear. Each wave drained back with a roaring rattle of stones being turned, pulled, rearranged. I stood until a wave pulled me in too, tumbling me down, my breath momentarily knocked from my chest.

Back on the beach, when an especially big wave came in we grappled for our stuff to keep it dry and there was a collective gasp and cheer. As the tide rose further, the usual polite gaps between towel towns was further compressed. We sat close to former strangers on the shrinking beach, our heads bare to the sky.

I'd been reading about monuments, cities and whole cultures that, like sunken ships, will likely be transformed into underwater relics by the end of this century. Lower Manhattan, Venice, Kiribati, Tokelau. Much of the infrastructure of the internet could be gone in decades. In a century: *any beach we've ever visited.*

How to imagine the scale of a human life against the scale of water? How to balance the value of each? How to inhabit the simultaneity of haunting dread and everyday joy? From this space of persistent oscillation, might we come to intimate the urgency for collective action and collective care?

Another body of water rushed towards us and we all laughed in wonder at the sea, even as it rolled in. The beach was a crowded grandstand. It was audience-participation theatre in which we would all be called upon. The kids joined us for handfuls of chips and watermelon, salt and juice. They pushed in close, and there was something stunning about the way we were all out there together, watching the waters rise.

REFERENCES

it's like sleeping or eating … Annette Lees, *Swim: A year of swimming outdoors in New Zealand* (Nelson: Potton & Burton, 2018), p. 7.

water is not a 'beachside attraction' … David Wallace-Wells, *The Uninhabitable Earth: A story of the future* (Auckland: Penguin, 2019), p. 94.

the silent, startled, icy, black language … Galway Kinnell, 'Blackberry Eating', in *Perrine's Sound and Sense: An introduction to poetry*, Thomas R. Arp and Greg Johnson (eds), San Diego: Harcourt College Publishers, 2001 (10th edn.), pp. 227–28.

Apocalypse comes swiftly and charismatically … Robert Macfarlane, 'The Burning Question', *The Guardian*, 24 September 2005: www.theguardian.com/books/2005/sep/24/featuresreviews.guardianreview29

ethical lotus-eating … Robert Macfarlane, *Underland* (London: Penguin, 2019), p. 15.

the perspective changes when history accelerates … Wallace-Wells, *The Uninhabitable Earth*, pp. 78–79.

hyper-object, a conceptual fact … Timothy Morton, *Hyperobjects: Philosophy and ecology after the end of the world* (Minneapolis: University of Minnesota Press, 2013).

the facts are hysterical … Wallace-Wells, *The Uninhabitable Earth*, p. 9.

the Waiwhetū Aquifer, the reserve … Nikki Macdonald, 'Underground water reservoirs at risk from seawater contamination', *Stuff*, 2 February 2019: www.stuff.co.nz/environment/109503698/underground-water-reservoirs-at-risk-from-seawater-contamination

cascading violence, waterfalls and avalanches … Wallace-Wells, *The Uninhabitable Earth*, p. 21.

Unladylike

When I think about power and womanhood, I think of my grandmother. She never had the sort of power that money could afford, but if you happened to be in the lounge of her retirement flat and she told you to sit, you'd sit down. People weren't afraid of her: my grandmother just had an unarguable certainty of her own worth and her right to be heard. People were also drawn to her kindness. When I took my infant son to meet her, she looped one arthritic arm around him and let him pull the loose skin on her face. Wrapped in a purple cardigan against the English autumn, she spoke to him softly. My son stared at her intensely.

Although my grandmother was kind, she often had a sharp tongue. On one visit when I was in my mid-twenties she turned to me, probably prompted by my self-absorbed moaning, and scolded me for wrecking my first marriage. She was not wrong, but I was so ashamed that I walked out and along the canal to where I was staying. Later she called to apologise. Although all was mended, I was reminded of the family saying: 'Grandma doesn't suffer fools.' I think that especially applied to foolish young women who couldn't take responsibility for their own lives.

My grandmother's stoicism was no doubt because of her childhood. Sheila was born in 1918 in Hednesford, a town in the English West Midlands. Her family lived in a flat above the bakery run by her father. She had many relatives in nearby towns whom she'd often visit. Her family were working class—seamstresses and miners—and although not poverty-stricken, they didn't have much to spare. It was common for one family to move in with another when times were hard; after her father lost the bakery during the Great Depression they moved in with his parents. When the house my grandmother was born in was pulled down for pit work, her mother showed her the empty space as if to say, there's no reason to be sentimental about this kind of thing.

Even though childhood gave Sheila an inner resolve, I don't want to fetishise hardship. There were opportunities my grandmother didn't have because she was working class; her parents couldn't afford to send her to university, so Sheila sat the civil service exam instead. During World War Two she worked at Telephone House in Birmingham. The offices were at the top of a building, and she worried constantly that they would be bombed. Each day she'd get the train to Birmingham and walk to work through the rubble of buildings damaged or destroyed the night before.

Sheila met her husband Len before the war. He was soon deployed, then captured, and was held in a prisoner-of-war camp before being repatriated to Britain in 1943 and then returned to war. When the war ended in 1945 he finally returned home. A few years ago my friend's husband went missing while walking in the North Island bush. By the time she realised he was missing it was dark; the search party had to wait until morning. There was nothing she could do but wait, too. To wait in this way is to understand human helplessness. Was her husband injured? Was it something worse? With nothing to do, the mind flips between dread and optimistic self-talk, unable to find comfort. In fact he had slipped and broken his ankle, and spent a wet night in a half-made tent before the search party found him. My grandmother—and other women like her—spent years waiting. Sheila would get up in the morning, fix her hair, dress in her grey uniform and catch the train, never knowing when or whether Len would come home. I make the comparison not to downplay my friend's fear, but to find a way to imagine Sheila's.

My strongest memory of my grandparents is from a visit to their house in the 1980s. It had a large rambling garden flanked with pear trees, where we scavenged for fruit that had fallen in the grass. From the back porch my grandmother would check on the figure of my grandfather as he moved beneath the trees.

*

My grandmother's self-responsibility and fortitude are qualities I never associated with her gender. If anything, I didn't experience my grandmother as gendered. We became close after she had gone through menopause and had stopped performing traditional womanhood. She often dressed in slacks, a loose T-shirt and comfortable shoes. She carried a curved walnut walking stick and wore her grey hair cropped short. During the day she tended the garden or watched sport on a boxy television. In the evenings she drank sherry before dinner. To me, she felt genderless, fluid, ambiguous.

I'm not saying that my grandmother didn't identify as a woman—I'm sure she did—and for much of her life she performed a particular type of womanhood. After Len came back from war she stayed at home to raise their three children. I have a photograph of her smiling on holiday in a summer dress, her hair freshly curled; and another where she has one hand lightly looped through my grandfather's arm. When I knew her best, though, her gender did not have the same immediacy that I experience with other people. Instead, in the space where gender would have been came my grandmother's unique *person*ness.

*

It is hard to write about gender and womanhood without mentioning Judith Butler, whose book *Gender Trouble*, published in 1990, changed how Western society views gender. In it Butler argues that gender is not an essential and fixed quality, but is instead 'an effect' created through repeated behaviours and 'stylization of the body'. For Butler, gender does not exist until a person's repeated behaviour 'congeals' into a gender identity—most commonly male or female in Western society. In short, gender isn't something we *are* but something we *do*.

Even though Butler's theory of 'gender performativity' has entered the zeitgeist, most of us still experience and think about gender as something that's fixed and innate. For instance, a web search of 'womanhood' defines the term as 'the qualities considered to be natural to … a woman'; the word 'natural' suggests attributes that are biologically given. The same search points me to 'femininity', which throws up definitions such as 'delicacy and prettiness' or 'gentleness, empathy, humility and sensitivity'.

I won't go too far into the arguments that surround Butler's work— conversations about the relationship between biological sex and gender, and the transgender experience. Those conversations belong to a different sort of essay. While theory is one of the ways that society progresses, it operates in the lecture hall of the mind and not the soft bed of the body, which is where, eventually, change happens for all of us.

So while Butler's work sparks many conversations, one is of particular interest to me. What I want to take from Butler is the idea that gender is something we *do*. I want to hold this idea up to the light; to take the back off the idea and tinker with its insides. I want to find a way to bring the idea into my body. Because if womanhood is not something innate, then neither are the qualities I've internalised about womanhood. To see gender this way gives me— and other women—the ability, to an extent, to define our own gender.

*

A few years ago women in my social circle shaved one side of their heads while leaving the rest of their hair long—a sexy subversion of the societal norm that women have long hair. The first time a friend described shaving her head my hands leapt protectively to my own hair. My delicate, pretty, gentle, empathic, humble and sensitive hair.

I've always had long hair, and not just any long hair but the kind one friend jealously calls 'princess hair'. My hair would only be closer to the Western feminine ideal if it were blonde—it falls in thick chestnut waves. Like Ophelia's in the famous painting by John Everett Millais, my hair has a delicate drama. Ophelia lies in the water gazing skyward, wildflowers strewn around her. Sinuous and heavy, her hair expands like a halo.

Although seeing gender as something I *do* allows me to challenge my gendered behaviours, I have found that success depends on how enmeshed those behaviours are with my identity, and to what extent they give me a sense of psychological safety. I'm more assertive than I was as a younger woman: I won't let men interrupt me in conversation; I won't apologise for things that are not my fault. Still, I can't cut my hair. Maybe that is because my hair is always loved, even when I am not.

In terms of our public bodies, hair might be the attribute most laden with gender expectations. When seven non-binary people were interviewed in 'Vibrant Colors, Buzzcuts, & Freedom', one theme emerged: hair was a way to step out of the gender binary and to prioritise self-acceptance over societal acceptance. As artist Katayoun discovered, though, expressions outside of gender norms are often read incorrectly:

When I had long hair ... I was always coded as femme and then after that, I made a move to a slightly more masculine style and people assumed I was trans masc. I want to be able to experiment with how I look and not worry about how I'm read … Interactions can make you feel really wrong or really right.

Butler wrote *Gender Trouble* in part to understand gay women's experience of stepping outside of gender norms and the resultant feeling—as Katayoun identifies—of being 'wrong'. Although the feeling is persistent for people who live outside of gender norms, many women experience that wrongness. As Butler explains, to be a 'woman' is to exist in a gender framework, and one is 'a woman' depending on how well one meets the expectations of the framework. While a woman may have a clear sense of her own womanhood, her experience is disrupted when others misread her gender or tell her she's doing it incorrectly, a behaviour known as 'gender policing'. As a child—usually when helping myself to food—I was often told my behaviour was 'unladylike'. To step outside of gender norms was to feel dislocation inside my own body.

A failure to meet gender norms leads to more severe outcomes than being scolded at the dinner table, however. When Indian-British writer Sharan Dhaliwal cut her hair, her social standing changed. In Dhaliwal's community, long hair signified 'being chaste, marriage material, whereas short or shaved hair related to promiscuity and shame'. 'No one's going to marry you now,' Dhaliwal's mother told her. And even more severe? The American civil rights organisation Human Rights Campaign reported that 'at least' forty-one transgender women were killed in hate crimes in the United States from 2018 to 2019; the victims were disproportionately women of colour.

Gender policing is layered throughout a woman's life. In her TED talk, Christen Reighter describes her decision to live childfree and the impossibility of getting an elective sterilisation. Even though she met legal requirements, doctors refused her surgery because her desire to be childfree did not fit with their idea of womanhood. Other women had similar experiences—those without children were told to come back once they'd had a child; women with children were told to have more.

Reighter felt disheartened and angry: 'I've always believed that having children was an extension of womanhood, not the definition … that strips [a woman] of her entire identity as an adult unto herself,' she says. 'It's so easy to forget the roles that society places on us are more than mere titles. What about … the fear associated with questioning them, and the desires we cast aside to accept them?' After years of persistence, Reighter finally convinced a surgeon to perform the procedure.

What I find most inspiring about Reighter's story is that she did not see her choice to live childfree as a failure of her womanhood. To not locate the problem in ourselves is to inhabit womanhood in expansive ways. It is also how women will change gender norms. As Butler says, 'The task is not whether to repeat, but how to repeat ... to displace the very gender norms that enable the repetition itself.' In other words, to make gender trouble.

*

To say I experienced my grandmother as genderless is really to say that she wasn't performing the behaviours that I associated with womanhood. My comment shows the limitations of how I understood gender at the time, rather than anything true about my grandmother.

While the origin of my expectations can't be reduced to a single moment, I cannot help but remember the crushed-velvet dress I wore to a school ball when I was fourteen. It was a hired off-the-shoulder number that fitted across my hips but constricted my ribcage and chest. My mother reached into her closet and handed me a pair of black heels. I stood in front of the bedroom mirror, a girl swallowed in maroon ruching.

I liked what I saw. I looked a little like Julia Roberts in *Pretty Woman* after she's been made over by Héctor Elizondo, the hotel manager. My wildness had been smoothed out and I suddenly felt acceptable. When my date arrived he pinned a corsage to my dress. 'You look so pretty!' he said. We stood in the kitchen while my parents took photos, his arm slung around my shoulders, my hands clasped neatly in my lap.

Taking off the expectations of womanhood has been like taking off that suffocating dress. I expand with space and air. Recently, for the first time since childhood, I've started tramping again. While staying in a wilderness hut my friend Leslie and I chopped kindling for the fire. We were high enough in the Ruahine Ranges for snow to still be on the ground in early spring. Beyond our hut's roof lay the misty expanse of the Manawatū. Lying in the grass beside the woodshed was an axe, its steel head corroded from years of alpine weather.

Leslie and I gathered pieces of wood from the dark shed and stood them up, their ringed faces flat to the sky. I lifted the axe across my shoulder, the muscles in my thighs tensed, my feet spread apart for balance, my teeth bared. I curved the axe down and smashed it through the first piece of wood. I know these details because Leslie, laughing, took a photograph. She wasn't laughing because I looked ridiculous—although I probably did—but from the surprise and ecstatic joy that had risen up between us, away from our domestic worlds, churning up the mud with our feet.

On that tramp I took *Flash Count Diary* by Darcey Steinke, a book that explores Steinke's experience of menopause, a phase I am also entering. What interests me about Steinke's story is the way she found menopause began an 'ungendering' process. This was because menopause meant the loss of 'female signifiers' such as smooth skin and shiny hair, and also because Steinke stopped performing traditional womanhood: she began to dress in androgynous clothing and go without makeup. Steinke found that stepping outside the 'brutal binary' of masculinity–feminity allowed her to experience 'a wider emotional sweep, a larger sense of the world, and a keener awareness' of herself.

While writing *Flash Count Diary*, Steinke researched other post-reproductive animals to make sense of the way ungendering makes her feel animalistic. She became obsessed with orcas, which are one of the few animals besides humans to go through menopause.

Steinke flies to Miami to see Lolita, an orca that has lived at the Miami Seaquarium since 1970. She is mesmerised by Lolita's show—the whale plunges down before launching her entire body out of the water. While the performance is impressive, Steinke feels Lolita's captivity: 'I recognize the feeling of being held captive, not literally, like Lolita, but metaphorically,' she says.

After seeing Lolita, Steinke travels to the Salish Sea where she hopes to catch sight of Granny, an orca matriarch born in 1911. In the wild, post-reproductive orcas like Granny lead their family groups and teach younger whales pod rituals, sexual techniques and how to find hunting grounds. If Lolita symbolises womanhood's captivity for Steinke, Granny symbolises the freedom that can come from menopause.

After Steinke's kayak tour clears the mouth of the bay, someone spots a pod in the distance. The group pulls together, gripping each other's paddles. Talking stops. The whales swim toward them, their dorsal fins high in the air. As the sea surges, Granny breaks the surface alongside Steinke—'*Kawouf!*' Granny's brown eye looks directly at her.

Later, Steinke tries to make sense of her experience: 'I felt a little as I had the night after my daughter was born … an event outside of human evaluation … What I felt was a dilation,' she writes.

*

On the day I return from the tramp I sit in the shower and let hot water rush over me. I think about Steinke and Butler and try to experience my body outside of my gender. The folds of my stomach, my uneven breasts, the pouches of flesh on my thighs. Hairless and tubular, I'm reminded of the naked mole rat my son and I once googled.

I think about when I went tramping as a child, one of the few situations in which I could escape the expectations of girlhood. Although I often felt cold and exhausted, I instinctively knew how to be in my body. When descending a scree I'd lean backwards; I knew how to avoid rabbit holes and matagouri. I felt so sure in the capability of my body that when my father organised a group of men to climb Ben McLeod—a peak in the South Island—I fumed at them that tramping was 'not only for boys'.

It took five hours to scale Ben McLeod, the dots of our bodies etching the mountainside. As we reached the summit the sun touched the far valley and the distant peaks turned luminous. Hot and vibrant, I flew down the descent. As I reached the lower slopes a hare darted along the fence line and paused, ears upright. The hare looked at me; I looked at the hare. For a second I felt the hare's *there*ness, and then it was gone into scrub. Of wonder, Buddhist Kittisaro says: 'One starts to get a sense of being part of something vast.'

Steinke's description of becoming ungendered reminds me of the presence of my grandmother. Like Steinke's 'dilation' it's an expansive feeling: an addition rather than a subtraction. A vastness I'm beginning to find in myself. Steinke's daughter sums it up well after her mother suggests there should be twenty genders: 'You don't get it,' she says. 'Each person is their own gender. There are as many genders as there are human beings.'

*

Just before my forty-second birthday I tramp with three friends to Waitewaewae Hut, a sixteen-bunk shelter on the Ōtaki River. We leave early on a Saturday morning, driving out of Wellington and up the Kāpiti Coast. The island glitters in the morning light. We turn inland toward the Tararuas and along a narrow road to Ōtaki Forks. At the carpark we adjust our packs and take a photograph: four women, ready. I stand on the right, my sunglasses pushed back on my head. My friend Kristina stands beside me, swamped in a grey waterproof. Next to her Rhiannon has been caught mid-laugh, her face bright in the morning sun. On the far side stands Kirsten, orange jacket zipped up to her chin, her hair haloed under a cap.

From the carpark we cross a swing bridge and climb to an exposed river terrace. Huge slips have gouged out the hillside. We stop on the edge and marvel at how the earth has fallen away. We feel a little dangerous—as though we're engaging in something taboo. In a way we are: to be absent from our families and duties is to be selfish. And women aren't meant to be selfish.

Soon the track turns into dense bush. We navigate by the orange trail markers nailed to trees. Sometimes we go for minutes without seeing one—the group stops to scan the bush then someone spots an orange flash among the green.

Our progress is hard and slow. The track works its way between knotted trees and around roots curled like snares. At times it's so steep that we climb on our hands and knees. After four hours we reach the halfway point—a forest plateau turned bog—and perch on tree roots to eat lunch. The air is damp and sweet. Occasionally a bird calls, and in the distance is the tumble of a stream. Rhi breaks up a block of chocolate and Kirsten hands around gummy snakes. We've formed the immediate camaraderie that I only experience with women. Most of the time we eat in silence. The bush takes me into itself. My body sinks into the mossy ground as though I've always been here.

Eventually we descend along a roaring stream and onto the bank of the Ōtaki River. A cheer goes up—we've walked for seven hours and the hut is close. We have to enter the river, cross to where the water is shallowest, wade downstream, and then cross back to the bank we've just come from. As a child I'd crossed rivers with my family, but I'd never attempted it as an adult. We decide to enter on the bend where the water is swift but only reaches our knees. We unclip our chest straps, link arms and step into the flow. Edging out, we turn on an angle to the current. It pulls at my feet and calves. My boots are immediately saturated and my toes burn with the cold. 'Keep going,' someone shouts, and we clasp each other until our eight-legged animal reaches the shallows. Here the water is slow and the rocks slippery, but we wade easily downstream. For a moment, I pause and look up. The mountains are huge above me. The sky unfurls vast and white. They enter my chest and I feel my heart beating with them. 'Sarah, you ready?' asks Kristina. We cross again.

*

When I tramp my shoulders burn from the weight of my pack; my legs become caked with mud; I grunt as I climb. Maybe that is why tramping didn't survive the passage from girl to womanhood: to tramp is to be unlovely.

Being unlovely in the company of other women has become a necessary ritual. It is one of the ways I am relearning my womanhood. To be dirty, tired and rough, outspoken and selfish and hungry. That is to be a woman. That is to be human. When I was younger, becoming a woman meant—in many small cuts—abandoning parts of myself. Now I'm taking them back and abandoning the parts that don't fit.

REFERENCES

'an effect' created … Judith Butler, *Gender Trouble* (New York & London: Routledge, 1999).

When I had long hair … Poppy Marriott and Tom Rasmussen, 'Vibrant Colors, Buzzcuts, & Freedom.' *Refinery 29*, 4 May 2019.

being chaste, marriage material … Sharan Dhaliwal, 'These Intimate Portraits Examine How Hair Connects to Gender Identity', *Vice*, 26 Oct. 2018.

'at least' forty-one transgender women … Human Rights Campaign, 'Resources: Hate crimes': www.hrc.org/resources/topic/hate-crimes

I've always believed … Christian Reighter, 'I don't want children—stop telling me I'll change my mind', *TED: Ideas worth spreading*, 16 Nov. 2017.

The task is not whether to repeat … Butler, *Gender Trouble*.

menopause began an 'ungendering' process … Darcey Steinke, *Flash Count Diary: Menopause and the vindication of natural life* (New York: Farrar, Straus and Giroux, 2019).

One starts to get a sense … Kittisaro, '#214: The Case for Devotion, Kittisaro and Thanissara', Ten Percent Happier with Dan Harris (podcast), 20 Nov. 2019.

Shelley Burne-Field

If the words 'white' and 'sausage' in the same sentence make you uncomfortable, please read on

My sassy mokopuna just started primary school. I'm not terribly worried about her. She's like her mother—aroha and kindness burst from their hearts. My mokopuna's skin is warm, milky-white, and she carries the sea in her eyes. Plus, she possesses legit antennae for bullshit.

I do worry about the books she brings home. Pulled from a pink canvas book bag, the thin booklets are slapped onto the kitchen table to be read immediately. My mokopuna's eyes are glittering by now. The power of her will to learn has gathered, gathered, and now floods into my sitting room. The stories are not 'See Jane Run', but are not far off. They have easy lines to learn by rote, and easier messages to absorb.

'I can kick the football.' 'I can throw the cricket ball.' These tales are complete with pictures of kids in a faraway land kicking soccer balls (old English leather ones) and other kids in the same faraway land bowling cricket balls (old English leather ones) in front of old pavilions, whitewashed and no doubt smelling of leather. My mokopuna dazzles me with every word. We high-five and whoop and holler. She'll be fine.

I do worry about my other mokopuna. His heart is the same—bursting with aroha and kindness. Yet his skin is velvet, chocolate-brown, and he carries the breath of kawakawa leaves in his eyes. At sixteen years old, he stands at 190 centimetres, tall enough to change lightbulbs without a ladder, lift his sister onto his shoulders, and play basketball—although he hates basketball and prefers to study Greek mythology and history.

I worry about my son, too. Also bursting with aroha. His skin is coffee-kissed coconut and his eyes churn like fire beneath the whenua. Being a growing tween, he chows down cheese by the 900-gram block, and is in the top

2 percent of the 2 two percent for giftedness in his age group. Before your eyes glaze over, that means he's smart. Smarter than me or his dad. My son told me last night he'd never experienced racism. That meant more to me than his first Christmas. I hugged him and told him I hoped he never would. We high-fived and hollered. Before he went to bed, he yelled out:

'Hey Mum, except for the sausage thing at school eh?'

'What sausage thing?'

''Member? At school that lunchtime?'

'Oh, *that* sausage thing.'

I'd forgotten about that. I remembered being worried before, but kissed him good night and said 'you've got this, times are changing'. Don't worry, I said to myself.

Why would I worry about the gentle souls of my tama and my mokopuna? Why should I worry about their lives?

Fear. Fear, because in Aotearoa the lives of the brown boys and girls in my whānau don't matter as much as the lives of white boys and girls. They just don't.

*

The 'sausage thing' at my son's primary school was like walking in on a cheating spouse. The signs had revealed themselves slowly. A stray receipt in a jacket pocket here, another chick's tights on our boat there. At my son's new school warning lights flashed, not about infidelity but about systemic racism.

Unfortunately for my son, my sunglasses were tinted with a colonised lens at the time. That specialised tint came with the label 'I-don't-want-to-be-the-Māori-mother-that-people-call-aggressive', so I didn't act decisively enough at the start. Aroha mai, my son.

When he was six years old we'd returned from Australia, where he had been treated like a famous All Black at his primary school. He loved it. We came back to Aotearoa and attended a generally wonderful country school, set under the Ruahine pae maunga. The parent group was generally welcoming. Lots of farmers and farmworker whānau. The roll was small, under thirty tamariki. A handful of Māori kids, but mostly white. When a person of colour enters an environment like that you're not completely unaware of racism, but there is always an element of hope.

After a few weeks my boy began crying at bedtime, saying he 'must be the bad kid'. He kept getting told off and he didn't know why. We would chew over the day's events after reading Orwell's *1984*, or Golding's *Lord of the Flies*— every night—and try to get to the bottom of my son's pain. I chatted with the teacher, keeping a practised, reflective air. I put on my nice scarf and visited the principal. She would look into it. That day he came home in tears, saying the principal had grabbed his arm, hard. She'd said he shouldn't go home and tell his parents everything that happened at school. My puku was beginning to churn, just like my son's eyes.

In October he hadn't earned a single certificate for the entire year. Not one. I'd already mentioned it to the teacher. Can you just find one thing he's done right? I asked. He really thrives on praise. 'That's not our policy,' she told me.

The kōwhai were blooming, golden and welcoming. Summer was aching to arrive, and the school began sausage sizzles on Thursday lunchtimes as a fundraiser. Kids could bring $2 and get a sausage and bread. The school might also cook other days, but they would let parents know.

Each Thursday my boy would trundle off to school with his $2 in a plastic zip-lock bag. This particular Thursday he came home with his $2 and said they had cancelled because one of the mothers couldn't come in. Okay, fine. No biggie. I rang the school. Would they be cooking tomorrow? I could cook if they needed, I told them. No, no, they said. Next week.

However, Friday rolled around—the very next day. A spare hour presented itself and I grabbed it, rushing to the school to spend lunchtime with my boy, and maybe to chat with the teacher about how he held him in class at playtimes and some lunchtimes so he could finish his interesting worksheets. More cars were parked at the school than I'd expected. Sausage sizzle smells rode the air. My antennae prickled but I shrugged it off. Then I saw quite a few white kids eating sausages in bread. The teachers' kids, the parent-group kids, the farmers' kids. The Māori kids were not eating sausages, including my boy. To be honest, a couple of the poor white kids didn't have a sausage either.

In a high, nervous voice, I greeted my son. I remember my throat squeezing in on my larynx, and I didn't mention the sausage thing at all. His eyes were welling. He really wanted a sausage, but they weren't allowed one. I asked the other kids who didn't have a sausage whether they had wanted one too. Yes they did, they said, but they didn't have any money.

A group of white mothers and teachers buzzed around the barbecue. My voice was squeaky, but I put on my best smile. Oh, sorry, I must have missed the pānui? My boy didn't have his $2, darn it all! They laughed and gushed. 'Just a last-minute thing,' tee-heed one of the mothers. Her kids didn't have any money either, but they just wrote out an IOU. He he. Ha ha.

I rushed out to the car to grab some gold coins for all the kids who didn't have a sausage, but when I got back they'd closed the lid on the barbie. There were no sausages left. The white kids and white adults were finishing, licking their fingers, tomato sauce coating their lips. My son and the other Māori kids, plus a kid with a permanent limp and some farmworker kids in holey T-shirts, ran off and played, laughing. What else could they do?

When I wrote a letter about it and met with the chair of the board of trustees, she said she didn't see a problem with it, really, and she truly thought I was overreacting. Maybe that's what some of you think as well. Tough. My son still remembers the feeling of being labelled a 'bad kid' and having to watch the white 'good kids' get a sausage.

I won't let you off the hook. My son was denied, and had to watch his Māori friends be denied too because they had no money that day, while his white friends were trusted to write with pencil on a piece of paper the $ symbol and the number 2. The brown kids were never offered this magical thing, these pencil marks showing '$2'. This paper strip wasn't a gold coin, yet it could act as a key to unlock an invisible door. This secret contract between white children, white parents and white teachers had been revealed, like a lover's note written in lemon juice and burned with a candle. Spelled out at lunchtime on a Friday, under the shadow of the Ruahine pae maunga.

*

Racism is wearisome. Literally tiring. It does not create a pearl after years of grinding. It creates sickness, fear, anxiety, sadness, resentment and worry. In society, racism is entrenched in our tired civil institutions. The worn framework that holds up our very way of life. I imagine the structure is affirming for white people. As affirming as breathing. For brown people it is debilitating. From the first sneeze of life to the final exhale. Day after day. Night after night. Our wairua becomes exhausted and frayed. The framework of our society isn't affirming; no, it becomes the bars of a prison cell, or worse, the snuff box of false hope. We sniff it, daily, trying to rally, knowing it will rot our septum as easily as a cocaine habit.

In the provinces racism seems worse. The Hawke's Bay-type provinces are paradise in my eyes. But they are also terribly racist, and therefore exhausting places to live and work if you're brown or black. I've worked in a few of those civil institutions. A prison. Councils. Hospitals. Power companies. Social services. I've done other jobs, too. Cleaning motels, orchards, in the guts room at the meat works. I've been a student in the university system too many times, with degrees out the wazoo.

Before those years of study and mahi, I left college as a seventh-former with a wonderful reference from my French teacher. I'd wanted to learn te reo but was made to take French instead. *C'est la vie!* At college, I was a 'good kid' even though I was brown. I was told this by a fellow student who is now a politician. I remember her saying in English class that I wasn't one of *those* Māoris. I was good. She actually said 'good', just like that, as if I was an avocado that she'd squeezed and found acceptable to her taste.

When I left school I was shy, but confident that, academically, I was okay. I sent out six CVs with my picture displayed at the top. 'Runner-up to Dux' was proudly typed in capitals. I posted the CVs to three banks, a pharmacy, an accountancy firm and a lawyer's office. They all had vacancies for what we'd now call interns, but I never got an interview.

I remember struggling a few weeks later with the idea of taking my photo off my CV. At the library I kept looking over my shoulder, embarrassed as I removed the image before photocopying a new CV. My cheeks felt slapped red. I was sweating. My trust in the community was leaking out of the pores in my skin. Lo and behold, I got two interviews at the same banks that had previously ignored me, but after the interview, no job offer.

At home I worried until the next year—second to dux—weeding Dad's gardens, preserving golden queen peaches for Mum and applying for more jobs. In the end my sister got me a job stuffing gherkins into a jar at the local pickle factory. I had to put up my hand to go to the toilet, but it was a job. Racism was already starting to grind, and I was only eighteen. To be honest, it hasn't changed much.

*

Luckily, I was made for school. Imagine a little boy, superhero crazed. Saving his whānau from evil. Now imagine this Māori child at an early childhood setting, mainstream, white. The secret contract writhes in the ether, protecting, protecting. There may be a whisper from a racist teacher, a glance, narrowed eyes or pinching fingers. Another amazing teacher may appear, but often not.

Then the boy goes to primary school, and he is older, wary, but hopeful. Still a beautiful tamariki full of life. The bus is loud with chattering pelicans and fireworks popping. The boy is told to stop making noise. Stop chattering. Yet only the boy is told off. The white kids keep chattering. He hops on the bus, day after day. Wanting to speak, but his eyes become downcast and he quietens.

The boy has a wonderful principal who helps him, but another white teacher can't pronounce this boy's name and simply calls him 'R' for short—it's easier, but it's not his name. It doesn't carry the meaning behind the name. Why his name matters. The same teacher says 'Mah-rees' instead of 'Māori', and doesn't flinch an eyelid.

Then secondary school, where the target on your back is either bright red or invisible. The mah-rees are revolting, sir. You are told not to take graphics and robotics but to sign up for cooking. You are given the option to go not on the ski trip but to the local pool instead. You are asked to perform the whaikōrero and kapa haka for all civil events to tick a box, yet you and your brown mates are never invited to have tea and tan slice. Then the boy hops onto the bus home, and he does this day after day after day after day.

And when the boy leaves school because he feels disenfranchised, isolated, so stink … when the boy leaves school to choose, let's be fair, anything other than the racist grind, then *he* is called the failure, the dropout, the statistic, the layabout, the no-hoper. Yet what a glorious and brave boy, to choose something that will ensure he is *despised* by those who hold the structures of our institutions so tightly: to leave school.

Just thinking about it makes me shiver.

What does this say about how racism conceals these boys behind a white lens? Let's change those glasses, shall we? Let's swap out that racist lens. That boy—what courage! What fortitude! What validity! Oh, to choose to be somewhere *other* than the place where your brown life does not matter as much as a white life. Oh, to choose to *matter*. You think this is a fictional mock-up?

Think again. My nephews. My friends' kids. My whānau.

From the cradle to the grave—and a prison stretch in between for the dispossessed, or a noose around their necks.

*

In Hawke's Bay, Māori and Pasifika boys and girls are three times more likely to commit suicide than white boys and girls. We have a higher rate than the rest of Aotearoa. We have a higher rate than the road toll. We have a higher rate than diabetes. I suspect the grind of racism plays a role. When I was at primary school, my ten-year-old friend hung himself. It is a tragedy unsurpassed, but not a surprise to me, when brown boys and girls kill themselves.

Suicide prevention plans are written. There is much gnashing of teeth but resources are scarce. Not enough social workers in schools, or counsellors, or psychologists, or mentors, or adults walking alongside. Not enough cash.

There is an equity gap between mental health resources provided for white people and those for brown people. A recent drought has amplified this unwritten rule. Farmers with million-dollar mansions sitting empty at Kinloch received food parcels during the drought. Not their farmworkers. Just the owners and managers. The money came—as it always does—from pulling local and central government levers. The old boys' network. The old girls' network. The white people's network. The levers were fully oiled. Consequently, fully resourced mental health teams were pulled together for rural folk, and are available, free of charge. Even for house calls.

I struggle not to bite a hole in my lip. We chew them endlessly, figuring out ways to help our Māori and Pasifika children who are *also* in pain. Not more. Not less. Also.

*

I often tell my husband that he is at the top of the food chain. He is in his sixties and white. (As an aside, at a bowling tournament in New Plymouth a white lady with soap-bubble hair sidled over to me. She said I must feel so lucky to have gotten myself a white man. I do feel lucky, but not because he's white. It's because we love each other, and he understands his big-cat status.) Conversely, I am near the bottom of the food chain. *Near* the bottom. Brown, wahine, educated and middle-class. I feel the grind, for sure. But my Māori sisters in poverty must ache. Their lives don't seem to matter in our society, sometimes *at all*.

There may be cries of—oh, but what about the netball stars, rugby stars, squash stars, softball stars, the newsreaders, our favourite musicians? Yeah, nah. I'm talking about the salt of the earth māmā who toils. The ones surviving in gangs, or she who keeps the ahi lit at the marae, or wāhine who work two or three jobs, or the ones on sickness benefits, or the ones in and out of prison, or the jobless, or the kuia looking after mokopuna alone, or the wāhine who have been middle-class or upper-class and have fallen onto hard times dealing with mental health illness or physical illness or whānau illness, the one who covers her toothless giggle, or the one bullied out of work or school or life, those who were never nurtured by a teacher, a coach, a boss, a supervisor, a doctor or anyone who may have given her a chance, a kind glance, a job, an opportunity, a smile. A meal.

I imagine the grind of racism when you're at the bottom of the heap must be worse than death. Utterly soul-destroying. These wāhine deserve a damehood for retaining the ability to smile and stay alive. Our sisters are pushed deep into the whenua, only popping out occasionally like mushrooms after a shower of rain.

A white friend told me that when she married her Māori lover it was the social capital racism that affected her. Let's call my friend 'Mrs White'. After she got married her name changed to 'Mrs Māori'. In the time it takes for Shania Twain to whisper 'From this moment', Mrs White lost a big chunk of her social capital and got a little taste of the grind.

Social capital is a Western academic term. Generally, it defines citizen success in a democratic society via advantageous human networks and relationships. Social capital may include a social contract (an understanding) within a local community: such things as paying on the twentieth of the month, knowing hidden pathways to jobs, easily accessing goods and services, leaving an IOU if you're $4 short at the dairy, a tab, access to trees cut down for firewood by the council along the grazing mile, a $3000 bull provided to the local school for a raffle fundraiser, the ability to access the hierarchy of needs—power, water, food, shelter, friendship, love.

When Mrs Māori rang up to get her washing machine fixed, she was told that she would have to pay up front, if they could get there at all. Remember, a few weeks ago Mrs Māori had been Mrs White. She explained her previous identity, aggressive and pissed off, and after profuse apologies her washing machine was fixed 120 minutes later, and she could pay on the twentieth of next month, just as before. Phew. Mrs Māori rebuked the service centre for their racist tendencies, and learned her lesson well. She is now Mrs White on the telephone, every time. To run a household well, social capital is as essential as money in the bank.

However, what about our Māori sisters whose skin is as black as the eye of a toutouwai?

What about our sisters who can't change their last names, wouldn't want to? Our sisters who can't change their black skin *would* want to, if we're honest.

Imagine a wahine running a household with three bright-eyed tamariki, uniforms needing to be washed. A black sister holding the fort—fighting the grind day after day after day after day. Your one washing machine breaks down. Your one washing machine that services your whānau, your sister, your sister-in-law, your niece, your brother's whānau, etcetera. You ring the service centre.

Hi, it's Mrs Māori here, I really need my washing machine looked at. Sorry, you have to pay $200 up front, and there will be a travel charge of $70, and you have to pay the rest on the day of service and, actually, we have an account in arrears for a person with your name *insert Māori name here* … yes but that's not me … I'm sorry, we can't help you. The shame of a stink uniform. The shame of a stink placed onto your skin, so baaaaaaaad that you cry that ugly cry, or stare pitifully into space, or *insert coping mechanism here*.

You think this is a mock-up? Think again. My sister. My friends. My fellow school mums. My whānau. I dare you to debate the hand-washing argument. I can smell the wet, mouldy home on your breath. If you've never dried work socks or a school uniform in the oven, with respect, please stay silent.

*

Recently I was a district councillor for a term. The racism, sexism, dishonesty, greed and double standards broke me. Thankfully, I have a husband, friends and whānau who armour me up. After I saved my life by leaving council, a black sister stood for mayor. Facebook comments compared her sacred moko kauae to a barcode for welfare. He he. Ha ha. At candidate evenings, during this wahine's speeches, white men and women laughed and scoffed. White business owners and white farmers guffawed and sniggered. I was there. I heard and saw.

At the end I stood and clapped, loudly. This mighty wahine confided in me that she knew she'd lose, but she wanted tamariki in our community to see her try. I cried for both of us.

When she lost by a landslide, she didn't hide, oh no. She went shopping to support local. A white woman was talking to the retailer. 'I'm so pleased that mah-ree didn't win,' she said. Just like that. 'I'm so pleased that mah-ree didn't win.' Not, hey I didn't agree with her policy on wastewater, or her thoughts on a new recycling centre. Just, 'I'm so pleased that mah-ree didn't win.'

Our black and brown lives matter. Our Māori and Pasifika lives matter. The lives of my tama and my mokopuna matter. They matter just as much as white lives. Not more. Not less. As much. The grind wears us down. Killing us. It all gets way … too … hard. Wearisome. Tiring. Usually we're supposed to ask for a call to action, some sort of social change, at the end of an essay or a speech. But I'm just too fucking exhausted. I'm going to kiss my husband and my tama and my mokopuna goodnight.

'It's okay darlings, times are changing. We've got this.'

In the morning I'm gonna whoop and holler and give them high-fives. Day after day after day after day.

Anna Knox

Ziusudra & the Black Holes: Rereading 'The First Essay'

I: Writing

Somewhere, at some specific moment, someone wrote the very first sentence.

Imagine.

Ancient Mesopotamia, a small settlement somewhere along the banks of the Euphrates, in a time before time is marked and when the past is the home of goddesses and gods. Today, the sun is pleasantly warm, the sky blue. Entering the courtyard after your morning ablutions you notice a falcon sweep the low hills to your right, scanning for gazelle. A good omen. After a breakfast of goat's milk and eggs, you enter the rear of the house and seat yourself on the floor by a low window where the light is good. In your hands is a reed stylus. Before you is a slab of damp clay into which you begin to press lines and shapes, tallying the quantities of items in your household for accountability, as is your daily task. The reed slips, slits open the skin on the side of your hand. Blood comes redder than any fruit, welling and dripping to the ground. You suck the wound, stemming the flow, while the blood on the dirt dries black and hard.

Later, as darkness moves over your household, you fall asleep with the shapes from the day's clay floating out above you, pointing to something in your half-conscious mind. In your dreams you remember your mother and, in the loop of your dreams, the shapes become like her name, and like your name, taken from hers—sounds that, spoken together in the air, refer to you.

Perhaps the goddess touches your mind, or perhaps time was always going to dictate that when you wake you feel something collide inside you and, half asleep, take the sounds of your name and try to cut something that approaches them into the clay, and with them, something else, a line of characters stating who you are, who your mother was—an introduction. You are reaching for something in the future, you realise as you cut, for your voice echoing forward in time, announcing you not only now but then too, making you a little like the goddess, enduring beyond a sound.

Maybe that is how writing started out—as a tiny etching unravelling all the way to this white tablet into which my own mind and fingers now command silent sounds. Maybe not at all. We'll never know. But in this imagined scene, is the protagonist male, female or neither?

*

When I found *The Lost Origins of the Essay* on a friend's bookshelf last year, I thought I had stumbled on something new. It struck me as something that promised to crack open the idea of the essay—a radical gospel excavating the world in words. 'I am here in search of art,' writes editor John D'Agata in his superb introduction. 'I am here to track the origins of an alternative to commerce.' For a writer, an irresistible undertaking.

After buying my own copy from Unity Books in Wellington I left it, like some kind of totem, on the kitchen bench for several days, admiring the cover and the rough, cream edges of the 700-odd pages that I thought, once read, were going to change something. One quiet evening when my daughters were asleep and I was otherwise alone, I sat down on a sofa facing the sea. I watched the city lights coming on one by one in homes and offices, and I opened the book and began to read.

It begins with a brief piece of Sumerian writing entitled 'The List of Ziusudra'. In suggesting this as the first essay ever written, D'Agata stakes a claim counter to most scholarly thought on the essay form, of which Michel de Montaigne is usually understood to be the father. (De Montaigne has a place in the book, but almost 5000 years later, after essays by Ennatum, Seneca, Li Tsung-yuan, Sei Shōnagon and De Sahugún, among others.) It seemed a good start.

D'Agata's evocation of ancient Sumer and the flood that destroyed it, of the accounting system on which that society built its prosperity and engineered its demise, and of the words of a supposed single survivor, Ziusudra, limping into existence after the waters had receded, was extremely compelling. When he described those words as 'the beginning of an alternative to nonfiction, the beginning of a form that's not propelled by information, but one compelled instead by individual expression—by inquiry, by opinion, by wonder, by doubt', explaining that Ziusudra was 'trying to make a new shape where there previously was none', my blood raced. *Yes! This is what the essay is!* I thought. *This is why I want to write in this form.*

But then I read 'The List of Ziusudra'.

*

Sumerian is a language our own culture's scholarship understands as once spoken by peoples living in ancient Mesopotamia between circa 5500 and 2000 BC. Most scholars also believe it was the first language to take written form. There is much academic thought on what constitutes writing, exactly, and therefore the first writing, but I am most persuaded by Jean-Jacques Glassner's description of writing as a conscious process, derived from an 'act of will' that marked a significant break in mental processes. As such, Glassner says, the first writing is most accurately referred to as an invention. And so, in his words, the Sumerians invented writing. Cuneiform, we call it—'wedge-shaped'.

On reading the first lines of 'The List of Ziusudra' I was captivated. By the voice echoing forward over millennia, by the unfolding of time in which tablets buried for centuries were unearthed then wrestled with by minds who learned the sense of their shapes and painstakingly eased them out of the clay, unfolding them, bending them, repeating them, until they were printed here:

Back in those days—in those far remote days—back in those nights—in those far-away nights—back in those years—in those long ago years—back at that time when the wise ones were wise, the wisest of all of them had given up hope.

Friends, let me share with you the advice those wise ones tried to offer.

I was eager for this 5000-year-old advice. I read on:

So first, don't ever buy a donkey that excessively brays, for this is the kind animal [sic] that will knock you on your ass.

Neither should you buy your prostitutes from the street, for they are the kind that will usually bite.

Also avoid the weekly sale of whores from the palace, for they are usually sold from the bottom of the barrel.

There was a slamming in my brain. Everything stopped. I could not keep reading. I can argue against that response intellectually now, but the feeling I had on reading those lines was like a bad dream in which I'd opened my mouth to receive a lover's kiss and then realised he was a stranger with a monstrous face.

This list was not written for me, I scrawled in my notebook. *I am not its audience. I am its whore and its prostitute.* I shared a connection with these ancient Sumerians whose textually outcast status I immediately inhabited, and whose timeless presence was summoned as I read, because they were (largely) women and I'm a woman, and Ziusudra and his imagined readers were men. Even with the vast space of centuries, our relationship had been planed to something that simple.

The third line raised a final imaginary being with whom I could identify, and placed me definitively not as a reader outside of this 'first essay' but as a subject within it:

And a weak wife will always be seized by fate

My sense of exclusion was complete.

*

Out the window it was properly dark now, and the interisland ferry was making its slow way into the harbour, its blazing lights reflected on the water.

What do you do? I wrote. *If your identity measures up against all of recorded human time as inferior? What do you do if even in the re-written histories of the world, in compendiums of their 'lost origins', in 2019, in the 'liberal West', you are still written out?*

How do you contend with that? How do you respond? As a woman, how do you read?

With questions. To find what isn't there. Fighting for a way in.

I decided to do some research.

II. Rereading

There is no doubt as to the gender of the supposed writer of Ziusudra's list, I learned. He is the Sumerian Noah, a king perhaps, and the apparent sole survivor in the Sumerian version of the ancient story of the Great Flood. This much has been verified.

But Sumerian scribes were not only male, I discovered. While most cuneiform is anonymous, attributable to no gender, of the several cultures of early antiquity in which writing first emerged Mesopotamia remains the only one with clearly documented evidence of female scribes as well as surviving examples of their work. Given this, and given that there are several thousand written documents from the late Urak period during which cuneiform writing is understood to have emerged, what stopped D'Agata choosing a piece of writing to open his 'new history' of the essay that could be attributed to a female, or even an anonymous source? Or, at the very least, from choosing one in which women were less objectified?

In 2017, Saana Svärd from the University of Helsinki and Charles Halton from Houston Baptist University published *Women's Writing of Ancient Mesopotamia: An anthology of the earliest female authors.* It includes over 120 translated cuneiform texts attributed to female scribes, none of which is perhaps as old as 'The List of Ziusudra' but many of which come close and could be said to have 'essayistic tendencies'. I read the book, cover to cover, in search of an alternative first essay.

Halton explains in chapter five that, as in our society, only a small portion of the texts produced in the ancient Near East were regarded as 'literature', and that hymns, along with prayers and poems, make up much of this body of works. And the person responsible for several of this corpus's most significant examples is also considered to be the first known non-anonymous author in the world and the first attested female author in history. Her name is Enheduanna. Could we not have had one of her pieces of writing as the first essay?

The daughter of Sargon I, King of Akkad, Enheduanna was installed as the High Priestess of Ur in the southern region of Sumer, into which her father's vast Akkadian kingdom had expanded during the twenty-fourth century BCE, and where the native Sumerian tongue was replaced with Akkadian as the official language. In her position as priestess she composed and/or collected many examples of writings around temples and deities, some of which survive today, including this one which Halton has translated as 'The House of Nisaba in Ereš' and which includes a description of the patron deity of all scribes, Nisaba:

> *The righteous woman who has discerning wisdom,*
> *… soothing and opening the mouth,*
> *always consulting lapis-lazuli tablets,*
> *giving counsel to all lands …*

It concludes:

The compiler of this tablet is Enheduanna.
My king, something has been produced that no person had produced before.

Is this essayistic enough? I wondered. While that last phrase struck me as convincingly so, I concluded that hymns—with their metrical structures and now silenced musical accompaniments—probably ride too close to the divine presence they sought out, for our modern minds, which would separate religious prayers from artistic questioning.

So could the body of proverbs attributable to anonymous women, or written from a female perspective, form an example of a first essay? Some proverbs in Svärd and Halton at least suggest the possibility. Like this one:

The wife of a man who cannot speak eloquently is a female slave.
Well, my mouth makes me equal to a man. My mouth gets me judged a man.

Still searching for an alternative, I wrote to D'Agata to ask if he had considered any other texts for the first essay in his collection. He mentioned early Sumerian letters. Several such letters attributed to female scribes and written from a female perspective are included in Svärd and Halton's book, such as 'Letter from an Angry Wife'. But although promising, none of these letters were as expansive as 'The List of Ziusudra', with its directness and breadth pacing stridently through time and space.

*

So maybe 'The List of Ziusudra' *was* unrivalled as an example of a first essay, I thought. But did it need to be this translation, which—as I have learned since my initial reading—is strikingly different to others that are also based on the same text, but which are significantly less sexist?

'The List of Ziusudra' is an example of what contemporary scholarship refers to as ancient Near Eastern wisdom literature, a genre to which the Book of Proverbs in the Old Testament also belongs. Most English translations of the list are titled 'The Instructions of Shuruppak' or 'The Instructions of Shuruppak, Son of Ubara-tutu', and are explained historically as a collection of important sayings written by King Shuruppak for his son Ziusudra. (In most extant copies of the 'Sumerian King List', Ubara-tutu is identified as the last king of Sumer before the deluge; Shuruppak appears in one copy.) In these translations the list is understood as being written specifically *for* Ziusudra, not *by* him for a general future audience—as D'Agata's poetic introduction suggests. Ziusudra is the reader, not the writer. This already changes the sense of the text significantly; but an even greater difference is that the collection of Shuruppak's sayings in most translations runs at around 280 lines, whereas the text in *The Lost Origins of the Essay* has only thirty-nine. The brevity lends an eloquence and creates something far more like a coherent, single piece of writing than a collection of sayings, which in turn reads more like an essay might.

I wrote again to D'Agata and asked him about the translation. In the book the translator is noted as a man called Joshua Barnes, about whom I could ascertain nothing in my research other than that he provided this translation. D'Agata said he recalled finding Barnes online in the early 2000s but offered nothing further.

That so much creative licence has been exercised through Barnes' translation establishes 'The List of Ziusudra' almost as a new piece of writing. But I don't take issue with this. In fact, it's more in keeping with the practices of the ancient Near East, where scribes signed their names to the texts they had copied—and likely often reinterpreted—from others.

Nor does D'Agata's inventive, beautifully envisioned account of these words issuing forth from the subsiding flood waters, or the translated text's misleading brevity, necessarily undermine the suggestion of this highly selective translation being the world's first essay. Recall that D'Agata is here 'in search of art', an endeavour on a par with the search for historical accuracy. And if our understanding of the essay is, as D'Agata puts it, of literature 'not propelled by information but compelled instead by individual expression—by inquiry, by opinion, by wonder, by doubt', then the list as presented in *The Lost Origins of the Essay* is legit as a first at least—as was suggested in our correspondence—in terms of its essayistic tendencies.

To regard the essay as an art form of tendencies, straddling the storyteller's divide between recounting and creation, is compelling. However, in a translation already playing fast and loose with meaning, the question, at least for this female reader, remains—why *these* thirty-nine lines? About prostitutes and whores and weak wives? In a translation that reconstructs multiple and largely disconnected phrases to tell a more singular story, why, at the very least, were those particular lines not preserved in their more balanced context? As in:

You should not buy a prostitute: she is a mouth that bites.
You should not buy a house-born slave: he is a herb that makes the stomach sick.
You should not buy a free man: he will always lean against the wall.
You should not buy a palace slave girl: she will always be the bottom of the barrel.

Or, instead of using those lines at all, why not:

You should not have sex with your slave girl: she will chew you up.

And:

You should not commit rape on someone's daughter: the courtyard will learn of it.

—lines which still clearly position female as subject (or object), male as reader, but at least shift her position to one slightly more improved?

Reading further in the alternative translations, I also found sections positively empowering of females in comparison to those Barnes had selected. Such as:

You should not speak arrogantly to your mother; that causes hatred for you.
You should not question the words of your mother and your personal god. The mother, like Utu, gives birth to the man; the father, like a god, makes him bright.

And:

The wet-nurses in the women's quarters determine the fate of their lord.

But most glaringly absent from 'The List of Ziusudra' are the final lines of 'The Instructions of Shuruppak', which critically frame the text with an acknowledgment of the deep-rootedness of cuneiform in female identity. The patron deity of all Mesopotamian scribes is the goddess Nisaba; in Sumerian myth Enki, the great creative force of the universe, gives the art of the scribes to his daughter Inanna, who also holds the function of a scribe as keeper of records in the world of the dead.

This gift of words is something which soothes the mind; when it enters the palace, it soothes the mind …

Praise be to the lady who completed the great tablets, the maiden Nisaba, that Curuppag, the son of Ubara-Tutu gave his instructions!

In Barnes' translation, all reference to this framework is lost.

III. Rewriting

5.51am EST, 11 April 2019. A moment in time, perhaps almost already lost to history. A photo, still very present on the internet, captures the expression on the face of the first-ever human to see the first-ever image of a black hole. The scientist in the photo is Katie Bouman, a post-doctoral researcher at Harvard who—thanks largely to that photo going viral—quickly became mythologised as the genius who developed the algorithm to capture the image and then, almost simultaneously, became quickly demythologised, as *Vox* put it, by 'an apparently small group of vociferous men' who endeavoured in the very public forums of social media to aggressively scrutinise her work for evidence of her contribution, or lack thereof, to the development of that algorithm.

Of course the discovery was collaborative, as it almost always is, and as Bouman and Massachusetts Institute of Technology immediately communicated in their own tweets and statements. In this case, a team of more than 200 researchers was behind the feat. But the story of the singular genius inventor/scientist/artist will usually catch anyway. Except, perhaps, in the case where the genius is female, and it is barked down.

How many such stories have been stopped in the telling?

*

In my own imagined version of the first writing, my imaginary scribe, to my disappointment, was male. And even once I knew a female scribe was a possibility in Sumer, I had to work hard to change his identity in my head. I still have to. Physically, I give my scribe a vagina, breasts, hips, children. I try to have her see the world from the perspective of someone with a cis-gendered female experience in ancient Mesopotamia, whatever that might have been. I try to change her mind. Still, she turns back into a man.

What stops me from imagining the anonymous writer as a woman? Why is it so difficult, when all my sympathies lie with her?

I think the problem is fundamental because the problem is history.

Even as I researched for this essay, the ghosts of millions of silent women rose then fell back into the pages. Because whichever version of the origin of writing was put forward in the scholarship I read, Adam was always its first author: Adam was given a script by Yahweh; Adam invented Hebrew; the angel Raphael revealed the scripts of the Chaldean alphabets to Adam; the Sumerian

Adams invented cuneiform. This is an old problem, but it seems like one we too easily lose sight of in scholarship and literature.

Five thousand years of telling stories in which men dominate means it *is* the way we think, and read, and write. It is in our blood.

What do you do?
How do you read?
How do you write?

*

Astronomy was an important area of study in the Ancient Near East. Thousands of astronomical and astrological cuneiform tablets, most of which were written by anonymous scribes, attest to this. In an essay about 'The Astronomical Diaries', some of humanity's earliest records of observational astronomy, E.L. Meszaros, a PhD student at Brown University in the US, notes: 'Even though much scholarly material from Mesopotamia lacks a named author it is assumed to have been produced by men. But the question of who wrote these texts is not so straightforward.' Meszaros rightly argues that while our assumptions about authorship are partly based on what we know about gender roles in the past, they are also heavily influenced by what our patriarchal tradition and scholarship culture assumes and thereby asserts about gender roles in the past. Because—history. Because it is in the blood.

'In a culture of anonymous texts, it is a mistake to discount women as observers or authors entirely and doing so paves the way for continued denial of the role that women have played,' Meszaros continues, calling up ancient generations of unacknowledged female astronomers whose connection to their work has been lost, as one day Katie Bouman's might also be. 'But,' she goes on hopefully, 'reasserting the possibility of their presence can allow us to view women as a part of astronomy from the start.'

Perhaps it begins with this.

Perhaps it begins when Glassner, in his authoritative text on the origins of cuneiform, writes about the Sumerian scribes going to training and imagines 'a boy placed under the control of someone other than its father'.

Perhaps it begins with rewriting that sentence.

REFERENCES

I am here in search of art … John D'Agata (ed.), Introduction, 'The List of Ziusudra', *The Lost Origins of the Essay* (Minnesota: Graywolf Press, 2009), p. 3.

the beginning of an alternative … Ibid., p. 4.

writing as a conscious process … Jean Jacques Glassner, *The Invention of Cuneiform,* translated and edited by Zainab Bahrani and Marc Van De Meiroop (Baltimore: Johns Hopkins University Press, 2003), p. 105.

Back in those days … D'Agata (ed.), 'The List of Ziusudra', in *The Lost Origins of the Essay*, p. 7.

So first, don't ever buy a donkey … Ibid., p. 7.

The righteous woman who has discerning wisdom … Charles Halton and Saana Svärd, *Women's Writing of Ancient Mesopotamia: An anthology of the world's earliest female authors* (Cambridge: Cambridge University Press, 2017), p. 78.

The compiler of this tablet is Enheduanna … Ibid., p. 79.

The wife of a man who cannot speak eloquently … Ibid., pp. 211–12.

literature 'not propelled by information' … D'Agata (ed.), Introduction, p. 4.

You should not buy a prostitute … I have used the translation available via the following link, which is largely based on Bendt Alster's translations and revisions: www.gatewaystobabylon.com/myths/texts/life/instructionshruppak.html

This gift of words … www.gatewaystobabylon.com/myths/texts/life/instructionshruppak.html

an apparently small group … www.vox.com/science-and-health/2019/4/16/18311194/black-hole-katie-bouman-trolls

Even though much scholarly material … E.L. Meszaros, 'Gendered Observation: The contribution of women to the astronomical diaries of Mesopotamia', *The New Inquiry*, 16 May 2019: https://thenewinquiry.com/blog/gendered-observation-the-contribution-of-women-to-the-astronomical-diaries-of-mesopotamia/

a boy placed under the control … Glassner, *The Invention of Cuneiform,* p. 197.

Himali McInnes

This Place

This place, south of the city centre, became so familiar to me it melted my bones like wax, leaving an awkward but warm imprint on my heart. This place, at times charming and sweet, at others frustrating and poignant, became a place that I cherished. With the passage of years I developed what environmental psychologists call 'place attachment' to this southern suburb of Auckland. My distinctive qualities, such as skin colour, a fondness for sushi, a love of animals and my Sri Lankan heritage, were subsumed into something larger, enabling syncretism with strangers despite differences in language, customs and diet. Given that we often focus on what sets us apart from others, it was an epiphany to find commonalities that crossed cultural barriers.

Over the last decade my attachment to South Auckland has solidified, and now pops up in other suburbs. While walking in a park in central Auckland I smile broadly when I see a group of young Pacific women, a sports team of some sort, giggling and back-slapping and bouncing to the beat of a portable bluetooth speaker. They don't make eye contact with me, however. I am just another stranger here and they owe me no recognition or camaraderie. In this park full of people intent on speed-walking, these young women are an anomaly, and their laughter has a nervous brittle edge to it. I nod and walk past.

Perhaps more potently, this place that is less affluent and full of need has led to my political awakening. In my eligible-to-vote but inert-with-apathy youth, I frequently did not make the effort to go to the ballot box. The legacy of Kate Sheppard and the suffragettes of 1893 was wasted on me. When I did rock up to a polling station I used the tic-tac-toe method of marking the voting slip, as there seemed no clear correlation between voting and perceptible changes in my life. The machinations of the Beehive were far removed from my medical student milieu. I was consumed with more immediate tangible concerns: turning up on time to lectures in the grey concrete warren of Auckland Medical

School; passing exams; trying not to faint during dissection classes or when we practised venipuncture on each other; re-learning the Krebs cycle endlessly because it never seemed to stick in my head.

*

Joan Didion wrote about falling in love with New York in her essay 'Goodbye to All That'. Cities like New York thrum with supernovae energy, they burst with the scents of a thousand lovers, they inspire music and art and flattery. They have gorgeous architecture, their skylines are iconic and they have distinct personalities, a mélange of vocalisations and victuals and vanities. Even the grime and dirt of such cities is quirky, an instance of Boho chic. Any mention of a visit to such places is dropped into conversation casually with the certainty of provoking envy and wanderlust.

It is more peculiar perhaps to admit to having a fondness for a place that is scuffed about the edges, humdrum, worn out. A suburb that some avoid, their perceptions warped by the presence of high crime rates and old vehicles belching unfashionable quantities of pollutants. The media is a negative Instagram for the undesirable parts of a city, stoking unease in the well-heeled, in those who believe the poor to be both culpable for their beggary and capable of reckless violence.

And certainly it is not well groomed, this place of which I am so fond. There are no topiary hedges or cream-brick houses, no organic wholefood markets or cafés selling raw vegan food. I was in my thirties when I started working as a general practitioner in South Auckland; a decade later there has been little cosmetic improvement to the area. The houses are thin-walled and small-boned, and umpteen little bodies still sleep in the same cold beds, smoothing the way for wastrel bacteria to jump from throat to ravaged heart. Fast-food joints dot the landscape like palaces for the poor. One day my husband met me for lunch and we wandered through the local shopping mall together. He was struck by similarities to shopping malls in developing countries—the cheap plastic trinkets spilling over pavements, florid clothes, all that flotsam with built-in obsolescence.

I sometimes rode my bike to work over the old Māngere bridge. As I crossed to the south the tarmac, eroded by hot sun and fierce rains, made my bones judder. Once a sloe-eyed, thick-muscled pit bull terrier chased me for fifty metres. I am normally sanguine about dogs and unflustered by them. That day I mustered every ounce of mana I had to get the creature to back off, yelling and eyeballing it to no avail. I did not cycle to South Auckland again.

Driving in this place has its own frustrations. Many times I have come off the motorway into Māngere and found myself crawling behind someone driving at thirty kilometres an hour. Sunny day, dry road, and a driver obeying the national speed limit of a faraway Island home. Each time I muse darkly about performing illegal manoeuvres in order to speed past but settle instead for being late.

Family violence is a creeping hidden stain in this place. One young woman I know recounted growing up in a cul-de-sac in Ōtara. Almost every child in that street, including herself, was subjected to physical or sexual violence. Although now a competent professional, the woman still bore the scars of that early trauma. Domestic and childhood abuse is prevalent in New Zealand and seems to disproportionately affect Māori and Pacific Island families. The reasons for this are complex and involve socioeconomic and cultural factors among others.

Despite the rawness of life in this place, I have nonetheless developed a deep attachment to it, due in large part to the overwhelming kindness and gratitude of its inhabitants. This love of South Auckland runs broader than just my personal predilections and infects many who work here. In fact, colleagues who have left and gone to work elsewhere often come back, citing as a reason the joy of working with those who have genuine needs and who show deep appreciation for their efforts.

'Thank you VERY much, doctor,' said any one of a number of delightful septuagenarian Pacific grandmas as they kissed me on the cheek after a consult. One spritely ninety-five-year-old often slipped me a twenty-dollar bill in thanks as she skipped out of my room—perhaps not exactly skipping, but walking unaided and with purpose, and likely to do so for many years as her mother before her had lived past 100. My protestations at the extra money fell on deaf ears, and over time I learned to smile and accept the gift before putting it into the staff tea fund.

There were also instances of sheer audacity that made me laugh. During one lunch break spent filing results and writing referrals, I heard a voice. It belonged to a young man outside my window, who dimpled his mouth until his smile spread to his chocolate eyes. 'Excuse me, Miss, can I have an off-work certificate, Miss?' Unable to obtain a traditional doctor's appointment, he thought to try his luck at an impromptu drive-through service.

The touching hilarious moments such as these are many. They come, I think, from a community that is on 'Island time', devoid of the hurry sickness that afflicts other suburbs. This is a community that takes time to indulge in small kindnesses. Cars stop to let pedestrians cross the road, even in the absence of a zebra crossing. People smile with friendly eyebrows and wave at strangers for no particular reason. Guitars are strummed at the local pool as belly-flopping teenagers send small tsunamis to the tiled edges.

The strawberry farm on Kirkbride Road is a fruity mecca during the summer months. Lines of people queue at the counter and watch as frozen fruit and ice cream are churned and dispensed into large waffle cones. Outside, a microcosm of society sits on wooden benches, slurping pink deliciousness. Police in stab-resistant vests and peaked caps on a short break, sticky squealing children, parents pushing prams, people with walking canes. The trestle tables inside the shop are piled high with fresh vegetables but the ice cream is the star attraction.

*

Children are cherished despite scarce resources. In my room they are polite and well behaved and often kiss their siblings, trading snot and bugs as siblings are wont to do. Older children help to babysit toddlers. Lost children are rescued by multiple strangers and swiftly reunited with their parents. Grandparents are brought in by teenagers who are solicitous and caring of their frail charges in a way that is genuine and heart-warming. Given that one in five of New Zealand's elderly report loneliness, and given that loneliness is an invisible burden that is worse for our health than smoking or high cholesterol, this whānau-centred care is enviable and allows the golden years to be truly golden.

The local shopping centre often holds free Zumba classes. The music is loud and peppy, heads are garlanded with 'ei katu of plastic flowers, and young and old alike jiggle and sweat it out together. The instructor wears a bandanna and a tight shirt, his salted skin shining as he pumps his arms and legs up and down the stage. As in any crowd of public exercisers, there are the show-offs who avoid eye contact as they flex muscles and twirl and strut with panache.

My consulting room becomes a soup swimming with stories. Sometimes it is a soup teeming with viruses, especially in the colder months, when patients who have been silent in the waiting room start to cough as soon as they see me. I call it the 'proving how sick you really are' reflex, an unconscious gesture that allows grown men and women to ask to be taken care of. I take to leaving my window open despite the cold.

Often patients' stories are plangent and reverberate in the room after they leave. There are stories of cancer, that most insidious of illnesses. The spouse who looks after a sick partner while ignoring their own health and who, without warning, becomes the first to succumb to death's veil. The intellectually disabled who are now in middle age and will need state care when their parents die. The grandma caring for five grandchildren at a stage of life when she should be unshackled from the constraints of work and school lunches. The stories of high blood sugars and kidney failure, rheumatic fever that has warped heart valves, the intractable coughing of chronic lung disease that turns lips blue and makes each breath a wheezy tight-corseted misery.

There are also bright stories that make me laugh with delight. Sometimes patients just want to talk, to connect with another human being, and there is profound healing in that connection alone. Some days I receive as much or more than I give out simply because the people I care for are so lacking in pretentiousness and are so utterly human.

There are unsolicited gifts. A Fiji Indian grandma brings me a pottle of tamarind chutney redolent with spices and tangy with heat, the best I have ever tasted. A Cook Islander brings me a succulent that she has grown herself over the last four years, a stunning plant with spiky rose-tipped leaves. There are words, words that cost nothing but which are priceless, emblems of gratitude that warm the heart and the soul. Kindness begets kindness; gratitude multiplies and seeds itself in a million little ways.

In spring I bring in heirloom tomato seedlings to give away to patients. The receptionists tell me of beaming faces as patients head out with their tender green gifts. Months later the patients tell me of the fruit in their gardens that is gold-yellow or black-cherried or pendulous red, and it makes my skin tingle to think of this propagation of heritage into the future.

This place south of the city centre has a multitude of heart-warming stories, yet at a macroscopic level it remains impoverished. In an ideal world we would all have the opportunity to flourish, but the world we live in doles out her blessings erratically. American business magnate and philanthropist Warren Buffett acknowledges that he won the 'ovarian lottery' by being born white and male in America, giving him a head start. The people of South Auckland, meanwhile, are afflicted by multiple stressors, and research indicates life-long sequelae from these.

Children exposed to chronic stress often become adults suffering from anxiety and depression with higher rates of suicide. Young minds exposed to trauma are permanently scarred, even if they do not experience violence directly. Being shunted into another room with the TV on while parents fight elsewhere can still have physical effects on the brain and body. As paediatrician Nadine Burke Harris explains in her TEDMED talk, childhood trauma can triple the rates of heart disease and lung cancer in adults and shorten lifespans by decades. High doses of adversity affect brain structure and function, the developing immune and hormonal systems, and even our DNA.

With exposure to chronic stress, the pre-frontal cortex of the brain is inhibited, reducing impulse control and executive function. Multiple areas of white matter do not develop properly, resulting in an inability to learn well. The amygdala, which regulates emotions, stays on constant alert for environmental threats, leading to a heightened flight-or-fight state. The nucleus accumbens, the reward centre of the brain, is affected, meaning that as these children grow into adults, pleasure-seeking behaviour becomes an imperative, a neurochemical salve that works to dull memories and pain. And with this, of course, come the consequences—drink-driving, imprisonment for drug-taking and so on—in an ongoing cycle of poor statistics and harmed lives.

Chronic stress, such as that born of poverty, can shorten the caps on our DNA known as telomeres. Shorter telomeres mean a shorter lifespan and greater morbidity. These altered genetics are found in eggs and sperm, meaning that parental deprivation can get passed on to children as a gift they did not ask for and do not deserve. Sometimes the perpetrators of childhood trauma may have little ability or insight and few resources to change their behaviour, and may have been victims of childhood adversity themselves. Notably, placing people into healthy environments where they can flourish has been shown to undo some of the damage to physiology imparted by trauma and stress.

*

My earlier political apathy was burned away in 2016 when I became aware of a number of patients who were sleeping in their cars. Despite sometimes holding down more than one job, many were still unable to afford skyrocketing rental costs. Other families were crammed into draughty emergency accommodation, and their children were developing chronic chest infections and missing school. The government at the time denied that there was an issue. Minister for Housing Nick Smith called the rise in homelessness 'a figment of some people's imagination'; the Minister for Social Housing, Paula Bennett, added, 'I certainly wouldn't call it a crisis.' Prime Minister John Key advised the homeless to apply for a benefit from Work and Income—ignoring the fact that one needs a valid address in order to get a benefit. My head reeled with incredulity. Had these people actually bothered to visit the suburbs where I worked every day?

I describe myself as a details person, as someone who can be struck still by the beauty of raindrops shimmering in a spider's web, the unfurling of grey-green artichoke leaves towards the sun, or the bright orange pollen dusting a bumble bee's bottom. As the deprivation in the community I worked in reached alarming levels I became incensed and indignant, and my scope of vision expanded upwards and outwards. How could people in power blatantly lie about the homelessness crisis when I was seeing it with my own eyes? I could reach out and touch the arms of people who were living in their cars, hear their stories first hand. My stethoscope on their chest could hear the rattle of their lungs as they strained against the cold air. I listened as parents described using public toilets in the morning before sending their children to school with empty bellies.

There was a groundswell of public disgust. People organised car sleep-ins. I took part in the Māngere Park Up for Homes one cold June night in 2016. It was organised by a group of Māngere flatmates: a lawyer, a graphic designer and a community law centre advocate. Almost a thousand people took part. Some were homeless—bona fide participants if you will. Others had been homeless in the past and understood the pathos and instability involved. Families turned up with children who played in the carpark dressed in their pyjamas.

I took my huntaway along for company. She is an SPCA rescue and thus a South Auckland girl at heart, but now very much a princess. There is a terrible irony in owning a dog that leads a better life than many people in this world. Two meals a day, her own beanbag to sleep on, a jersey on cold nights, plenty of fresh air and exercise. Suffice to say she was unhappy at having to sleep in a cold car with condensation on the windows. She sighed and groaned in that soulful, human way that dogs have. She fidgeted from front seat to back, trying to make herself comfortable. She burrowed into my side, waking me up several times. I had a sleeping bag and was warm enough, although my face chilled as it fell to six degrees. In the morning when I awoke bleary-eyed and tired, I simply drove to my house in order to use the toilet. I felt achy and fatigued after only one night in a car. That day at work it was hard to concentrate. All I could think about was heading home that evening to my comfortable warm house and falling asleep in my bed. The contrast between the two sleeping situations was simply enormous. I felt a huge sense of privilege, and with it came a sense of responsibility.

Many will argue that the privileges they hold are their right to enjoy as they please: they have earned them and hence deserve them. There are also those who believe that anyone in New Zealand can succeed if they work hard enough. There is of course some truth to these opinions, but only a partial truth. It is difficult to have insight into the unearned advantages with which we have been blessed. Blaming the poor for their situation or suggesting it exists because of faults of character or behaviour displays a fundamental attribution error: the poor are poor because they are lazy, because they spend money on luxuries such as cigarettes, because they don't care. We are more likely to explain failures in our own lives in terms of external factors, but are resistant to giving others the same benefit.

*

Understanding how chronic stress and deprivation affect us on a physiological and neuroanatomical level is important, because it should and must deserve empathy. Everyone has choices they can make, but some people's choices are limited by circumstance and environment. I work one shift a week as a prison doctor seeing inmates who are disproportionately Māori. Their past stories are chillingly similar: broken families, violence, abuse, chronic stress and deprivation. There are reasons why some end up in prison. It takes a Herculean effort for people in such situations to pull themselves out. Where one has succeeded despite the odds, you will often find that someone has intervened in some small but significant way. In this smallish island nation the importance of who you know is paramount.

South Auckland has given me many gifts. It has helped me to identify with and care for people who are strikingly different from myself. It has removed the ignorance that could so easily exist if I only kept company with those in my own socioeconomic stratum. It has made me aware of the importance of large-scale as well as personal solutions to people's issues, and has set me on a path of advocacy. It has made me aware that for some, the ability to change their life circumstances can be hampered by invisible but nonetheless pertinent influences.

It takes a nation to help a nation, a village to raise a child. Even at a fundamentally self-serving level, it makes sense that all New Zealanders should flourish, as this begets prosperity for all. The children of today are the workers of tomorrow, when many of us will be in our dotage and in need of kindness and a strong community. It is far easier and more cost-effective to build strong children than it is to fix broken adults. So much creativity and intellectual vigour could be unleashed with relatively simple inputs, such as improved housing and healthier food.

The words of Martin Luther King Jr, the American Baptist minister and civil rights activist, seem apposite for this place that I care for: 'Our lives begin to end the day we become silent about things that matter.'

REFERENCES
place attachment … Leila Scannell and Robert Gifford, 'Defining place attachment: A tripartite organizing framework', *Journal of Environmental Psychology* 30 (2010), pp. 1–10.
Joan Didion wrote … Joan Didion, *Slouching Towards Bethlehem* (New York: Farrar, Straus and Giroux, 1968).
Domestic and childhood abuse … Marie Dannette and David Fergusson, 'Ethnic identity and intimate partner violence in a New Zealand birth cohort', *Social Policy Journal of New Zealand Te Puna Whakaaro* 33 (2008).
American business magnate … www.cnbc.com/2018/05/04/warren-buffett-says-the-key-to-his-success-is-luck.html

Children exposed to chronic stress … Maria Cohut, 'How childhood trauma affects the brain', *Medical News Today*, 30 Sep. 2017: www.medicalnewstoday.com/articles/319566.php

childhood trauma can triple the rates … Nadine Burke Harris, 'How childhood trauma affects health across a lifetime': www.ted.com/talks/nadine_burke_harris_how_childhood_trauma_affects_health_across_a_lifetime?language=en

High doses of adversity … V.J. Felitti and R.F. Anda, 'Relationship of childhood abuse and household dysfunction to many of the leading causes of death in adults', *American Journal of Preventive Medicine* 14 (1998): 245–58.

Chronic stress, such as that borne of poverty … E.S. Epel and E.H. Blackburn, 'Accelerated telomere shortening in response to life stress', *Proceedings of the National Academy of Sciences*, 101:49 (2004): 17312–15.

'Our lives begin to end' … Martin Luther King Jnr, Selma, Alabama, 8 March 1965.

Derek Schulz

Kiwi-Made

We were taking home $9.20 an hour so we weren't in it for the money. We cooked, we drove, we dressed, showered, toileted, entertained, learned how they spoke without speaking, disputed with their doctors, eased them through their furies and their seizures, cleaned them up afterwards, administered the drugs, sat with them in the ambulance. We fitted the catheter, tucked them into bed, fretted through the night then came back in the morning. We became the everything that no one could bear to be.

That kept them all together.

Sex was a problem the manual sorted for you. Encourage them into their room. Close the door. If they're doing it by the window, keep a blanket handy. Throw it right over. It wasn't any help at all, but my female workmates were experienced, deadpan, ribald and indispensable. They never missed a trick and would giggle all the way back to the lounge. 'Harry's back in the bathroom, do you want to join him?' they would enquire, then hive off to conference in the garden. I tried things: the long walk, chocolate cake on the garden swing, the knucklebones that he always loved to roll in his cupped hands and shuffle round the table. After which he'd head straight back in. Finally, I got the message and left him alone. Then went back to clean up the mess.

Harry was deaf, blind, mute and sixty-one years old. He remained one of life's mysteries. Rubella had gone through his mum like a bushfire. He walked like he'd been on the sauce for a week, but when you took his arm you found he was balanced and true. It set up a curious rhythm between you: a foxtrotting pas-de-deux. Blind and ID'd though he was, within twenty-four hours he would figure the layout of a house he'd never been in before. He went around each room, arms splayed up against the walls, tapping the spatial arrangement into his memory. He'd had a boyfriend before he came to us so we assumed he was gay, but he would try and force it on the women just the same. They'd talk it through among themselves and never made a fuss. When he wouldn't eat his veggies we mixed them in with his chips. That isn't in the manual. He'd sit there picking out the beans until you knew just what he was thinking. He was a choke risk and everything went into his mouth. You had to watch him like a kāhu, and the older he got the worse it became. Much later, when I heard the news, I went around to support his supporters. They had found him sprawled on the floor. It was no one's fault yet they blamed themselves anyway. You can't help it. 'I should have done this.' 'If only I had …' 'How can I live with it?' They churned it over and over.

All for $9.20 in the hand.

Women are a lot more complicated. Brenda caught me once with her fist, right between the eyes; the second time, when I saw it coming, I jerked my head back straight into a cupboard door. She was blind too but could break her bedroom windows, strip off and lie yowling on the lounge floor while filleting her arms. She'd keep it up for six hours straight and you'd get resentful. You couldn't leave her, and there were five others in the house.

Gena was forty. She had no language and would stand in the bathroom, back turned against the world, screaming at the wall. You knew it was only a matter of time and hoped it wasn't on your shift, but when I got back one morning she'd smeared faeces right round her room. Gem cleaned the floor and walls, I did the sheets, the blankets, the pillows, the clothes. It wasn't easy because you had to scrub it off first in the bath. But it sorted out the staff. You could see it in their eyes. Some never came back the next day. Then the accountant would ring. 'You used too many rubber gloves last month!' Did he get the raw end of Leah's tongue! 'I'm sending that twerp the used ones!' she said as she came steaming back to the kitchen.

It helped having men in the house. Gena started to become a woman again: offhand, touchy, curious, sunny, good-humoured, irate. Her notes carried the warning that she could micturate on your feet if she didn't like you. One day in the bathroom she gave me a bold, decisive stare, then turned, shuffled away and pissed all over the floor instead. It came out like the Huka Falls. She'd bagged a few of the others so it felt better than winning the lottery. We had to put her back in overalls during the night. But there was one worker I never could trust. She'd pitch Gena into the shower, bundle her into bed before seven then clear off home early. I'd go straight in to check. One night I found Gena choking, the cord of her overalls tightened round her neck—but only so much. It was deliberate. I was pitched into a fury, but managers are knock-kneed and duplicitous. They would sit on trouble like that then turn it round, so I handed it back to the women. They knew how to get rid of suspect workers.

The psychologists had rated these guys as children and Gena came in around the age of five. It was intellectual marsh gas; the dilettante musings of a smug Behaviourism. Once you could see past the disablement, she would swing back to her age. But how difficult this was to gauge, for she was a born mimic and would effortlessly acquire the tics and follies of her housemates so she wouldn't stand out. She would give her doctor a curious stare—Who does he expect me to be today? But then the world would get too much again and she would disappear into herself for days at a time. Her behaviour was typical of severe brain injury and her notes spelt out the tragedy: she had fallen from a swing as a three-year-old. No one believed that.

Aroha was working around the clock. She slept over in a rest home then came in for a morning shift. She'd sit in the lounge watching Prince Tui Teka hamming it up on Māori TV. It was all in te reo and she'd be beside herself, chortling on the sofa with the boys, but if I asked her to translate she wouldn't. 'It's too rude for the Pākehā,' she would rule, magisterially. Then try to look ashamed of herself.

She and her husband never missed a Sunday service and would take along the guys who were up to it. One night one of her pōrangi'd souls at the rest home contracted norovirus. He'd dragged it through the house and it had taken her all night to clean up. 'I've showered,' she said when she came in, 'but can't get rid of the stink.' I sent her back to the bathroom, then home, and covered for the rest of the day. You'd get sacked if they found you out, but fuck them. She never forgot. From there on I'd get the big kai breakfast anytime we shared a shift. Nothing was too good. She'd wait till we'd got the guys away then fry up the chips, bring in the fish, show me how to marinate it the Māori way, grill it and drop as many poached eggs on top as she thought I needed. Blue cod. The kina was for afters. It cost as much as caviar but was mana for the soul. You scooped it out of the jar with a spoon. 'One for me,' she would say, then 'one more for me,' before stopping to offer me some. She'd give me a meaningful look, meaning: she didn't want to share.

When I said I liked it she wouldn't believe me.

*

For seventy cents less you could work in someone's home, but you paid for the petrol and the wear and tear on your car yourself; seven days on a rotating shift, 400 kilometres a week. They put you to work like the self-employed while the taxpayer pocketed your expenses. Then there were the rest homes you had enabled them to shut down. I was learning what government had become: a preening ground for wide-boy traders; a treasury stacked with hard-boiled nuts. They demanded everything for nothing but it was never going to be enough.

Out here in the suburbs it was even more of a wilderness because they sent you to their incorrigibles first. I soon felt right at home. Deb was in her sixties and looking after her husband Jeb. He'd had a stroke, a bad one. No language, no movement in his arms or legs, but he was all there just the same. They always are. But in Deb I found another. She had filled herself with an allure she couldn't bear to part with. There was no gentleness to her touch. No softness in her mind. She knew exactly how to get him back: through the sheer force of her will. He couldn't move but would fall out of bed at night, or she'd slap him a little, right in front of me. I tried to show her a better way but she wasn't having any. The bruising was the last straw and could have been pinned on the worker, so I let her have it, both barrels. Jeb couldn't speak but he began squirming and squawking for Deb. I was blindsided. Was he enjoying it? Fortunately, I had an 18-year-old student with me. Management wouldn't believe me, but when the company got her wide-eyed report they dropped the Care from their books.

I was beginning to learn the trick of it. Leave well enough alone. It's their minds you're being paid to work with. Even where they're assessed as not having one.

*

Now that I'd got a name for backing into trouble, they sent me along to their next incorrigible, Sayl, a brawly millionaire. He'd deliberately leave cash on the dresser to try you out, and ran his bathroom like he'd run his company. 'Straighten the towel.' 'Clean that fucken mirror.' 'You leave on my say so.' 'You call that clean …?'

The tempo rose and rose until you had to have it out. I dug out something from inside I didn't know was there and looked him back, straight in the eye.

'You can stop that bullshit right now!'

He was stunned *and* pleased, but when I got back in the morning I found him still in his bed. He hadn't slept and had grown purple through saving up what he had to say. 'Now you listen to this,' he said. 'I'll say what I fucken like in my own fucken home. You got that?' 'Absolutely, Sayl,' I assured him, then set out his grunds for the day.

We'd both won, so we started to get to know each other.

I was an E Tū man, steadfast and staunch, yet I liked him immediately then tried to work out why. He was phlegmatic and soured and had a brand-new wardrobe—Icebreaker jacket, Barkers trou, silk shirts, show-day shoes, Vivian ties and a bottle of eau de cologne, thrown back into his drawer. Slowly the story came out. His previous support had been thirty-one years old, leggy and ambitious. She'd dressed herself to prove it and would help him out in the shower then take him to London's to flash him up again. She thought she was getting $40 million. He thought he could get it for free. There'd been a sorting out. He missed her brash conceit and was furious with himself for falling. But it went a lot deeper.

The stroke had taken out his left side and he would kick himself along on his right with the walker, dragging the leg. Day by day, week by week, he'd punch out the miles from lounge to hallway to bedroom to hallway to lounge, clawing the movement back. But I could see something he couldn't—a rising organic disorder, the struggle to recall, an accruing distress. There'd be a week of irascible tantrum then he would have the turn that would restore him to himself, mostly during the night I suspected. The change was barely perceptible, but there was always that little bit missing. It was affecting somewhat more of his brain than the machinery that controlled mobility. A little less stress with the walker might have helped, though you had to admire him. But as the months rolled by, you sensed a grudging acceptance. The hard graft and my gritted teeth were paying off.

It took one of my queer dreams to find him out. They switch on like a light then off again just as curtly. In this one I found myself watching him tooling round in one of my other Care's bathrooms. He seemed quite at home until his legs suddenly scissored from under him. It woke me with a start. I have these dreams all the time, but how are they cooked up? Is that the right question?

Does it even make sense to ask? Where to start? How to start? At first you overthink them, but then just go with their flow—while keeping the news to yourself.

This one seemed even loopier than usual until I got to work. Sayl was staying in bed for the day. He'd come a cropper in the bathroom and blamed himself. He wasn't saying, but I could see he'd had the turn and it had dropped him to the floor.

'I'm staying in bed,' he said. 'I'll bring you some breakfast,' I argued back. But he wasn't having any. 'I'm a fool,' he confessed, 'come back tomorrow.' I left my home number beside the bed and explained how pissed I'd be if he didn't use it. We all did it sooner or later with Cares like Sayl. You'd get sacked if they found you out, but fuck them. He signed my sheet and sent me off with a grin. My next stop was Brett. It was her bathroom the dream had shanghaied Sayl into, but she wasn't there. She'd had the turn too and been rushed back into hospital. So I had a day to myself on full pay. Twenty-five in the hand, minus petrol.

All on the taxpayer's largesse.

At Christmas Sayl sent me down to his wine cellar to fetch myself two bottles of his wine. I drank only beer and knew nothing about the vino, but managed to lift two of his rarest years despite myself. He nodded approvingly then chipped in half his ham. Only toward the end did I discover why we got on so well, despite the bluster. It came seeping out. He was Spanish-born, from Barcelona; salty, open-minded, and intensely moral. Family was everything and everything became family. His housekeeper had seen him through the death of his wife. I would watch them playing together. It was sparky and amusing—a brother with his youngest sister. She only got the minimum wage too, but it was under the table. He would send her to Queensland with her grandchildren every year.

'Okay then,' I finally prodded, 'why have you never gone back to Spain?' 'Franco!' he barked at me, as if it was my fault and had only happened yesterday. His father was a socialist and very active so they were hunted down. The children and their cousins had been scattered throughout the world: Canada, Melbourne, New York, Wainui. So was he the one closest to his dad? An autodidact, meticulous and serious with razor-sharp intelligence and an unforgiving tongue. One morning I watched him examining his slippers. He raised his jowly face in distaste. 'Look at the money wasted on this,' he argued. 'They make an upper to last six months; the sole ten years. Whoever designed this, I'd have fired the fucker!'

He never stopped trying to groom me. I never stopped pretending he could.

*

Sel was another. You walked into the house through the library where Thatcher and Reagan bookended a local history of the rebel All Black tour to South Africa. This was going to be hard, but you were only there for the stroke. It had taken out his language, stiffened his right arm and teased away at some vital functions. Arrhythmia of the heart mostly. He could walk okay, but would suddenly turn far too white and you'd have to prop him back in a chair. But it wouldn't stop him for long. I'd do the lifting in his garden where his tomatoes were a month ahead of ours, though we had the edge on his sweet peas. After a while you stopped noticing the deficits. He'd put on his hat and gesture toward the car and I'd drive him into town. You'd get sacked if they found you out, but fuck them.

Christmas Eve I took him down to Pak'nSave but his bankcard wouldn't work. I marched him into the bank, determined to sort them out. 'Hello, Mr Quick,' the teller said, floating her breeziest smile right past me before buzzing in the manager. She waited till they were in his office then turned her screen toward me. There were five accounts, only one under $40,000. Then the empty one: he was using the bank's money and they had started to mind. A couple of weeks later he left a folder out and nodded for me to leaf through. It headlined a statement from his broker. The yearly income alone totalled $50,000 plus. It was all being shovelled into the Quick Library Trust. The money was going to the poorest schools in the district, including the one that had started him off. He had me sussed within an hour. I'm still bewildered.

*

Leni had cancer. It was right through her but you wouldn't have known. Sometimes it's like that, returning you to the fullest bloom of health just before the end. She was a farmer's wife who'd had to turn into the farmer when her husband didn't return from the war. She already had her children and never remarried; then she'd retired into town and her garden. You would cook tea, shuffle her down for a pee and a wash then get her ready for bed. She'd prop herself up on the La-Z-boy in the lounge with a duvet. The government would only pay for an hour, but it took as long as it took—two hours some nights. My workmates were the same, only more so. Kora was from Sāmoa and would pay a babysitter $15 to mind her kids then get to Leni for $9 minus the petrol. She'd leave her children. She wouldn't leave Leni.

Then there was an industry crisis. A bloke in another company in another town was accused of untoward behaviour by an elderly woman with about 60 percent of her neurology still working. She should have been in twenty-four-hour care, but the government was busy saving its taxpayers the $140 a day. It was he who was judged the victim, but the media had its field day and outraged a lot of viewers, and didn't want to know how it had wrecked his family. So male staff were segregated from the women. But Leni got straight on the phone. She gave them such a scolding. She'd go straight to the newspaper, she told them, unless she got her way. My supervisor Pati sent me back the next day. She was Te Arawa, from Rotorua, and the best supervisor we ever had. She set aside a back room for the workers' Christmas party, then rang to call it off. We were paying for it ourselves but the managers had found out and threatened her with the sack.

Leni was a good Catholic, and on Sunday a female priest would drop by to minister to her. I didn't think there were any, but there you go. I was brought up at the opposite end of the doctrinal spectrum then walked away from it all. So the rituals were an intrigue to me—solemn and distant and binding and yet somehow warm-hearted. Perhaps because they were women. It seemed to rekindle her, to return a surer sense of balance. Others could see it too. Her granddaughter would ring. 'Nanny, can you say a prayer for me? God doesn't listen to mine but he always answers yours.' The woman was in real estate and facing a holdout. She needed one more house before turning them all into flats. Leni lost me on that one; still, being a good Catholic, she kept a bottle of whisky under the kitchen bench and fostered a passion for the turf. We'd watch the Melbourne Cup together—she always ran five bucks each way. She had the inside gen on a local horse and cajoled half the neighbourhood into backing it. When it ran home fourth, she was distraught and wanted to refund all their cash.

Then one morning I arrived to find her incoherent and near comatose. I knew exactly what it was—diabetes—so spooned in the antidote: blackberry jelly. She soon revived, but the diabetes was starting to run out of control. There was more going on than that but I tried not to see it, and fetched a pot of honey to place beside her chair. Finally, she agreed to leave the garden she loved. I visited her only once in her new digs at the rest home. She was sitting beside her bed, dressed like next spring, sunny and engaging and absurdly grateful. Somehow, we'd got her through.

*

Kora rang to try and get me to the funeral. 'We'll all be there!' But I prevaricated and prevaricated. When you find yourself avoiding the funerals, it's time to get out of the job.

Which left me all those dreams to unpick.

Una Cruickshank

Waste

It's difficult to hold the size of a sperm whale in your mind's eye; people often resort to describing them in terms of industrial products like cars or buses. The largest males can measure twenty metres—the length of a standard shipping container—and weigh 54,000 kilograms. Females are much smaller but still spectacular; like humans, they live more than seventy years if they don't meet with an accident or violence. The sperm whale's enormous blunt head, which comprises one third of the length of its body, houses a large organ or 'case' filled with a pale waxy liquid called spermaceti. It seems to have something to do with sound amplification, as sperm whales both echolocate and communicate through clicks that traverse hundreds, possibly thousands of kilometres underwater.

Spermaceti may also help protect the males' brains—the largest in the world—from concussion when they ram their massive foreheads into one another, and occasionally into boats. On 20 November 1820, a male sperm whale twice rammed the *Essex*, a whaling ship whose crew had just harpooned several members of its pod:

> I was aroused with the cry of a man at the hatchway, 'here he is—he is making
> for us again'. I turned around, & saw him about one hundred rods directly ahead
> of us, coming down apparently with twice his ordinary speed and to me at that
> moment, it appeared with tenfold fury and vengeance in his aspect.

The *Essex* sank, leaving its twenty-man crew adrift on the open sea in three small boats. One boat became separated from the others and disappeared; suffering 'outrageous thirst' and starvation, after two months the remaining survivors resorted to cannibalism. Owen Chase and two others published their recollections the following year. The incident of the ramming whale directly inspired the climax of *Moby Dick*.

Sperm whales require about a tonne of food per day to power their enormous bodies. They dive from the surface world of sunlight, birds and men down into the mesopelagic or twilight zone, where there's almost no light and the pressure on their bodies is so extreme that their lungs are compressed like squeezed accordion bellows. A feeding sperm whale is a holy terror of appetite, a vast mouth tearing through all in its powerful downward path. Most of the creatures that live in the mesopelagic zone are cephalopods (squids, octopuses), and the unfussy sperm whale swallows them whole.

Some whales wear visible scars from doing battle with large prey, including giant squids, and about one percent will suffer the cephalopod's revenge internally. There are three hard, indigestible parts to a squid's soft and delicious body: the beak, the eye lenses, and an internal organ called the pen or quill. Occasionally these get stuck and become an irritant in a whale's intestinal lining, where it slowly accretes layer upon layer of mucus, backed-up faeces and squid parts until it forms a coprolith—a stone made of shit. Eventually, the whale either passes the blockage or dies of an intestinal rupture. The result is ambergris, and is 'worth' between 10 and 14,000 euros per kilogram.

Ambergris is often misdescribed as whale vomit, but this is just prudishness or wishful thinking. It has always been a confounding substance, a luxury in search of a purpose. Even the name reflects a history of uncertainty about what it really is. The Arabic name for ambergris, *anbar*, was diverted through French and split in two to produce *amber gris* and *amber jaune*; grey amber and yellow amber. Sharing certain qualities—both were found on beaches after storms, and both made a fine incense—they were commonly assumed to be similar substances, if not exactly the same. Several medieval Muslim scholars theorised that ambergris spouted up from underwater fountains or springs, and in later centuries some Europeans adopted this belief. A Chinese writer in the mid-thirteenth century, Chao Ju-Kua, stated that ambergris was the hardened drool of dragons that slept on rocks in certain seas. Other writers guessed it was plant material, droppings from large seabirds, a fungus, an undersea fruit, bitumen, pitch or sea foam; or whale dung, sperm or vomit.

But the world's few modern experts are unanimous: ambergris is sperm whale shit. Robert Clarke uses the vivid term 'fecal concretion', which is both deliciously alliterative and nastily tangible. Its primary use today is as a fixative for perfumes. Chanel No. 5 and Shalimar by Guerlain contain ambergris, as do certain small-batch and custom perfumes available only to the fashionable rich. A modern recreation of Marie Antoinette's perfume, Sillage de la Reine, contained ambergris, as per the original formula, and sold at $US500 per twenty-five grams. Those perfumers willing to speak on the record agree that the animalic note of real ambergris is essential. Artificial replicas like Ambermore, Cetalox, Synambranc and Ambrox, though molecularly correct, will not do. The smell of luxury is, on a near-subconscious level, the smell of shit.

*

For complicated reasons involving weather, tides, gyres and terrain, certain beaches seem to attract specific types of flotsam. For example, Mason Bay on Stewart Island is jealously watched by professional ambergris hunters, who comb the shoreline for pieces spat up by stormy waters. The Roman historian Tacitus, writing in about 98 AD, described a Germanic tribe he called the Aesti collecting amber from beaches in their territory, somewhere along the Mare Suebicum or Baltic Sea:

> *They call it* glesum*, and find it amongst the shallows and upon the very shore. But, according to the ordinary incuriosity and ignorance of Barbarians, they have neither learnt, nor do they inquire, what is its nature, or from what cause it is produced. In truth it lay long neglected amongst the other gross discharges of the sea; till from our luxury, it gained a name and value. To themselves it is of no use: they gather it rough, they expose it in pieces coarse and unpolished, and for it receive a price with wonder.*

What's true of such valuable flotsam is also true of the worthless kind, which is why several beaches in Cornwall in the UK are known as Lego beaches. On 13 February 1997 a huge wave overturned the *Tokio Express*, a container ship en route from Rotterdam to New York, washing sixty-two shipping containers into the sea. One of these contained 4,756,940 plastic Lego pieces, and because reality gets away with some awfully cheap gags, many of them were ocean-themed. They included 13,000 red-and-yellow spear guns, 26,600 yellow life preservers, 97,500 grey scuba tanks, 4200 black octopuses, 418,000 pairs of diving flippers (assorted colours) and 26,400 ship's rigging nets.

Freed from their container, the Lego pieces rose, billowing around unobserved beneath the waves until, weeks later, they began washing ashore at beaches on all sides of the Cornish peninsula: Perranporth, Gunwalloe, the Lizard. Like inverse amber or ambergris, bright smatterings of cheap, scentless Lego continue to be thrown ashore whenever there's a storm, to be collected and traded by beachcombers as novelties. The University of Plymouth used the *Tokio Express* Lego to study how long plastic might survive in the ocean, based on wear and decomposition, and announced in March 2020 that the answer is somewhere between 100 and 1300 years.

*

Ambergris was one of three substances extracted from sperm whales that caused humans to hunt them to near extinction during the Golden Age of whaling (roughly the 1770s to the 1870s). The other two were blubber, which was converted into whale oil, and spermaceti, from the head case. Spermaceti made an amazing skin lotion and was once sold as a cure for tumours of the breast. A dreamlike, curious passage in *Moby Dick* has whalers squeezing the lumps out of a tub of spermaceti with their hands:

> *No wonder that in old times this sperm was such a favourite cosmetic. Such a clearer! such a sweetener! such a softener! such a delicious mollifier! After having my hands in it for only a few minutes, my fingers felt like eels, and began, as it were, to serpentine and spiralise.*

Ambergris, too, has been a coveted luxury product for over a thousand years, and has been traded internationally since at least the ninth century AD, when Nicobar Islanders began bartering lumps of it for iron goods from passing ships. Elizabeth I used it to perfume her gloves. Charles II liked to eat it with eggs. Suleiman the Magnificent drank it in his coffee. It has long enjoyed a reputation as an aphrodisiac and also as a highly effective all-purpose medicine. However, it's the unique smell of ambergris that has exerted the most enduring fascination. When freshly expelled, whether from a live whale or a decomposing one, ambergris is viscous, black, heavy and foul-smelling. To become valuable—almost literally worth its weight in gold, depending on the market and the quality of the lump—it needs to age like an oceanic cheese. Having risen to the surface it will float for months or years, moving with the currents. Perhaps it finds its way into a near-freezing subpolar gyre, or gets drawn into the Great Pacific Garbage Patch for a circuit. The salt water and harsh sunlight oxidise and degrade it, gradually transforming it into a greyish lump of matter that looks like heavy pumice and has an odour unlike anything else. It has been compared to: fine tobacco, the wood of an old church, sandalwood, the tide, freshly turned earth, seaweed drying in the sun, Brazil nuts, ferns, new-mown hay, cow dung, violets, old musk, a grandmother's perfume, furniture polish, leaf litter, mushrooms, grass, vanilla, mulch, pine, and rubbing alcohol without the sharpness. If carefully preserved, a piece of ambergris can retain its scent for 300 years.

*

In January 1992 the container ship *Ever Laurel* spilled a consignment of 28,800 plastic Floatees bath toys at precisely 44.7°N, 178.1°E, near the international date line, en route from Hong Kong to Tacoma: 7200 red beavers, 7200 blue turtles, 7200 green frogs and 7200 yellow duckies.

In August and September of that year, hundreds of Floatees beached near Sitka, Alaska, 3500 kilometres away. Next they appeared in the Aleutian Islands, then Japan, then back to the US, their path tracing a large crescent around the North Pacific Subpolar Gyre. They were an accidental boon for oceanographers, who have used them to study the speed and direction of invisible ocean currents for almost thirty years now. As each Floatee washes ashore its long journey can be roughly sketched by where it was found and how long it took to get there. The intrepid little toys vividly illustrate how no accident that takes place in the ocean can be considered isolated: the waters have their secret connections and pathways, their own logic, which we've barely begun to understand. Because only a few hundred Floatees have been found and reported, leaving thousands of plastic beavers, turtles, frogs and duckies unaccounted for, they will continue doing this job for centuries.

*

Whales have been viewed in terms of their cash value since at least the eighteenth century. Between then and now they have been processed into: vitamins, tennis racket strings, candles, fertiliser, livestock feed, soap, glue, watch and clock oil, fishing rods, shoe horns, hoop skirts, corset stays, lamp oil, buttons, parasols and umbrellas, brush bristles, wool cleaner, dye, industrial lubricant, tongue scrapers, bonemeal and margarine. In the 1840s, when Herman Melville was a whaler, it was already apparent that sperm and right whale numbers had become depleted to an alarming extent. Traditional mating grounds and nurseries were empty, and rather than months it now took three or four years to fill a whaling ship's hold with oil and spermaceti. In *Moby Dick*, Melville dedicates a chapter to the question of extinction and, in the voice of Ishmael, draws the comforting, fallacious conclusion that whales would live forever. They were too old, too numerous, too free to roam the world to be hunted to extinction as the buffalo had been and the passenger pigeon soon would be:

> *Wherefore, for all these things, we account the whale immortal in his species, however perishable in his individuality. He swam the seas before the continents broke water; he once swam over the site of the Tuileries, and Windsor Castle, and the Kremlin. In Noah's flood, he despised Noah's Ark; and if ever the world is to be again flooded, like the Netherlands, to kill off its rats, then the eternal whale will still survive, and rearing upon the topmost crest of the equatorial flood, spout his frothed defiance to the skies.*

It took a further century for whaling regulations to be established, by which time blue, right, humpback and sperm whales were almost extinct. The International Whaling Commission's declared purpose is to 'provide for the proper conservation of whale stocks and thus make possible the orderly development of the whaling industry'; it is both the largest bulwark protecting whales against whaling and a body concerned with the economic future of whaling. Its convention is couched in terms of allowing whale stocks to recover so whales can be hunted responsibly; their dollar value is the justification for killing them and for letting them live. It's unsettling to discover that the 1982 moratorium on commercial whaling—which though imperfect has been critical in helping whale 'stocks' recover to a viable fraction of their pre-Golden Age numbers—will end whenever the balance between conservation and profit is deemed to have corrected itself. The god Capitalism is only napping, barely resting its eyes, and if the whales recover it will begin demanding their slaughter again, demanding its tribute of blood foaming in the water, a great sacrifice to ensure another year's harvest of hairbrushes and margarine.

A 2019 report by the International Monetary Fund suggested that live whales should be valued at two million dollars each in recognition of the large amount of environmental carbon they capture. For the first time, a live whale would be worth more than a dead one (though still less, gram for gram, than its own impacted shit). The revised price tag implies a compliment; it's the apology from a species that hasn't learned enough from its mistakes.

*

Sometime in the early 1980s a shipping container was lost overboard off the northwest coast of France and became lodged in a sea cave only accessible at the lowest of tides. Crushed like a shoebox by the awesome force of the ocean, for the next thirty-five years it slowly disgorged its cargo: hundreds, maybe thousands of novelty telephones shaped like the cartoon cat Garfield. A pair of beachcombers found the shipping container shortly after it came to rest in the cave but didn't report it until 2019, when a newspaper ran a story about a plague of shattered Garfields that had been washing up in Iroise Natural Marine Park for years. The smashed container is wedged too tightly among the rocks to be removed, so shards of phones continue washing out into the sea and toward the nearest beach where they are tediously picked out of the sand. They'll take many times longer than a human lifetime to break down, first into fragments and then into molecules. Bowhead whales in the Arctic can live for 200 years, but the Garfield telephones will outlast them, too.

*

If, half-remembering a story you've heard, you Google something like 'dead whale plastic in stomach', you'll find that whales die from eating plastic all the time. In addition to plastic bags and vast amounts of squid, whales' stomachs have been found to contain shoes, rubber boots, toy cars, toy guns, bundles of insulated wire, dolls, cosmetic jars and fishing nets. You may also learn that, like cows, sperm whales have four stomachs, and that most of what we know about their diet has been reconstructed through posthumous dissections. Nobody has ever filmed or photographed a sperm whale feeding; nor has anyone ever seen one pass a piece of ambergris. It's unknown how often that particular blockage proves fatal; certainly a lot was found inside dead whales during the whaling era, and it was once believed that it was only produced by diseased-looking specimens—what Melville describes as blasted whales, dead of 'a sort of prodigious dyspepsia'. Robert Clarke was working on a whaleship in December 1953 and witnessed a 420-kilo 'boulder' of ambergris retrieved from the large intestine of a male sperm whale the crew had just slaughtered. Contrary to Melville, Clarke records that the 14.9-metre male was in good condition and had food in its stomach(s). The modern shipping container, which made possible the Lego, Floatee and Garfield telephone spills, was invented two years later.

*

At a pivotal moment in his narrative, Owen Chase describes his crew as 'twenty men; six of whom were blacks'. This seems to have been significant, but it's not clear what the reader was expected to infer from their race. It's possible Chase meant that the six were slaves; enslavement was common in the American whaling trade during its antebellum Golden Age. Until they are named in the appendix, most of the crew members are interchangeable, faceless, sometimes drawing nearer in their flimsy boats, sometimes becoming lost in the foggy distance. The reader could easily forget the presence of those six might-be slaves, but to do so is to miss a clear analogy thrown up by nature. Although whales are normally quite mild-mannered, the freakish ramming of the *Essex* demonstrated that they could destroy their tormentors any time they chose to deploy their full strength.

*

One last improbable fact about whales is that they haven't always lived in the ocean. More than 300 million years after the earliest four-legged creatures emerged from a swamp, before diverging or splitting into countless new species, at least one mammal returned to the water. Fossils tell the story. Fifty-two million years ago there was dog-like *Pakicetus*, in whose villainously hunched form I think I see the hyena. *Ambulocetus*, an amphibian, looks more like a cross between dog and crocodile, and *Dorudon*, with its ridiculously small hind limbs, was completely aquatic and equipped with tail flukes. Thirty million years ago came the first toothed and baleen whales, the two groups into which all modern species fall. From these descended all the present species of whales, dolphins and porpoises, whose live bodies are filled with souvenirs from their ancestors' long adventure on land. Their embryos wear hindlimb buds and sometimes fur or whiskers. Whales still breathe oxygen into lungs not dissimilar to ours, and hidden within their broad flippers are curiously hand-like bones.

    The whole history of life on earth is recorded in whales, in their bodies and their tribulations. They spurned the world as they found it and made the seas their own, until humans built a boat big enough to destroy them and a god big enough to destroy everything else. Who would have thought such evolutions were possible?

REFERENCES

I was aroused with the cry of a man … Owen Chase, *Narratives of the Wreck of the Whale-Ship* Essex (London: Golden Cockerel Press, 1935), ch. 2 (ebook version).

fecal concretion … Robert Clarke, 'The Origin of Ambergris', *Latin American Journal of Aquatic Mammals* 5(1): 7-21, June 2006, p. 9: https://doi.org/10.5597/lajam00087

They call it *glesum* … https://en.wikipedia.org/wiki/Aesti

No wonder that in old times … Herman Melville, *Moby-Dick* (Knoxville: Wordsworth Editions, 1999), p. 344.

Wherefore, for all these things … Ibid., p. 381.

a sort of prodigious dyspepsia … Ibid., p. 339.

twenty men; six of whom were blacks … Chase, *Narratives of the Wreck*, ch. 3.

Mikaela Nyman

Through a Glass Darkly

It is December 2019 and across the Tasman Australia is burning. I am deep into my explorations of materiality for an artwork for the local 'Scapes' exhibition at the Gables at Brooklands Park. A historical building in Anglo Gothic style, the Gables is a treasured local art venue. Four cramped rooms downstairs—or five, including the repurposed surgery that is now a toilet—with many doors and a dangerously steep staircase. It is impossible to imagine this was one of four colonial hospitals commissioned by Governor George Grey in the late 1840s. Would it have been even remotely functional?

According to historical accounts the hospital was invaluable in its early years and mainly frequented by the local Māori, to the point where it was referred to as the 'Native hospital'. Originally located on Mangorei Road, it may have been considered a bit remote for New Plymouth's Pākehā residents. But it is equally true that the hospital was a pawn in a wider strategy of cultural assimilation.

Out of a total of fifty-five inpatients and 570 outpatients in the 1849 hospital records, only four are listed as Pākehā. Three hundred and twenty smallpox vaccinations were administered that year. The mention of smallpox captures my attention. I can't recall ever having discussed the disease other than in a historical context or in relation to terrorism. Yet the eradication of smallpox on a global scale is fairly recent, as certified by the World Health Organization in 1980.

Smallpox carries flu-like symptoms followed by a rash. The virus is spread by saliva, airborne respiratory droplets, blood, hugs and handshakes. Extremely contagious, disfiguring and often deadly, it has no known treatment or cure. But there is a vaccine.

New Zealand historical records pinpoint 1913 as the year of our worst smallpox epidemic. The culprit who introduced it was identified as a certain Richard Shumway, a Mormon missionary who arrived on a steamship from

Vancouver carrying the variola virus. Upon arrival the weary traveller was apparently not feeling well at all and suspected he had measles.

I would like to think that Shumway briefly reflected on Christopher Columbus's legacy some 400 years earlier; that he recalled cautionary tales about the diseases the European crew carried and swiftly spread, including measles. Or that he paused to ponder the fate of King Kamehameha II and Queen Kamāmalu of Hawai`i, who in 1824 travelled to London for an audience with King George IV. The pair quickly contracted measles and were dead within a month.

But no sooner had Richard Shumway arrived than he proceeded to attend a large hui where he pressed his sweaty forehead and dripping nose against the faces of iwi representatives from all over the North Island. The variola spread like wildfire and claimed fifty-five lives, all of them Māori. I have no idea how many fell sick and recovered, or what their faces looked like afterwards. Words like 'pockmarked' can only evoke so much.

Authorities and the media were quick to point a finger at the victims and their communities, blaming crowded living conditions and poor personal and communal hygiene. Nationwide travel bans were introduced and checkpoints for immunisation certificates were set up. The sick were carted off to rural isolation camps. The 'yellow jack' of pestilence—used in maritime shipping and to mark infected houses during the great plague epidemics in Europe—was hoisted across New Zealand. The stigma of having that yellow flag hoisted on your roof: would you ever be able to live it down?

And we know what happened in 1914. The fear of smallpox was overtaken by the ravages of World War One, to be followed by a devastating influenza pandemic that struck at the end of the war. Within two months, 9000 people died in New Zealand alone.

*

A certain conviction, even doggedness, is required for any creative pursuit that entails a race against deadlines. It helps to turn a blind eye to the chaos and disruption school holidays and Christmas inevitably bring. At times ignorance is your best friend.

By 5 January my print will have to be finished, framed and ready to be hung. The day after, I will start working at a contemporary art museum. A couple of weeks later we will be on our way to the Coromandel for a camping holiday. In the months that follow there are promises of writers' festivals, international residencies and paid overseas engagements—the reward for years of solitary work. The shine and glitter to make up for the hard slog.

But no matter how invaluable these opportunities are from a professional development and networking point of view, it's the thought of a Nordic summer and a rare family reunion with my remaining three elders in Sweden and Finland that has my heart dancing like a fantail. This includes my dad, who doesn't believe in phones and has never used Facebook, Skype or Zoom. The last time he phoned of his own volition was to say that my grandfather was dying. That was in November 1998. I long to spend time with my uncle, my aunt and Dad, to visit places together, to take the opportunity to conduct field research into our chequered family history.

'The first task of memory is to forget,' Finnish poet Ralf Andtbacka wrote in my copy of his latest poetry collection, *Potsdamer Platz*. The date was 25 October 2019 and we were still making plans for the next writers' event, the next book fair after Helsinki. His poetry collection went on to be awarded a prestigious literary prize. Seven months after the ink on the title page has dried, I will hold up the page to the light and his words will seem prophetic.

But for now there are summer skies and bees droning in the sage. It is before we become obsessed with sourdough, bubbles and hand sanitiser. The thumbnail draft concepts are kept deliberately playful and bright in colour and tone. But the prints rebel. And as soon as I pick up the brush—bristles stiff from lack of use—an alternative reality reveals itself. The colour scheme dominated by eerie ochre and dioxazine violet. Leftover printing ink, oily and tacky, finds its way across the knobbly bits of the repurposed canvas, leaving charred branches and bluish smoke among skeleton trees. Burnt trees were never part of the original concept. Yet how could they not be?

Across the Tasman the bushfires have been spreading at an alarming rate since June, causing loss of homes, lives and livelihoods. There seems to be no way to extinguish the blazes once and for all. Later, when other things have overtaken the bushfires in competing for our attention, we will learn that an area the size of Syria was scorched, more than 18 million hectares of land and 3500 homes burnt to the ground. Thirty-four people lost their lives.

Almost as soon as the initial shock has worn off the devastation will be forgotten. Flushed away by the next calamity.

The canvas landscape seems biblical in its starkness. It is painful to behold. The oil-based ink refuses to dry. Ink travels to the most unlikely corners of the house leaving a smoky trail.

*

Memory is a vast basket that contains the collective and the individual, the personal and the painfully private, as well as the repressed. The reconstruction of memories, versus the deliberate reconfiguration of memories, is a long-standing preoccupation of mine. 'The first task of memory is to forget.' Can there ever be a singular truth where humans are concerned? Truth is always subjective, and profoundly so in the wake of emotional injury.

In between bike rides up and down the same strip of country road, I come across the concept of the 'absent determinant' in a journal article on W.G. Sebald, a German writer and academic renowned for his preoccupation with the impacts of trauma on memory and the way lives are shaped in its aftermath. Paul Sheehan draws attention to the much-cited 'absent determinant', namely the Holocaust—deemed an 'unrepresentable event'—that has been identified as a driving force in Sebald's writing. 'Absent' in the sense that it is the constant that shaped Sebald and his writing, yet he refused to write about it in a traditional way, avoiding sentimentality and commemoration at all cost. And here again, a hint of smoke: Sheehan highlights gaseous matter and fire as constants in Sebald's work.

Fire and rupture—particularly violent disruption—inhabit my thoughts over the next few days. The effects of colonialism and intergenerational trauma; how they cause fragmentation of people and lives. Violence. Such a suggestive and subjective word, it exists in so many shades. In the warped zone between sleeping and waking, I once again hear the familiar moans of my maternal grandfather reliving the nightmare of fighting the Russians in the Winter War. He never spoke about it but his subconscious deceived him in his sleep. The 'absent determinant' an invisible hand that pushes many of us, momentarily at least, towards the edge of a precipice of which we wish to remain blissfully unaware.

Which is to say: it is perfectly acceptable to lose your footing when your world tilts.

*

Finnish author Tove Jansson gifted her Moomintroll characters with the ability to hibernate during the long Nordic winter. All they required was a stomach full of pine needles and a comfortable bed. Spring greeted them when they eventually awoke.

I confess I have always been attracted by this idea, but never has hibernation seemed a better prospect than at the present time. Sleeping as a way of countering fragmentation, as a way of resetting life and, perhaps, memory. Sleeping as a way of escaping a world that makes little sense. A creature of comfort, my choice would be the soft needles of the casuarina, the she-oak, a nod to coastal habitats and our Pacific region.

Over the past decade reports have circulated about seemingly healthy but apathetic children lying in a comatose state for months on end, earning them the nickname 'Snow White children'. It is curious that the reports predominantly emanate from Sweden. The majority of these children are asylum seekers and seem to have withdrawn from the world. They refuse to move, speak or eat. They have to be fed, some intravenously. Dormant and deeply traumatised.

Anne-Liis von Knorring, a Swedish professor emerita in child and adolescent psychiatry who has encountered over fifty Snow White children since 2003, is adamant that these refugee children have lost hope. They are stuck in an asylum seekers' limbo, waiting for a verdict, waiting for their lives to begin. Until they can feel safe again there is little prospect of them waking and reconnecting with the world.

In 2014 the Swedish National Board of Health and Welfare formally named the condition 'dejection syndrome'. More than eighty children in Sweden were diagnosed in 2015 and 2016 respectively. Having a name for the condition renders these children visible.

It surprises me to learn that dejection syndrome has a history that spans more than a hundred years. Descriptions of the condition, albeit rare, can be found in medical records dating back to the late nineteenth century. It seems a perfect indicator of the times in which we live.

*

We tumble out of lockdown and soon emerge at level two, the unruffled and the frazzled alike, hiding behind equally joyful façades. Our first walk on the beach is a deeply sensuous affair, soaking up the warmth of the black sand through the soles of our feet, the ocean now a couple of degrees cooler than when we were last here.

The older generation complains about acquaintances taking liberties and phoning at all hours of the day, causing chaos to normal routines. My own experience is the complete opposite. Within my circle people seem to have retreated into social distancing by phone as well as in person. Emojis are an unsatisfactory means of communication, leaving me desperate to talk to real people, to hear their voices in order to ascertain whether they are actually coping. I want to respond to something directed at me personally, in real time, without looking at a Zoom screen and multiple faces.

To make matters worse, friends and relatives in Sweden have gone quiet. A terrifying silence. It takes me a while to figure it out. Something a Swedish friend lets slip when I finally get hold of her leads me to believe many are weary of being judged, perhaps even held responsible, for a national policy they support that goes against the grain of other countries' policies. That insight carries so much pain.

Before long my partner is coming home with daily stories of road rage whenever he adheres to the speed limit in the city. His mother, inexplicably, tells his sister that he only helped her with the shopping once or twice, when in reality he has shopped for his mother every three days since late March. A graceful retired librarian ends up in an altercation with the mechanic at her local garage, whom she's known for years, simply because she responded with a firm 'No' to his repair suggestions. A friend and her husband are stonewalled at their local eatery when they query whether their expensive vegetarian main is in fact the standard side dish of roast potatoes and pumpkin.

I experience my own version of going postal and nearly end up being escorted out of the local post office. All because I use strong language—directed at no one in particular and open for interpretation—when I discover that I *still* don't have the necessary documentation with me when I return to the post office for the same errand for the third time on the same day. Things come to a head when I ask the woman behind the counter to refrain from reading my tax certificate and bank statement. She was only going to confirm my address, after all. I haven't even finished the sentence when she slams my money order down on the till and raises her hands in the air—as if I am holding a gun to her head—and shouts for help, yelling she can no longer serve 'this person'. Everyone stares at me.

We are clearly out of practice.

Even those who at first seem relaxed are on edge. It is all too easy to rub up against one another, to incline towards misunderstanding rather than seeking to understand what someone is trying to say or do. In a matter of weeks we seem to have forgotten how to navigate human relationships, how to interact with the least amount of friction.

From a practical point of view, it is annoying now to have to bike all the way to town to post a parcel.

*

A friend whose husband suffered a brain injury in a motor vehicle accident recently described her status as one of 'abstract loss' and 'abstract grief'. Since her husband is not dead and because, to the uninitiated, he seems fully recovered, people tend to forget that he was terribly injured a few years ago. Yet the reality is that the life he used to have, the life she had, and the life they shared before the accident no longer exist. The trauma persists and is indefinite. He appears perfectly fine. He is still a kind and gentle soul with a magnificent beard, only with a permanently damaged brain. It manifests itself in short-term and long-term memory lapses, among other things.

The extent of the physical damage is not something my friend tends to dwell on, but on this rare occasion she spoke of the difficulty of grieving for something that does not exist, the loss of something that could have existed. The loss of their future, as they perceived it: intangible and at the same time utterly real.

I hold on to those words. It seems to name what it is I can't quite grasp.

Years ago I visited the Pancake Rocks at Punakaiki. I still remember the sucking and spraying from the blowholes, the sound of the ocean breathing below us, the loud boom and the surprise as compressed water and air shot up into the sky, pressed through caverns in the limestone.

The past months have felt similar to traversing that rugged terrain peppered with blowholes. Jobs are here and gone in the same breath. Applications stack up like pancakes, written and discarded, revised and submitted. Whenever some funding is secured it feels like a spectacular win, unexpected rather than deserved. We buy a bottle of wine, we celebrate. Nothing is routine. Home schooling is a failure but the children seem to thrive, which is a small relief. So many other things spill like Indian ink over a wet page, thinning and blooming, only to run off in unexpected directions.

The peace and quiet of April cupped us in suburban hands. The flipside is the speed at which the dial is instantly turned up the minute we return to 'normality'—knowing well that this is a new normal which we have to learn to navigate—as if we have to make up for time lost. Despite not knowing how, or what, making it up as we go. Our why is all about survival. In front of our children we keep up pretences. In the provinces there is a real shortage of decent jobs for those who opt to leave the cities. Everything migrates online, so why not decently remunerated policy, teaching and management jobs? People don't lose their skills simply by moving away from the crowded urban spaces.

The borders remain closed, which should be reassuring. Yet withdrawal, dejection and rejection manifest themselves like so many paper cuts and hairline cracks. We think we are standing on firm ground only to realise it's more like a sheet of ice.

Winter arrives with drifting West Coast rains. The children are back at school in more capable teaching hands. Perhaps it's the changeover, the shedding of responsibilities: all at once it's as if someone has clicked an immobiliser in my body. I can barely scrape myself off the couch. My heart is a bruise that radiates pain into my back. I force myself to write, insist that I feel normal—whatever that is. In the middle of the night my burning heart bangs against its ribcage. Days later I end up in the emergency department with all the hallmarks of a heart attack.

I have plenty of time to stare at the ceiling and ponder bats, civets and pangolins. I dwell on the consistency of things that don't naturally mix, like oil and water, the fact that the variola virus was brick-shaped.

My heart proves to be as strong as the proverbial ox. The oxygen in my blood is plentiful. Pericarditis is the final diagnosis: an inflammation of the heart lining, perhaps a virus of a more benevolent kind. It takes weeks to recover.

'You look like shite, and I mean that in the kindest possible way,' says a friend when we meet at a café two weeks later. She is studying to become a Jungian analyst and counsellor. I'm glad she doesn't have access to my dreams.

I tell her a family member, a doctor, is sceptical about the pericarditis diagnosis and has suggested more exercise. (Two pairs of raised eyebrows, an exhausted smile from me.) She looks at me with eyes that are wide and caring and very much present, the kind of eyes I have missed lately, and says: 'Maybe it's a broken heart.'

The café noise recedes into a sound-tunnel. I melt against the wall, feeling how solid it is, the coolness of the plaster against my back. A sense of relief pouring over me.

Researchers say the reason so many people feel exhausted after too many Zoom meetings has to do with the fact that we keep staring at our own face as we interact, reading ourselves while at the same time trying to read everyone else. It is not ourselves we need to see. It is a basic human desire to be seen, and I mean *truly* seen, by those who matter to us.

Who is to say for what a person should grieve and how? Who knows what constitutes the final drop that makes all the fragments tinkle in disharmony? Empathy seems to have taken a back seat again with the return to normality, and with the scale of terrifying events in the world at an all-time high. When the loss of lives is held up as the measure every day, any emotional response seems insufficient. And there is little patience for those who mourn lesser things, including ghosts of promises never realised.

This is not a competition, I feel compelled to say again and again. There is no comparison.

It is about all the things great and small that coalesce into a whole, that nourish us; myriad ways of being that contribute to individual and collective wellbeing and consciousness over time. The pace with which we move on to the next monumental thing is frightening at the moment. The connections between global and local matter. #MeToo matters. Who deserves a statue and how we choose to tell our history matters. Black Lives matter. Climate change matters, even though it appears to have been momentarily forgotten.

Then there are the small things: the fragments and disconnects, the dreams and hopes. The flotsam and jetsam that appears useless to anyone but the individual concerned, for whom it harbours intangible connections with land and with people, both the dead and the living. And there's the open-endedness that renders our grief abstract, turning what was within reach into something intangible. At once both utterly real and non-existent.

REFERENCES

the eradication of smallpox on a global scale … World Health Organization, 'Smallpox': www.who.int/health-topics/smallpox#tab=tab_1

The first task of memory … Ralf Andtbacka, *Potsdamer Platz – En dikt* (Helsinki: Förlaget, 2019).

absent determinant … Paul Sheehan, 'A History of Smoke: W.G. Sebald and the memory of fire', *Textual Practice*, 26:4, 2012, pp. 729–45, DOI: 10.1080/0950236X.2012.696492

these refugee children have lost hope … Upsala Nya Tidning, 'Barnen har tappat hoppet', 4 November 2018: https://unt.se/leva/barnen-har-tappat-hoppet-5115203.aspx

Matt Vance

Lines of Desire

Whether they are imagined or real, we leave traces of ourselves in places.

From the rooftop of the George Forbes Memorial Building at Lincoln University, it all became clear.

Below us, in the space in front of the Memorial Library, lines crisscrossed the lawn. There were two distinct types: those prescribed by design and common sense, and a more ephemeral set created out of the need to get somewhere important, a shortcut to the social order.

The first type was laid out in concrete and led righteously between the formal, ornate entrances of important buildings. There was no hesitation or enjoyment in these lines; no opportunity for chance encounter. They were ruthless and efficient and, for that reason, were largely ignored by pedestrians on fine days. These were the paths ordained by a designer under the steely gaze of a building committee, and were mostly used only when exams were looming, or when it had been raining and the need to keep your feet dry was paramount.

The other set of lines was only visible from on high with an eye-of-God approach, some time on your hands, and a good lecturer to show you where to look. Graham Densem was my lecturer. He wore large glasses and a constantly genial grin, and had time to answer even the most ill-informed questions from his students. His mix of enthusiasm and eccentricity was infectious to young minds, and he thought nothing of spending the entire scheduled lecture on the roof looking at the grass below. To some it would have been a field trip, but to us it was an illuminating relief from the stuffiness of the lecture room. The eye-of-God bit was provided by the rooftop of the Forbes building, which did an adequate impression of a red-brick deity.

We were a small class of five. This was in the days when universities let small classes like this happen and did not condemn the study of the quirky and insightful in their desire to get bums on seats and inadvertently rid the world of artfulness. Landscape Awareness was the name of the paper. It sounded like one of those courses that would give you an easy pass and Fridays off. Nowhere in the prospectus did it say it would change the way I saw the world.

We stood on the roof deck of the building for an hour and watched the comings and goings of students on the patch of grass below. It was like a view into a secret world that had been whirring away under our feet all along, a world we had failed to notice. Even the unenthusiastic Nicki was fascinated. She had taken the course thinking it would be a few easy credits to bring her a step closer to extracting herself from a career as an insurance saleswoman. She puffed on her cigarette and fell into the same reverie as the rest of us. Not many insurance companies allow you to sit and observe the world for an hour from the top of a building while smoking a cigarette. Nicki seemed to revel in it, her awkwardness at such frivolity quickly dissolving into curiosity.

'What do you call those, Graham?' she asked, waving her cigarette at some faint tracks in the grass.

'Oh, those,' said Graham peering over the top of his glasses. 'Those are desire lines.'

Once pointed out by Graham, the desire lines became intriguing to watch. Some walkers paced with an erratic swerve across the space; others skirted around the edges with a slow country gait. A few were taking shortcuts across the grass to a lecture they were late for, others bee-lined to the cafeteria for distraction, and some were legging it to the carpark. Where these lines intersected, the possibility arose of chance meetings of friends. Only the administration staff seemed to be using the prescribed paths, as the sobriety of command dictates. Walking in a series of straight lines and right-angled turns, they looked as if they were navigating a maze.

Canadian writer Rudy Wiebe observed the way many Inuit understand the landscape around them: 'For the Inuit, as soon as a person moves he becomes a line.' To find other humans or to hunt quarry, the Inuit lay a line of tracks through the white expanse of ice and look for signs of other lines that might lead them to their goal. As Wiebe notes, 'the entire country is perceived as a mesh of interweaving lines rather than a continuous flat surface'. Ice has a habit of receiving trails and keeping them in frozen stasis for months. In the temperate world, grass is as close to ice as we get. It takes more than one walker to make a lasting impression, however, and the grass tends to grow back if left for a while. But for the most part it is an effective medium for the recording and projection of desire. The hallowed university grounds with their lines hard and soft became our own version of the Arctic.

The concrete paths would take you quickly and comfortably to a destination like the library, but the desire lines were more than just shortcuts: they were an experience. None of us would ever look at the world around us in quite the same way again. Nicki puffed on her cigarette and Graham grinned as we peered over the edge, thinking up half-baked theories, and watching a wonderful collision between the disjointed modern landscape and the richness of the ancient world in the traces people left of themselves.

*

A few years later I moved south to Dunedin. The lesson from the top of the Forbes Building had stuck with me but was now shuffled to the back of my mind under a layer of work commitments and deadlines. When I first arrived in the city I knew no one, and substituted socialising with wandering the streets and beaches of this compact town that has just a whiff of single malt whisky about it.

One of my favourite places to wander was Dunedin Botanic Garden, set firmly at the university end of town. The garden straddles a popular pedestrian route between the University of Otago campus and the affordable student flats of North East Valley. Like any space that has a flow of people, especially younger ones, the lower garden has a vibrancy normally associated with downtown urban streets or well-designed laneways. Botanic gardens are normally the locale of horticultural groups, rhododendron buffs and family parties—but not here, among the manicured lawns, gravel paths and specimen trees. In Dunedin Botanic Garden the walkers are mostly students, many of them preoccupied with essays, tests, tutorials and the angst of youth, interspersed with the occasional lone elderly resident making their way to the nearby supermarket.

The garden is an orderly sort of place and provides a refreshing break from the roar of traffic and the lay of concrete; a place where you might slow your step after a particularly tortuous lecture on the finer points of financial management; a place where the landscape is easy to understand. The paths and clusters of trees are in keeping with the hard-wired instincts gifted to us by our distant ancestors from the African savannah. There is plenty of visibility, trees to run up if danger presents and no dark spots where you might be ambushed. In its picturesque form the garden is easy to read; it tells us, 'All is well, come on through.' More than the botanical collections or the detail of the stone walls, this point ensures its popularity.

Here and there in the lower botanic garden, words can be found. They are the ultimate landscape symbol, their meaning requiring no guesswork. Words do not come from the deep primitive mind that the African savannah theory bubbles from. Words are from what psychologists call our 'higher mind', hovering somewhere in our frontal lobe—the thinking and artful part of the brain. The obvious ones at eye level tell you where the toilet is or that your dog is not welcome here.

Other kinds of words are present too, mostly hidden down at shoe-level and for me, an unread part of the experience. They are confined to small plaques on specimen trees and provide the common and Latin names, like *Quercus rubor* and *Fagus sylvatica*. They sound like characters in an obscure Latin pantomime.

Higher-minded or not, the walkers of the lower botanic garden ignore the plaques and the signs denoting the toilets. Their landscape consists of open vistas, specimen trees and asphalt pathways. They avoid eye contact with other walkers. They are using their savannah-honed instincts to read the landscape symbols that tell them this place is safe.

In between doodling in my sketchbook, I watch the walkers from a park bench on a winter's afternoon. It is okay to sit and sketch but not to sit and stare. Pretending to sketch allows me to observe behaviour without appearing to do so. What I notice is that once the passers-by have done their quick primeval assessment of the place—is it safe?—they go into a landscape version of autopilot, steering around obstacles like errant toddlers, oblivious to everything and absorbed in their thoughts.

*

All this sketching and observing came about through an invitation to join a sculpture exhibition that was to be staged in the garden. Most of the other sculptors had headed to the more cloistered upper garden with its prominent vistas and shady grottos that delight and surprise the more curious patrons with time to wander. Like a hawker on Main Street, I had become fascinated with the lower garden, the one that has the foot traffic and the specimen trees with Latin names.

My focus settled on an old kōwhai, one of the last remnants of the native forest that once stood in this place before the Scottish settlers arrived. It had the gnarled character of age and defied all the features of the exotic specimen trees planted around it. Like most noble quiet achievers, it was largely ignored, being too small to compete with the mighty oaks and beeches. It was my kind of tree.

The day before the exhibition was due to start, I turned up with a ladder, my dad and a small roll of building paper with a poem printed across it. The other exhibitors had already installed their works and were celebrating their efforts in the coffee house. With the aid of my dad and the ladder, I wrapped the building paper around the trunk of the kōwhai and spiralled it upwards to the first of the branches where we tacked it in place. Dad took photos as I formed four root-like structures in stones, radiating out from the trunk and over the grass. A few pedestrians darted the odd look our way, but for the most part we were granted some legitimacy by the fact that we looked like a father-and-son team of arborists. Our only contact with the audience was from a confused woman who thought we were protestors saving the old tree.

The exhibition opened with cheap red wine and sterling speeches. The next day I got a call from Alan, the garden manager.

'Somebody has moved your stones,' he said.

'It's all right, Alan, we will just let them move and see what comes of it,' I replied.

Alan managed a very tidy botanic garden, and it did not get that way with ideas as loose as 'we will see what comes of it'.

'If they disappear, we are not responsible,' he muttered.

'That's fine, Alan, there's always a risk some bugger will flog everything with public art,' I said. Alan did not sound reassured.

Two days went by before I got another call from Alan. 'Your rocks have disappeared and the buggers are wearing tracks in the turf around that tree.' The 'buggers' Alan was referring to were the students who used the botanic garden as a shortcut to lectures. The poem required the observer to walk around the trunk in order to read it. Readers were deserting the safety of the path and the old straight line for the uncertainty of a tree wrapped in a poem. I mumbled some promise about reseeding the grass around the kōwhai at some unspecified future time.

The exhibition got a lukewarm review in the newspaper from the local art critic, and a week later it was over. Dad and I went to remove the poem. We found the walkers were still at it, deviating from the path and circling the kōwhai. The artist's delight was a groundsperson's nightmare. There were well-worn tracks in the grass around the tree as well as to and from the path. They were the most unusual of desire lines.

A quick trip up the ladder and the poem was unfastened and rolled away into a neat tube. Removing the very thing that had made the tree a symbol was like observing the death of a friend.

For a few days after that I sat and watched from the nearby bench, pretending to sketch once again. Initially there was still some memory of the tree that had become a poem. People pointed it out and wondered aloud where the poem had gone. But bit by bit over the next few days the memory faded and people went back to walking the straight path and thinking of other things. The tracks in the grass faded and began to regrow until no trace remained.

*

Tina's look was a mixture of disbelief and revulsion. It was as if I had said something uncouth to the vicarage committee. There was a brief pause during which she looked as if she might be sick. I unconsciously stepped back, not wanting to spoil my best work shoes.

It finally erupted out of her.

'You can't draw something you can't see … You can't draw sound!' There was a finality about that statement, a God-like decree uttered from the rooftop of a building. It was not the kind of statement you are supposed to grin at. I grinned. It made things worse. Tina's face reddened with rage.

Tina was one of five graduate students taking my class on landscape analysis. It was decades since Graham Densem had regaled me from atop the George Forbes Memorial Building at Lincoln University and set in motion a different way of seeing the world. As life would have it, I now found myself in his shoes teaching a different generation.

Graduates like Tina usually have a passion for education. Most have worked in the world of commerce and have come away with a curious dissatisfaction, an 'is this all there is?' feeling. They come back to university to follow their hearts and not their wallets. They understand the value of education and know exactly why they want to be here. Every year is different, however, and Tina's small cohort of grads had perhaps left it too long before returning to follow their hearts. They had become stiffened by the world; the elastic bands of their minds had become rigid fire doors against the world of ideas.

I had just tried to float an idea under the fire door and had come up hard against a brick wall. The idea was to sketch the desire lines of the space in front of the same George Forbes Memorial Building, by drawing a blind soundscape on our pads. When I mentioned the idea of desire lines and lead the group to the roof to discuss them, Tina looked skeptical.

'People will just follow the path,' she said, 'like that guy there.' She pointed at a chap in an expensive suit who was late for a committee meeting in the administration building and could be seen striding purposefully along the neat-edged concrete path.

'If you wait a few minutes until the end of lectures, you will see what I mean,' I replied. The minutes moved on and the lecture theatre doors opened. The patch of grass in front of the Forbes building was flooded with students, each following the desire lines rather than the formal paths. I turned in triumph to Tina and found her absorbed in her phone.

To draw desire lines purely from sound was pushing it. The next week I had the students bring or borrow a hooded garment to wear so they would be able to see the page of their sketchbook and nothing else. It would allow them to draw but they had to observe with their ears. I issued a sketched plan of the area and directed the students to position themselves in a rough grid around the site. I asked them to sit and listen for ten minutes before the changeover of lectures in order to get used to using their ears and not their eyes. More than a few of them became bored and started looking around—that was, until the post-lecture crowds arrived. Then they ducked their heads and focused on their sketchbook lest they be recognised by their friends.

Looking over their shoulders, I saw that all this movement and sound was converted into a kind of a graphic shorthand: a large group of people going by was a thick pencilled barrier in zig-zag lines; a piercing whistle became a circular pulse of sound across the page; a single person walking was a series of dots that marked their footsteps.

We are permanently in a soundscape. It is a part of our world that we intuitively accept without question. Only rarely are we without it: in a silent desert like the Mackenzie Country, perhaps, or in the world of the profoundly deaf. Sound is usually the result of movement and, for this reason, is a vital part of our perception of place. For most, sound is also secondary to vision and for that reason is shoved firmly down the back of our perception broom cupboard.

To be blind is to incur sympathy for the loss of our most vital sense. The deaf are treated less sympathetically and at worst are confined to the realms of a freakish minority who talk with their hands. To pull sound to the top of the spectrum and force a reluctant grad student to confront it is to mess with this sacred hierarchy. It is also, as it turns out, asking for trouble.

I searched for Tina in the group of students, all with their hooded heads down and looking for all the world like a satanic sect. Her head was down like the rest of them but she had replaced her sketchbook with her phone.

Ignoring the prescribed paths, the crowd departed on their way to libraries, carparks, cafeterias. My class retreated into the Forbes building to compare notes in their studio. There was the usual hum of excitement that groups of students seem to be overcome with as they return from a jaunt outside. The sketchbooks were scattered on the table as discussion ensued. Many admitted it was hard to go from seeing to listening for the idea of desire lines. 'It's like changing language mid-sentence,' said one.

Afterwards, as the class departed, I noticed Tina sitting at her drawing board looking at her blank sketch plan. Her right elbow was on the desk, her hand supporting her chin in a manner I usually associate with bored teenagers. The look of boredom was a cover for anger, however. As I approached, her chin came off her hand; her eyes lit up but remained fixed firmly on some indefinable point in the distance.

'That desire line stuff is bullshit. Why can't people just follow the path? The path is real and what you're talking about is pure fantasy,' she hissed at me. 'You can't draw something you can't see … You can't draw sound!' That was the point at which I grinned. It made things worse. Tina refused to draw sound and desired no lines.

REFERENCE

For the Inuit, as soon as a person moves … Rudy Wiebe, *Playing Dead: A contemplation concerning the Arctic* (Edmonton: NeWest Publishers, 1989).

John Horrocks

The Certainty of Others: Writing and climate change

In January 2019 a group of people dressed as zombies appeared at Wellington Airport. 'REBEL FOR LIFE' read the placard of one hollow-eyed zombie, her face streaked red with the fake blood of victims. Along with other members of Extinction Rebellion Pōneke, she was protesting against the plan to extend the runway into Cook Strait, a plan that would allow larger planes to fly into Wellington and add to the city's carbon emissions. Other people in the airport shrank away from the unwelcome and alien challenge to their own concerns about boarding passes and getting to departure gates on time.

The great optimist and self-promoter Walt Whitman had no such qualms when he described another group of travellers, the commuters on the Brooklyn Ferry. In his poem 'Crossing Brooklyn Ferry', published in 1856, he described his ecstatic feelings as he stood beside New York's East River and looked at the waves in the twilight and the seagulls high in the air. He was confident that those who had come before him had shared the same experiences, as would the generations who followed. 'What is it then between us?' he wrote. 'What is the count of the scores or hundreds of years between us?' There was, as he put it, 'the certainty of others, the love, light, sight, hearing of others'.

Whitman's work has survived so far. More than a century later, readers of his poem can download a travel pack that includes an interactive tour of the Brooklyn he knew, or zip across the river in a water taxi described as a modernised form of Whitman's own travels. Modernity, however, may not be enough to safeguard creative works in the future. Movements such as Extinction Rebellion and Birth Strike—members of the latter pledge not to have children—are signs that many people no longer believe in the 'certainty of others'.

The arrival of Covid-19 has shown how a settled future may be suddenly disrupted. Similarly abrupt societal change was experienced by South African writers after the end of apartheid. At the 1996 Toronto Writers' Festival, novelist André Brink talked of how authors had to re-think their role and face the loss of their comfortable moral authority as critics of a totalitarian regime.

In 1996, however, Brink could still rely on the prospect of future audiences for his work as he searched for new themes. Such certainty is no longer there. In March 2019 at the Wellington School Strike 4 Climate, several of the students who spoke to the crowd outside Parliament Buildings questioned whether they were being left a liveable planet. Should they have children? one asked. Many of the placards challenged older generations and the parliamentarians in the nearby buildings: 'WE ARE MISSING OUR LESSONS SO WE CAN TEACH YOU ONE' … 'FOSSIL FOOLS' … 'WHY SHOULD WE GO TO SCHOOL IF YOU WON'T LISTEN TO THE EDUCATED?' A speaker from Pacific Climate Warriors pointed out that, for them, the ocean is not just a resource. It is an ecosystem on which their lives depend.

On the morning of the march, as the crowd assembled in Civic Square, there was a happy confusion as students from all over Wellington found their friends and took photos of themselves under signs with messages like 'THERE IS ONLY ONE EARTH'. Later in the day the news came through that a man had shot people at two Christchurch mosques. A fine day that started so well finished with a reminder of the effects of malign ideas. It is possible that those who have blocked action on climate change will one day be seen to be as dangerous as the Christchurch gunman or supporters of genocide. Among them may be politicians. Turning towards the Parliament Buildings, one speaker for Te Ara Whatu said that we should not just look there for the leaders we need: we all have a duty to be kaitiaki to the land.

*

During the environmentally disastrous 'Think Big' energy projects of the 1970s and 80s, there was already awareness that the world was nearing a turning point over carbon dioxide emissions. There were jokes about 'killer' trees after the famous comment in 1981 by US President Ronald Reagan, that trees cause more pollution than cars. That year, at an afternoon of poetry readings at Denys Trussell's place in Parnell, I read a short poem about Mobil's synthetic petrol plant at Motunui, the theme of which was the lack of thought about use of the country's gas resources and the implications for climate change:

Now the Earth is warming up and ozone holes
hunt me in summer like unseen searchlights
I'd like to believe in THE ANSWER.
Who wants to end like the dinosaurs
—illustrations in the picture book
of some galactic juvenile?
In SYNWORLD why have trees at all?
Better still a flawless ball
glistening in a new syncoat
across which flickering words could float.

'Have a nice day, hello, goodbye.'

And in the synclouds in the sky
if there were an atmosphere
could hang, for us, a huge syntear.

*

What might have been seen as a mordant exaggeration in 1981 now appears much closer to the visions of the future in several local works of fiction. Climate change is a central preoccupation of novels by Chris Else (*Waterline*), Jeff Murray (*Melt*) and Lawrence Patchett (*The Burning River*), all of which were published in 2019. They followed Tim Jones' novella *Where We Land* (2015) and James McNaughton's *Star Sailors* (2017).

This flood of new titles is remarkable. There has been little like them since Geoff Murphy's 1985 film *The Quiet Earth*, which is based on a 1981 novel of the same name by Craig Harrison. It has similarities with the *Left Behind* film series inspired by Christian fundamentalist Tim LaHaye, in which millions of people suddenly vanish. In Murphy's film the devastation has been caused by a bungled attempt to set up a revolutionary energy grid, while in the 2014 *Left Behind* movie believers in Christ vanish in mid-flight, their clothes left neatly on their seats. The less worthy are left behind in a world dominated by the Antichrist, who happens to be the murderous secretary-general of the United Nations, Nicolae Carpathia.

In both films aeroplanes are used as symbols of humanity's misplaced faith in technological progress. In *The Quiet Earth* scientist Zac Hobson finds

JOHN HORROCKS

a crashed aircraft with a mysterious absence of dead passengers, while the disappearance of people during LaHaye's version of the Rapture is followed by chaos—the sudden loss of partners and children, robberies, car crashes and other accidents. By contrast, Zac Hudson wanders alone through an empty world. Believing that he is the last man left alive, he becomes increasingly lonely, erratic and distressed. Hudson is played by Bruno Lawrence, a great part for an actor who had a knack for expressing mournful disintegration. His sense of his own identity fragments as he tries on a negligée, then dresses in a toga-like gown to give a speech from a balcony to an assembly of cut-out figures of famous people, among them Khrushchev, Nixon, Hitler and Alfred Hitchcock. During his delivery he claims he has been 'condemned to live'. The speech is accompanied by applause that is orchestrated by him and played on banks of tape recorders.

This bizarre effort to simulate contact with other people is less striking than the fact that his meanderings throughout the North Island never include contact with any forms of creative work. He never reads, watches films or listens to music. Without people to share his experiences, these activities are as pointless as his responses to the cornucopia of material goods he finds in a deserted mall. He can now take or consume anything he wants: a new suit, cakes, even a giant model of a moa that he tries to wrestle onto the tray of his pickup truck.

American philosopher Samuel Scheffler asks how our attitudes would be affected by a scenario very like that in *The Quiet Earth*. How would we behave if, for example, we knew that a giant asteroid would destroy the Earth thirty days after our own deaths? Apart from the grief and dismay such a prospect would evoke, he considers how this might affect people's plans and activities. The motivation to take on creative and scholarly projects would be diminished by the knowledge that there will be no future audience for them. Scheffler argues that the prospect of a life after our own might matter more to us than the continuation of our own existence. His imagined asteroid is part of an improbable thought experiment, but the possibility of irreversible climate change could prompt similar conclusions.

Science fiction allows authors to take hypothetical situations like this to extremes. In Ian Banks' *The Hydrogen Sonata*, the humanoid Gzilt population is

191

only a few days away from the Subliming, a mass removal from their present life to another state of existence. Vyr Cossant, one of those who think of themselves as the Last Generation, debates whether she should spend her remaining time practising an extraordinarily difficult piece of music: is it a meaningless way of filling time before her life is to be abruptly transformed?

The recent New Zealand post-apocalyptic novels are not as bleak as this (or even Murphy's *The Quiet Earth*), in part because they are about survivors. 'What if you had an apocalypse and nobody came?' was the comment of a reviewer of *The Quiet Earth*. The presence of people in fiction is a narrative requirement, quite apart from any sense that there could be a survivable future. The characters in these local novels are like those in other dystopian works, such as the isolated defenders of a flooded world in John Lancaster's *The Wall* (2019), the few remaining fertile women in Margaret Atwood's *The Handmaid's Tale* (1985), and the father and son who journey through the ashes of a ruined United States in Cormac McCarthy's *The Road* (2006).

The New Zealand works introduce many of the possible results of climate change. These include the arrival of climate refugees, food shortages, contests for remaining resources (such as those of a thawing Antarctica), a brutal division between the well-protected few and the rest of the population, a collapse of central government and a loss of national autonomy. In some of these scenarios the principal damage caused by climate change comes from a rise in sea level. In Murray's *Melt*, for example, the main character, Vai, wants New Zealand to resettle the people from her own Pacific island before it disappears. Jones' *Where We Land* also takes up the forlorn prospects for refugees from countries that are going underwater. An overcrowded river ferry from Bangladesh that has made it as far as the New Zealand coast is torpedoed by the New Zealand Navy; the novella is the story of the sole survivor, Nasimul, who manages to swim to shore.

McNaughton's *Star Sailors* has more of a sociological/sci-fi flavour and introduces a mysterious alien who washes up on a beach near New Hokitika. It begins with a description of Wellington's south coast, where a huge seawall called Freedom's Rampart soars above the ocean. At Lyall Bay it is eight metres high. The physical barrier that expresses the battle against the sea has a social correlative: a wall around Mt Victoria, which protects privileged Inners against the population of downtrodden Outers who subsist in windswept outer suburbs. The Inners enjoy not only better living conditions but also medical enhancements that allow them to live longer, and have grotesque bodily modifications such as new sets of well-defined abs.

The Inners know that in other countries there are floods and crop failures caused by droughts and diseases, while in New Zealand waterways have dried up and soils are contaminated by heavy metals. Yet readers might regard even this scenario as unduly benign when our world is facing the prospect of unbreathable air, dying oceans, wildfires, pandemics, hurricanes, the release of methane as the result of the melting of the Arctic permafrost, and heat waves that lead to an explosive increase in crimes like murder, rape, assault and robbery.

Melt is the most darkly premonitory of the New Zealand perspectives, as the character Vai is offered only one option for resettling her people: in abandoned Balclutha, where mouldy houses are rotting after repeated floods. After a number of disappointments at the hands of cynical politicians, she finally realises that nothing will be done for climate refugees.

Vai's failure, despite her forthright struggle to protect her own people, is like that of the Spartans who died defending the pass at Thermopylae in 480 BCE. The Greek poet C.P. Cavafy (1863–1933) wrote of the honour due to them even though they were betrayed to the Persians. In doing so, he assumed a future in which past deeds would be recognised in the same way that he himself had recalled the literary ambitions, loves and political intrigues of Greece and Hellenistic Asia Minor two millennia before. Poems by Cavafy such as 'Thermopylae' and 'Waiting for the Barbarians' may seem less satisfying if climate change implies that there may be no future audiences. They still testify, however, that humans can behave well despite knowing they have no future.

Each of the recent post-apocalyptic works described here also shows some people behaving well, rather than simply finding ways to survive in a ruined world. A policewoman chooses not to report Nasimul, the refugee in Jones' *Where We Land*, and a shopkeeper hides him. Moral choices like this are absent in *The Quiet Earth*, where Zac Hodson is little more than the hapless victim of an industrial accident. The sudden transformation to the environment caused by this event also differs from the worlds of *The Burning River* and *Waterline*, in which ruinous changes have already happened.

The Burning River opens in a clearing beside a swamp. The man who lives there makes his living by fashioning goods from the plastic he salvages from the muddy, polluted water. The scene is identifiably set in a future Aotearoa: mānuka logs burn on his fire and he talks to an unseen intruder in Māori. The rest of his world is entirely fictional. It is like the ironically named town of Byte in *Waterline*, a miserable place dominated by a fanatical religious sect and BORIS, a capricious AI programme that makes decisions for the local urban authority. Sea-level rise has forced a family to move there from their perfect home by the coast, but Brian, the father, has been extradited to another town, where he is now stranded in the Jolly Jesus hostel.

At the heart of these two novels are the responses people make to their predicament, and both involve journeys in which they develop strengths they never expected. *The Burning River* is very much the story of a quest in which Van, the swamp dweller, learns he has been chosen to lead other survivors on a journey to find a new place to live. Stella, the mother in *Waterline,* not only sloughs off an inept and domineering husband but starts a new relationship with the leader of a group that seems at first to be no more than a gang, the members of which have names like Red, Slaughter and Scumbag.

Religious fanatics, groups of predators, failures of technology, bodily enhancements, robots, impossible truths, the search for safety, talk of the End of Days—all are staples of post-holocaust fiction, but *Waterline*, *The Burning River* and McNaughton's *Star Sailors* also demonstrate in a more positive fashion what might be. This is true, for example, of the eco-friendly community founded by Geordie, the 'Boss' in *Waterline*. It is embattled but is still managing to fight off neighbours who want to take it over. Geordie explains that the settlement was established on land that once belonged to the 'Ancestors' before it was grabbed by the white man. His family has long since been cut off from its whakapapa, and the deliberate absence of this word in the novel becomes an indicator of the degree to which people in the novel are no longer sure of their origins.

Star Sailors concludes with an idyllic epilogue in a small Hawke's Bay settlement that has survived the collapse of the consumption-led life of the Inners. Jeremiah, reformed communications man and formerly a needy social climber (though still taking a drug to restore hair growth), delivers a valedictory speech about love, taken from 1 Corinthians 13.

The Burning River also finishes with scenes of reconciliation. Van finds the courage to speak to a sceptical crowd from the community where he and his companions have sought refuge. In a mix of Māori and English, he asks to be accepted and recognised by his own relatives who are present in a long building, very like a wharenui, in which the tikanga echoes a distant past. The bonds of ancestry have survived here. In *Waterline* Geordie describes to Stella a community with a very different composition:

> *We don't know who we are. In any case, there's too many different sorts here for that to matter now. We're all just survivors, basically.*

However positive the endings of these novels might seem, they are all stories of people who are 'just survivors'. There is no denial of potential catastrophe. There is also little evidence in these novels of creative activities or cultural memory, apart from the ornaments Van fashions from plastic, the great image of Whaea and the shrines of her people in *The Burning River*, and the role of fashion design, culinary skill and events to mark important occasions in *Star Sailors*. This creative poverty seems the result of the struggle for survival. The lives of the people in these post-apocalyptic existences are not ones in which there is any 'certainty of others'.

Such prospects are so dire that it is handy for readers to be able to laugh as well. *Waterline* includes passages based upon the impossibility of challenging the judgements made by AI programmes and the Kafkaesque entanglements of the former IT specialist, Brian, who finds himself charged with supposed crimes like vagrancy. *Star Sailors* satirises another aspect of modernity—the dominance of spin and communications specialists in public life. The amorality of these operatives reaches its climax in the faking of supposed messages to humanity by the alien, Samuel, who has been in a coma for years in a New Hokitika hospital.

Without more action on climate change within the next few years, those who were at the Climate Strike marches will see some of the consequences pictured in these post-apocalyptic novels. A fictional presentation allows readers to anticipate what responses they may have to make and the ethical choices that go with them. Authors like Else, Jones, Moss, McNaughton and Patchett show there can be humour about the most extreme of circumstances, that there is still a place for courage, and that there are possibilities that people may still be able to live together in a devastated world. Given the uncertainties of a planet affected by climate change, that seems enough.

REFERENCES

What is it then between us? … Walt Whitman, 'Crossing Brooklyn Ferry', first published in 1856 in the collection *Leaves of Grass* as 'Sun-Down Poem': https://whitmanarchive.org/published/LG/1856/index.html

readers of his poem … Jesse Merandy, 'Walking with Whitman: A downloadable walking tour': http://msr-archives.rutgers.edu/CBF/walking%20tour/index.html

novels by Chris Else … Chris Else, *Waterline* (Christchurch: Quentin Wilson Publishing, 2019); Tim Jones, *Where We Land* (Wellington: Cuba Press, 2015); James McNaughton, *Star Sailors* (Wellington: Victoria University Press, 2017); Jeff Murray, *Melt* (Auckland: Mary Egan Publishing, 2019); Lawrence Patchett, *The Burning River* (Wellington: Victoria University Press, 2019).

Scheffler asks how our attitudes … Samuel Scheffler, *Death and the Afterlife*, ed. Niko Kolodny (Oxford: Oxford University Press, 2013).

Vyr Cossant, one of those … Iain M. Banks, *The Hydrogen Sonata* (London: Orbit, 2016).

What if you had an apocalypse … 'Apocalypse now and then: 10 great end-of-the-world scenarios', *Nerve.com*, cited in R. King, 'A Perspective' (November 2008): www.nzonscreen.com/title/the-quiet-earth-1985/background

We don't know who we are … Else, *Waterline*, p.197.

Tim Grgec

Drinking More Fruit Juice Won't Help

Mum used to walk along the beach with our dogs Minty, a Jack Russell, and Rudolf, a springer spaniel. A beach access at the end of our street led to the Matua shoreline. From there, at the right tide, you could walk along the peninsula to Fergusson Park to watch the kiteboarders and the kids playing cricket. Where endless clumps of seaweed dried, not quite green. Sometimes Mum walked all the way to Pillans Point, the spot where the port began and the Mt Maunganui peninsula arched its spine towards Mauao—a mountain stranded at the water's edge. In summer people came to Matua to watch the cruise ships slip through the tiny gap at the harbour entrance. You could see everything from that side of town: to one side Matakana, the stretching sleeve of an island that enclosed the entire harbour, and to the other side the port. Every evening those ships sailed calmly past it all, like floating buildings, eventually disappearing into the small gap where the Tauranga moana spills into the Pacific Ocean.

Years later I walked behind a woman along the same beach. Wind blew against her brightly coloured hat. For the first and only time since my mother's death, just for a moment I genuinely thought I saw her. It happened all at once. While fishermen launched from the boat ramp, this woman's feet made soft, temporary marks in the sand the way Mum's used to. The woman looked towards the lines of trees on Matakana Island, each one tall against the pale sky—the same view Mum looked at. I felt sick from the smell of seaweed. The tide was coming in slower than it should have—or was it because I was following a woman down the beach as if she could be Mum? Too scared to look, too scared to walk any faster.

*

Mum was first diagnosed with cancer in 2003 on my eleventh birthday. My brother Petar and I didn't find out for a few months, until after I'd settled into

Year 7 at my new intermediate school. It was the first time I had to wear a uniform—a grey shirt with grey shorts and stiff brown Roman sandals.

Perhaps the grief started then, when I didn't even know, in the conservatory at home where most evenings I'd interrupt Mum's reading to tell her about the myriad things on my mind. She often read as the night pressed in at the side of the house, her thoughts encased in glass. There I told her things before she found out some other way. Some were trivial, like how I'd fallen in with the cool guys at school who smoked cigarettes and looked at porn mags at lunchtime. Or about the detentions I'd had. How once, for example, I was placed in a different class for a morning under strict instruction to sit silently in the corner until the bell rang. I was punished for being talkative, and punished again when I broke my silence to explain how Greek and Latin roots served as clues to the meanings of words. The next day I found a five-dollar bill under my muesli bars and Nutella sandwiches with a note saying, 'there for just in case xx'. In the conservatory I believed in her fully. It was the place where we shared the kind of conversations in which each cumbersome worry becomes a little bit smaller.

If things were more serious, we would talk into the night. She told me about the specialist cancer lodge in Hamilton she had to go to for weeks at a time, where she had a specially made mesh mask that fitted so tightly that she couldn't keep her eyes open. Every day at the lodge Mum sat with this mask on as the radiation treatment killed off her brain cells. She worried that she couldn't concentrate or read like she used to. Worst of all, she said, was the fear that she would no longer be able to drive.

Years later we stayed up talking about metastasis, the way cancer breaks away from the main tumour and travels through the bloodstream into other parts of the body. After about five years of treatment Mum's tumour had moved into her bones and organs, her spinal cord and even her blood. It was no longer just a single tumour refusing to leave. With every heartbeat it was slowly enveloping her body from the inside out. The dim reading lamp next to the chaise longue held the glow of her eyes, glassy and strained from the effort, when she told me this. All the darkness of the house seemed to sit behind her. And it was then, late on a school night, right there in the conservatory, that it hit me: she was going to die. The cancer was in her blood and she was going to die. I had just started Year 12.

*

That year, not knowing how much longer she had, Mum wrote diaries for Dad, Petar and me. 'Tim, I don't know what I'll write in here,' mine began, 'but I feel I should share my thoughts with you, worthless they may be.'

In it she told me things I'd never known, such as how she and Dad first met. Dad was the eldest of four in a family of Croatian immigrants. He was born in Graz, Austria, after his parents escaped from communist Yugoslavia in 1957. By chance they ended up in New Zealand as refugees, living to begin with in Whanganui and then in Auckland. Dad was the first to go to school and taught his family English each afternoon. He went on to complete a master's in history at Auckland University, then started a master's in philosophy at Cambridge.

'Your dad and I are opposites in many ways,' Mum told me. 'I don't know how we got together. I was too much like Petar, loved to drink, smoke and leave work as early as I could.' She first noticed Dad in a lecture on something to do with the origins of World War One. He was well liked by the professor. Mum dropped out of the paper, thinking it was too academic. They met again years later, in 1983, in a queue at a bank in Wellington. Dad was working at the Department of Trade and Enterprise and needed a chequebook; Mum was a low-paid clerk at the Department of Labour and needed an overdraft. In the diary she talks of Dad's adopted English style of dress that day. She saw something in my Croatian father, who wore 'his favourite corduroy mid-green jacket with a thick black moustache'. She wondered if this was his way of trying to negotiate his heritage. A way of fitting into the English-dominated culture at university.

Mum was born a year after Dad with her twin brother Mark, in Dunedin in 1959. Her Presbyterian father was studying theology at Knox College before becoming a minister and eventually taking up a parish in New Plymouth. Mum grew up in a strict religious household and was expected to be the model minister's daughter. Her liberation came at university in Auckland where, like Dad, she completed a master's in history. In her first year of university Mum shared a room with her best friend Kay, who placed a line of tape exactly in the middle of the floor between their beds to prevent Mum's messiness overrunning the whole room. Mum wrote of how she won the Tequila Olympics in her hall of residence that year, out-drinking the boys; of how she helped organise anti-Springbok Tour marches in New Plymouth when home for the 1981 holidays; and of how she became the president of the history students' association just to spite Dad's friend Paul, who desperately wanted the position.

In her diary she also wrote of things she struggled with. One entry began, 'Today I found out definitely that the cancer has gone into my brain and I have no idea when or how to tell you. Only 6% of breast cancers go to the brain so yet again I've had bad luck. I'm scared about how I'll be affected and what you'll have to witness. If there was any way I could change the outcome I would.'

*

One morning I spoke with Mum as she planned her funeral. There was absolutely no way, she insisted, no way her father Reverend Tom Woods would take over as celebrant. Instead she chose her aunt Joan, who knew Mum's aversion to the sombre preferences of the Presbyterian church. We talked about how everyone expected me to say something at her funeral, because that's what you did: 'You have to speak,' my friends told me. 'You just do.' There would be eulogies from Dad, Petar and Mum's best friends, but I didn't want to add anything. I said to her that morning, 'I've told you everything I ever needed to, Mum, and that's enough.' And it was. All the conversations we shared in the conservatory, the evenings of reassuring chatter—it was all enough.

Her funeral was on New Year's Eve. I'd come back with my friends after three nights of partying at Whangamatā. We were silent that whole winding drive, listening to the static of the aux cord. Mum had been an English teacher at Otumoetai College, the school my brother went to. Her pink casket sat on the stage of her school hall; the aisles were lined with friends, former students, people I'd never seen before. She left the hall to ABBA's 'Dancing Queen'. My right hand gripped her casket tightly.

*

I sometimes talk about Mum with Dad and Petar. We wonder what she'd make of certain situations, of the three of us finally visiting Croatia when I was eighteen—Dad's homeland, the place she visited with him in the late 1980s; how the men still drank shots of rakija every morning at breakfast just as they did back then. Sometimes we even talk of how proud she'd be. But we never go as far as to say we miss her, never say anything about the emptiness, there's no way we could ever risk that.

When she passed away Dad suggested we each see a psychologist to help process our grief. I was seventeen, heading into my last year at a traditional all-boys' school—the kind that's full of rugby analogies, where everyone seemed to communicate through grunting. I might have enjoyed reading and writing poetry but I'd still spent four years subscribing to its atmosphere of guarded vulnerabilities. Not only did I refuse the suggestion of counselling, dismissing it as a weakness, I ridiculed my older brother for taking up Dad's offer. I couldn't bear the thought of explaining myself to a stranger, a stranger who couldn't bring Mum back.

Our inability to communicate, however, stretched beyond my adopted stoicism. The risk, even now, is a return to the void—the very place inside us in which we confront how meaningless our lives are without her. Each of us offers a different take on the past that the other two thought they'd let go of. All it takes is the return of one repressed memory to suddenly deflate our bodies once again.

*

Although the three of us became closer after her death, we also drifted without Mum glueing everything together. In a way I envied my devoutly Presbyterian grandparents, who had a higher power not only to justify the loss of their daughter, aged fifty, but also to anchor them to something beyond themselves. Dad sold the family home in Matua, Petar moved to Melbourne and I to Wellington, as if our family dynamic had been rebuilt upon shifting foundations, now absent of any recognisable centre. Perhaps it was this absence that made me try to revisit her world in any way I could, ascribing meaning to things that weren't necessarily there. I wanted to know everything about her. What was she like as a teenager? How did she view the world at the age I am now? Sometimes I looked at old photos of her. Sometimes I read Mum's favourite books—Janet Frame and Katherine Mansfield—where she'd scribbled in the margins, as if I could actually read what she was thinking. Every dog-eared corner was a special insight into her mind, something she had left behind. Occasionally the exact tone of her voice came back, and in those moments the words spilled out of their pages and I couldn't do anything but miss her.

Without realising, I did everything I could to see parts of my life reflecting parts of hers. I started making my bed a certain way: her way, with the

pillowcase openings facing inwards and the top sheet folded over the duvet.
I read more. Mum was an English teacher, after all. She made me memorise
Shakespeare when my teachers didn't go into enough detail. She recited to me
Hamlet's most famous soliloquy, without sharing his dread of the afterlife: 'The
undiscover'd country, from whose bourn/ No traveller returns …' There was the
time she asked to see my Year 13 subject selection for the next year. I was over
English by that point, over school. She was dying when I showed her the form,
and I couldn't believe she cared. But there she was at the kitchen table, calmly
replacing 13PE with 13ENG with only a month to live. The next year I topped
Year 13 English. I went on to complete a Master of Arts in English literature
followed by a Master of Creative Writing. Without realising, I'd constructed
an entire identity from that one moment. I'd held onto that piece of paper the
whole time, as if it was still crumpled in my pocket.

*

But what if my construction was a misreading of her world? Frame's
autobiography *An Angel at my Table* and Mansfield's *Selected Stories* were only
two of the hundreds of books on my parents' bookshelves. Everything I ever
needed to read I could find at home: from Shakespeare to Tolstoy to the 2001
edition of *Essential New Zealand Poems* that I pored over time and again, trying
to imitate every single one. I so desperately wanted her world to become mine
that I dived into everything she'd ever read. I found myself reading Austen
and Woolf. Critical works. Bestsellers she kept at her bedside. When I'm sure
of myself, feeling buoyant, I act like I did this of my own accord, as if I always
would have ended up here, underlining words with a pencil.

 For a long time I questioned whether, without realising, I'd just invented
my own version of her. Whether this was all simply a coping mechanism,
an elaborate construction of her world to help me to deal with the everyday
sadness of mine without her. She had that master's degree in history. What if
she preferred books about things that had actually happened, things that drew a
line between the past and present? Next to Frame sat Hadrian, a man caught in
between, ruling at a time when the Roman gods were no longer believed in but
before Christianity took its hold on Rome and the Western world. What if, in
the end, it was all for show? Perhaps she secretly preferred television to reading,
or drinking wine with friends? History is, of course, just the emphasis of certain

facts over others. What if my emphasis was an imitation of misremembered qualities—leaving me with a love for literature, for female writers, trying to find their pockets of wisdom I thought my own mother lived by and gave to me?

Maybe the foundations have become less and less recognisable, blurring the lines between where my mother's influence left off and my life began. 'What do we have in common?' Mum asked in her diary. 'Both of us have untidy bedrooms. We enjoy socialising but enjoy reading. I also think you'll be a good cook.' It's hard to know at what point I started thinking for myself, sharply and clearly as she so often demanded. Mum was strict because she saw herself in me—capable but lazy, always leaving things to the last minute. I prided myself on doing well at school while putting in the minimum amount of effort, sunbathing by the pool on exam leave rather than planning my essays. From my father I inherited a preciseness, a love for history and his ability to memorise important facts and dates. 'Those who cannot remember the past are condemned to repeat it,' he once told me, citing George Santayana, when I asked for a defence in studying history. My father and I share an intellectual curiosity about the world, constantly searching for new perspectives.

But there's no way I'll ever know how much I'm a product of my mother and how much a product of her absence. Whether my identity was something predetermined or something more malleable, made up of all the bits and pieces of people and stories and experience we inherit over the course of our lives. At seventeen I tried as hard as I could to model my identity on the memory of another human being, someone who could no longer model these things herself. What started as an evening walk across the border to her interests turned into entire years spent trying to recreate the characters and settings of her imagination. Entire years spent trying to recreate her. I will never know how much such a grief distorts and inhabits the individual, forever disrupting the natural order of things. Whether it causes one to always look forward or backward, caught between the temperaments of missed and missing.

*

Mum's diary ended abruptly. The last entry was on my seventeenth birthday, 19 November 2009. A Thursday. That afternoon I'd finished a Level 3 stats exam and we were going out to dinner to celebrate. Harbourside, probably. Our favourite restaurant as kids because the wait-staff gave us bits of bread to toss over the balcony for the fish to gobble up below. We'd grown up since then. Mum no longer needed to shake her head as we ordered pork spare ribs from the kids' menu, or warn us that we wouldn't be allowed out for dinner next time if we didn't use a knife and fork properly.

Earlier that week we'd found out that the cancer had spread to her spinal cord. I came home after school to find Mum vomiting. We talked through her closed bedroom door about how she was too unwell to go out but how we would celebrate properly soon enough. She wrote in my diary that evening, 'You didn't even get to go out for your seventeenth birthday because I ended up sick. Losing your mother to cancer is wrong, unfair and I feel anger and grief. But some things we can't change. Drinking more fruit juice won't help, Tim.' It wasn't long before she was admitted to the hospice, the point of no return. Our harbourside dinner eluded us.

That night, for the first time, the tone in Mum's writing shifted into something more instructional. In urgent syllables the sentences became shorter and snappier, as if she was scrambling to get it all down in time. The last paragraph ended:

> I refuse to say cancer is a journey that makes us stronger. It's one I'd rather our family wasn't on. So you need to take care of yourself. You are bright. You have a great group of friends. But soon you'll face the hardest situation yet. I've wasted many opportunities, but I think many of us do, thinking we have all the time in the world. Our lives would be so much different, Tim, so much different, if we had all the time in the world.

The diary still sits in the top drawer of my bedside table. Her large sprawling loops only made it through twenty pages or so before the writing got too much, before her days started to loosen, to become too hard to keep hold of. For a long time I could barely open it because it was the closest thing I would ever have to her actual thinking. As she got further in, her sentences read like they were taking on water. Towards the end, inconsistencies and odd grammatical mistakes became the sign that she was struggling to come up for air, each one mapping the coordinates of a sharp mind finally losing its grip on the world. Her last line hung at the top of a page with dozens of white pages waiting on the other side beyond it—the blank space she would never fill.

*

Tauranga's Waipuna Hospice lies on the Wairoa River off State Highway 2. Thousands of people drive that road every day and don't even realise it's there. The hospice sits alone on a plain overlooking the water, surrounded by empty paddocks. Whenever I'm hitching a ride with a friend from Auckland, I look out for it on the left as we enter the city. I never say anything. I don't really know why I do it. She wasn't even there for long—a few weeks, perhaps? Months? But I can't help it. Right there, I think, the last spot on earth where she stood.

*

Her eyes were either open or closed, I can't remember which. No one seemed to notice. My dad, brother, uncle and I were silent as we each held her hand for the last time. It was a strange feeling, holding my mother's lifeless hand. But it's not as if it came without warning. For days she had barely held back. For days we waited, hoping it wouldn't happen on Christmas. It was one of those hot Tauranga summers, a real summer where the days seemed stretched at each end. I can't remember it with any clarity. Only that on Boxing Day afternoon, with the dark yellow sunlight creeping through the gaps in the blinds, her hand was still warm. She'd been dead for about half an hour and her hand was still warm. Nothing could have prepared me for that.

*

It's been over ten years since she died, and still I often dream about my mother. Even though it's the same dream over and over—Mum and me at our first family home, a large powder-blue villa in the Avenues—the surprise afterwards always gets me. It gets me every single time. In it she twirls my hair as she did when I was a child, lightly so her fingers never tangle, firmly enough so the knot never falls. Strange light filters through the leaves outside, hazy in the late afternoon, latticed with flecks of something that my brother would have insisted must be dry leaves swirling around in the wind or even bits of dead cicadas that had shed their loose skin. Maybe both. Mum doesn't say anything in this dream. She can't. And no matter how hard I try to warn her about what's coming, she just sits there indifferently twirling my hair. Her face is a shadowy blur of itself, perfectly distinct and muddled at the same time.

Every time I wake from this dream I think it's actually possible to call her or write. As if there's an opening, a brief moment when I really believe she's never left. 'Just one more conversation, Mum,' I think to myself. 'One more.'

Character-Building

A character can grow through making the correct move, as well as the incorrect one—but he must grow, if he is a real character.

—Lajos Egri

One afternoon in early September 1996 I was sitting in Union Square sharing my lunch with a squirrel. With a plain bagel and a pottle of yoghurt, two carefully budgeted-for purchases from D'Agostino's across the road, I was rewarding the russet rodent for its company on my first full day in New York City.

Spring in Manhattan was hotter than expected and after lunch I'd be on the hunt for a fan to cool the room at the Roberts House on East 36th, where I'd slept the night before and would be staying for the next ten months. While helping me haul my cases up four flights, a girl in Daisy Dukes and flip-flops had recommended stores where I could purchase a windowsill fan. As we wended our way, she introduced me to other residents, told me their states and countries of origin, and gave me a run-down of mealtimes, laundry facilities and other new-girl need-to-know-isms.

Manhattan was an Advent-calendar city from my chamber with its bed, desk, closet and sink. From my little life I could peer out and into the frames of others' little lives. On my fifteenth birthday I'd watched Hitchcock's *Rear Window*, the film in which a convalescing Jimmy Stewart spies on his neighbours while waiting for his girlfriend, Grace Kelly, an ice-cool blonde about to become a princess. There's many a princess dream in the Big Apple, whereas the truth is a city grittier and more multicultural than Hitchcock's imagining. You don't need to visit the United Nations headquarters to get a feel for all-over-the-world. It's a city that invites curiosity about others' business, while simultaneously schooling you in staying out of others' business if you wanna know what's good for you. A city that can be both lonely and crowded, or a place to be who you want, to grow a new you. A place where, in your interactions with others, you try to suss out who they are versus who they claim to be. And what they want from you.

It's also a city that fosters a resourcefulness from paucity. A crash course in making much from what you have and sticking it out despite any tremblings of doubt. In such a loud-hot-cold-fast metropolis, everything and everyone is trembling around you all of the time, so any of your own doubt you read as an assimilation of this. The energy propels you to keep moving and picking up where and when you can.

I was eighteen years old with my own room in the most exciting city in the world.

Sitting on the grass under a tree in Union Square I fed my little friend, the squirrel. A lady walking past barked, 'It'll bite ya!'

In New York, you need to decide fast what you're doing there.

Why you *need* to be there.

*

Before leaving home I had bumped into my former history teacher in the street. Miss B was a no-nonsense spinster with a pudding-bowl haircut and brogues. She was an expert on antiques and succinct in her instructions: if I was going overseas then I owed it to myself to seek out some Fabergé eggs.

That first week in New York I walked north up Fifth Avenue perusing some of the big-name stores—cursorily, because I was clearly not one of their clientele and could take only so many withering glances in the heat. At the southeast corner of Central Park I spied A La Vieille Russie. Recalling Miss B's lessons on the antagonism between the ground on which I stood and the former Soviet Union, I decided to gamble on the Russian antique dealers being more accommodating than the staff at Bergdorf's or Saks.

Once inside I enquired after their Fabergé inventory, ready to cut a deal. The sales clerk explained that the few they had in stock were of the more discreet variety. This was fine by me because I wasn't ready to blow my meagre finances on postage, and a smaller one would be less likely to break in transit than a Romanov edition. Nevertheless, I expected something more significant than what appeared to be a marble starling's egg nestled in a vitrine among far grander and gaudier baubles.

'How much?'

'Eighty thousand.'

'US?

'We do take foreign currency.'

It didn't take a master of subtext to realise that the clerk wasn't open to haggling down to the region I had in mind, tax or no tax. With what little dignified artistry I could muster, I informed her that I'd ask my acquaintance if this was in fact what they had in mind then took my leave, fooling no one that I wasn't a right double-yolker.

*

I first met Michelle, my friend-to-be, in screen-acting class at the Lee Strasberg Theatre and Film Institute. A native of Astoria, Queens, she could read a phoney on the flip of a dime and was a loyal, no-bullshit, savvy support in a land of singular go-getters. Michelle had been a part-time student at Strasberg for a number of years, between running her own dance school and doing acting gigs when she could score them. Our first scene together was from Tennessee Williams' *Summer and Smoke*. I was a guileful, sassy Nellie to her repressed Alma; textbook against-type casting. Michelle played a poised vulnerability that ached with what was not said.

Occasionally, on Sunday nights, Michelle and her mother would invite me to their house with its small garden—a rarity for a working-class family. I'd catch two subway trains to the nearest station, where they'd pick me up in their car on their way back from evening church. Dinner was at the local Italian (my first real cannoli! *Don't forget the cannoli!*) then we'd go to their place. Michelle's stepfather lived in a ground-floor room, reliant on oxygen but with enough air in his lungs to holler complaints and demands.

Michelle and I would 'fix snacks' of Graham crackers then descend to the basement to rehearse. One night we were among piles of tulle, Lycra and spangled headpieces, costumes she was sorting for her dance school's upcoming concert. One item was to be a tribute to *Evita*, and Michelle was concerned the fifty black umbrellas she'd ordered wouldn't arrive in time. When I reminded her that it was bad luck to open an umbrella inside, she threw up her hands and said, 'Now you tell me! You wanna tell these kids who've been practising for months they can't do the umbrellas? Anyway, it's gonna look amazing!'

Another night we watched *The Devil's Own* at her local cinema, sneaking in sandwiches we'd bought at a store beforehand. After the lights went down we unwrapped them and started eating. The first bite was tough, and I tore at the bread with all my delicate might. As I tried to chomp down a mouthful, Michelle whispered, 'Sweetie, make sure you remove the cardboard.' She chastised the other patrons for exiting before the end of the credits. How could they not want to know who did the cinematography, the sound, the lighting? The genius of the craftspeople behind the work?

You could have all the flair you wanted, but you had to appreciate the craft and the work.

At Strasberg we were taught to show up and do the work. To know our lines ('you better know those lines *as they were written*'). To prepare, to know, to re-prepare. Don't work until you get it perfect. Work until you can't get it wrong. One teacher drilled us in this more than anyone else, and you had to complete a semester at the institute before you could make a case for being in his group. He didn't suffer fools who thought they could drop by and audit his class, where the main infringement was 'acting'.

'You're fucking acting!'

'Fucking acting' meant you were preening your performance, you cared too much what your audience thought of you and not enough about the work as required by the text. I witnessed someone new to the class taking their first tentative entrance steps when he yelled: 'YOU'RE FUCKING ACTING! YOU SELF-CONSCIOUS PIECE OF SHIT! IF YOU WANNA ACT THEN ENROL IN SOMEONE ELSE'S CLASS!'

By the grace of some thespian deity, I managed never to act in that room.

The method expounded by this teacher was not to take from or create unnecessary additional work. First and foremost, it was a means to get you and your baggage out of the way, and only carry in what you needed to embody and realise the text. The text was paramount, and the methods were the means to serve it and your reading of it, whether this meant dancing around and in and out of the words or the entire reduction of any extraneous movement. It was this teacher who directed me to Lajos Egri's *The Art of Dramatic Writing*, the classic scriptwriting manual first published in 1942.

About once a week I visited the Samuel French bookshop around the corner from the Flatiron Building. The front of the store was manned by a short, rotund, camp man who revelled in matchmaking actors with scripts, and couldn't help but perform excerpts for customers no matter how unlikely his casting. It was pure scriptural love and the weeks when I could shell out for a new text were heaven.

I learned how to read plays in script analysis class on Tuesday nights while car alarms wailed from the street below, as if in a round, or as a clarion call to be always on high alert. The alarms are a rhythm of the city, just as each play text has its own rhythm and ebb and flow of energy. We students had to resist the temptation to merely scan the dialogue, and instead learnt to read and interpret the spaces between the words; the beats and pauses that actors sometimes fear will swallow them like sinkholes.

The script analysis teacher worked in theatre and film casting and production. He'd show us the headshots that had landed on his desk that week and rate the standouts against those who didn't have a hope. He told us that if we got an audition, we should approach every script as if it was Shakespeare. Anything less would guarantee nil chance of a callback.

*

Enter RUMOUR, all painted with tongues:

> RUMOUR: Open your ears; for which of you will stop
> The vent of hearing when loud Rumour speaks?
> I, from the orient to the drooping west,
> Making the wind my post-horse, still unfold
> The acts commenced on this ball of earth.
> Upon my tongues continual slanders ride,
> The which in every language I pronounce,
> Stuffing the ears of men with false reports.

And so we'd recite with one breath, first lying on our backs and again while standing.

In voice and dialect class, time and focus were split between placement of vowels and consonants and projection, and the forming of characters in relation to different accents.

We were born on the prairie … Dropped there by British Intelligence … And what sense are we to make of the wreckage? … They had to turn over to get their mouths at you, to bite you … All of this was long ago, Vladimir.

Most of my classmates, in particular the Americans, had trouble distinguishing New Zealand from Australia. Especially the accent. They simply could not hear the difference. Voice and dialect classes were fun except when being *made* fun of. A student from the UK asked me why people (by which he meant Europeans) had moved to New Zealand, to which I replied, 'for a better life', which came out as 'a bitter life'. I was going to be no one's laughingstock and set aside thirty minutes every day for speech practice.

The teacher instructed us in how to use the International Phonetic Alphabet to parse and map out dialects, and to train ourselves to speak à la 'neutral' Upper East Coast, an accent that floated somewhere in the mid-Atlantic, possibly where the *Titanic* went down. He was non-judgmental and curious about how we spoke and assured me that rolling rrrrrs are a boon for speaking different dialects. He even recorded my thick, flat vowels on cassette tape for his dialect library.

Ten tin pens were kept in Ben's tin bin.

Tin ten pins werrrrrr kip ten Bin's ten ben.

*

The script analysis teacher put out a call for extras to act in an independent film directed by one of his friends. The agent said on the phone, 'You're booked for the job', which sounded snazzy and showbiz, except I wasn't being paid. None of us extras were. It was our opportunity to show the real pros that we could be trusted to show up and do the work and not act like fucking amateurs.

Being an extra was also an opportunity to learn how to go through the on-set motions, most of which in this case involved little motion at all. We waited on the shady side of a West Village street early on an autumn morning to play protesters, dressed as if it were mid-summer because continuity doesn't care about chilblains. It's all material, as the saying goes, so we used our shivering and blue lips for the thirty-second takes of us shaking our fists at the actor playing a porn film baron. During one of the many breaks a Brazilian woman, also from Strasberg, said to me in front of everyone, 'You're a pretty girl, but you should do something about your skin.' During every tape playback in screen-acting class I so wanted to believe that I was the only one distracted by the eruptions of acne on my face.

*

Most of my fellow Roberts House residents would emerge from their rooms for breakfast fully made-up. A full face of slap while they filled their faces with coffee, juice and sultana flakes. Portions and presentation were handled with precision.

The Roberts House was established after the Civil War as a place for single Christian women to live respectably together in Manhattan. Sylvia Plath had lived in a more up-market version of this, but as in any cast of characters here, too, were young women fighting similar internal catastrophes and journeys of self-destruction despite their best intentions on arrival. Others had more hopeful and stable plans, such as postgraduate study or internships at the United Nations. Everyone appeared to believe in something and themselves on arrival, and yet the unfolding of time and circumstances revealed many to be something else.

The night when a news anchor announced from the TV at the far end of the dining room that Timothy McVeigh had been sentenced to death for the Oklahoma bombings, the US residents around me cheered. When I queried this sentiment, one replied, 'We're taxpayers and we're not paying for that asshole to live.'

There was a formal lounge on the ground floor. A grand piano was the room's centrepiece among chintz settees and lamps, and Maya, a jazz singer and music conservatory student from Sweden, taught me to sing 'Blue Eyes'. The singing class at Strasberg was my bête noir. The accompanist worked nights at the Blue Note on West 3rd Street and was sunk in cynicism from seeing so many try to make it over the years when only a handful were up to task. He'd arrive at the third-floor classroom puffing and wiping his sweaty brow before fishing out scores from his messenger bag and thudding onto the piano stool with a sigh of resentment.

We could 'entertain' guests in the Roberts House lounge, and here, on Friday or Saturday nights, Michelle would meet me to run scene lines before she headed downtown for dancing. She'd wear a clip-on peroxide Madonna ponytail and motorcycle boots, explaining their suitability for dancing: 'I'm not having anyone step on *my* toes.'

Not stepping on toes or having your own stepped on was part and parcel of getting around and about each day, both literally and metaphorically. You didn't want to lose your footing, especially in inclement weather. New York is a big weather city. The first time I scuttled home after dark in a thunderstorm I feared the skyscrapers would be scuttled by the lightning strikes zapping across the indigo sky. On the days that bucketed with rain, vendors peddled umbrellas in the morning that would be mangled, lacerated and discarded in trash bins by evening, no longer needed or wanted. The onus is on you to remain wanted in Manhattan.

Madonna lived on popcorn when she first came to New York, or so I read. It's cheap and it fills you up! There was a popcorn machine at the Roberts House. We'd unwrap little cakes of white butter from their foil casings, melt them in the microwave and pour them onto popcorn, followed by a generous dusting of salt. I became a regular drinker of coffee and eater of peanut butter and jelly. A substitution of food from your homeland transpires when you stay long enough in another country:

Saltines with soup.
Tuna salad sandwiches.
Bread noticeably sweetened with sugar.
Angel cake.
Hazelnut coffee.
Turkey, turkey, turkey instead of chicken, chicken, chicken.
Cranberry juice. Cranberry everything (especially for the turkey, turkey, turkey).
Eggnog (in milk cartons) for Christmas.
Knishes from Russian Jewish delis on the Lower East Side.
Fat-free Häagen-Dazs (sugar galore!)
Bacon bits and blue-cheese salad dressing.
Milk fresh from New Jersey cows (a bit off, to my nose).
Most dairy tasting a bit off.
I CAN'T BELIEVE IT'S NOT BUTTER! Oh yes, I could. I really, really could.

*

On my nineteenth birthday I sat on my bed and snivelled, looking at the photographs of far away, so familiar, in a copy of Grahame Sydney's *Timeless Land*, sent by my family. As if a shard of schist had entered my stomach I was torn, debating whether or not to stay and fight the churning rat-race with its portents of limited sustenance or satisfaction. In the early 2000s I would spot one of my Strasberg classmates in a small role as a detective in the sequel to *The Silence of the Lambs*. There was a shot of the back of his head when he crouched down to pick up some evidence, giving more exposure to a bald patch than his face. I never saw him in anything ever again. Two of my closest NY female actor friends lied about their age, and they were barely thirty. It was a salutary lesson in the pitfalls of body and appearance as career currency. However good, clever or charismatic a performer may be is immaterial if they're shoved on the shelf with more and more continuously stacked on after them, like chipped and faded Matryoshka dolls.

*

'My advice to you is not to enquire into why or whither, but just enjoy your ice cream while it's on your plate.'

In the spirit of testing another strategy, I auditioned for two London acting schools. My contemporary piece was the opening monologue from Thornton Wilder's *The Skin of Our Teeth*, and Cece, a Roberts House actor friend, helped me rehearse. Having studied and worked professionally in Costa Rica, she'd moved here to audition for The Actors Studio as a last resort.

Out of the blue, Cece had to return to her homeland. She promised to be back soon. I stashed her extra suitcases in my wardrobe and she arranged for me to take over her babysitting job. The first night I arrived at the Upper East Side apartment, the elder of the two boys who were to be my charges answered the door clutching his pet snake's freshly shed skin and asking if I wanted to hold it.

The boys' mother was a slight, frenetic woman from the UK. She told me that when she was a student at Oxford she'd kept a python, which she'd let out for a 'roll on the grass to scare the tourists'. Her remarkable home library included many playscripts. I read *Under Milk Wood* one night after the boys were in bed. Catching a flicker out of the corner of my eye, I looked up to see their snake hissing at me from a glass cabinet next to the sofa.

The weeks passed and there was no sign of Cece, just a note in my pigeonhole in the Roberts House lobby telling me to take whatever clothes I wanted and to have her cases stored in the basement. In an age before the internet, so much corresponding was done through intermediaries. Scraps of dashed-off information, easily lost or misplaced.

At weekends that summer I walked up to the Lincoln center library to borrow scripts and lay on the grass in Central Park to read, just one body in a sea of strangers and aliens. You could slip away so easily in New York. I travelled alone to the Bronx Zoo, stopping on my walk back to the station to stand under the spray from an open fire hydrant while neighbourhood kids darted and danced around. All they knew of me was that I did not belong.

Egri writes, 'In conflict we are *forced* to reveal ourselves.' The conflict of choice reveals the foundations of our character. It reasserts the courage to rebuild, shift and grow in an alternative direction, seemingly correct or connected or not. With this determination in hand, I took my cue to slip away to another land.

REFERENCES

A character can grow … Lajos Egri, *The Art of Dramatic Writing* (New York: Touchstone, 2004), p. 77.

Rear Window … directed by Alfred Hitchcock (USA: Patron Inc, 1954).

A La Vieille Russie … In actual fact established in Kiev in 1851. See https://artdaily.cc/news/98276/A-La-Vieille-Russie-moves-to-new-5th-Ave--showroom#.XemXXpMzai4

Summer and Smoke … Tennessee Williams (New York: Dramatists Play Service, 1977).

Evita … directed by Alan Parker (Hollywood: Hollywood Pictures, 1996).

The Devil's Own … directed by Alan J. Pakula (Los Angeles: Columbia Pictures, 1997).

Enter RUMOUR, all painted with tongues … William Shakespeare, *Henry IV*, Part II, Prologue.

Timeless Land, Grahame Sydney, Brian Turner and Owen Marshall (Dunedin: Longacre Press, 1995).

my advice to you … Thornton Wilder, *The Skin of Our Teeth* (New York: Samuel French, 1942), p. 12.

Under Milk Wood, Dylan Thomas (London: Dent, 1954).

In conflict we are *forced* … Egri, *The Art of Dramatic Writing*, p. 191.

Elese Dowden

half-gallon quarter-acre pavlova pretext

We must not be deluded: limited in its action, its dynamism halted, the civilization of the colonised society from the first day enters the twilight that is the precursor of the end. Spengler, in his The Decline of the West, quotes these lines from Goethe:

> *So must thou be. Thou canst not Self escape.*
> *So erst the Sibyls, so the Prophets told.*
> *Nor Time nor any Power can mar the shape*
> *Impressed, that living must itself unfold.*
> —Aimé Césaire

This is a is a story about Governor Grey, René Descartes and Mike Hosking: the blood-spattered carpenters of history. It's a heart-warming tale of shame, botany metaphors, and the intricate golden-dawn streetlamp silhouette of the evergreens—against the violent, creeping-violet construction of innuendo. In writing, I practise the art of connecting. If connecting is equal to constructing, I am the Auckland Unitary Plan. I draw cards as ideas, cards as communal fate. Like Madame Sosostris, I speak with a bad cold (and a mangled accent). Édouard Glissant calls history 'a highly functional fantasy of the West', and in the paragraphs that follow, I paint a purposeful imaginary of my own. I write what I think, and hope you'll believe me (because to write is to hope).

*

Stories are metaphysical. They permeate every sacred crevice of existence, winding their way across longitudes, latitudes and lineages as determinedly as māwhai over stone walls. *Dirty Politics*, the Mercury bill, your DSM diagnoses, that time your cousin rolled a fire truck out in Hūnua: they are all stories, and none of them authored in isolation. We're in lockdown again in Naarm, but no matter how I arrange the cards I can't shake the feeling that I'm not the only one reading them.

There's this jumping spider that hangs out behind my monitor, and I like to think she's involved in the authorship process too. As we write, the threads of the narrative's neural network light up in silkworm sepia. The worn-out web metaphors we spin scaffold the togetherness of time, growing and repairing like a spidery Ship of Theseus. Historical fantasy allows us to create new worlds in six-word sentences. *Did you leave the oven on?* I had to run downstairs to check, in case I'd accidentally authored a new timeline in which my kitchen looked like a 'Don't drink & fry' ad.

I. Creation myths

The flipside is the geometric rule that all angles in a right-angled triangle add up to 180 degrees. People love useless pieces of information. We call these good words 'facts'. If they form a narrative bridge, we call them 'bon mots'. When a Pākehā writes down a bon mot, we call it 'science'. In 1979 two guys called Stephen and Richard wrote about the spandrels of San Marco. Spandrels are the ornately embellished right-angles you see at the intersections of arches and walls of bridges and cathedrals. Like bones under flesh, spandrels bear the inertia and the permanency of time; they put the *arch* in architecture. Just as Marmite is a side-effect of beer, a spandrel is a side-effect of biological construction.

When I was a baby philosopher at Auckland Uni, Robert Nola taught me that religion was a spandrel. I was a Young Nat, so I believed him. He also taught me about Blaise Pascal, a French gambler who took a punt on God-belief by drawing a punnet square over which Kierkegaard still turns in his grave. Given the upsides, Pascal figured the old church thing was worth a crack. Perhaps *religion* is a spandrel but *spirit* is not, and that is the scientist's mistake. He forgets he is trained not in the art of narrative reflection but in the science of narrative observation. Galileo learned that one the hard way. Day and night exist simultaneously; the earth both brightens and darkens as it turns.

As above, so below.

We carry the weight of our ancestors in our bones because in reincarnation, energy finds its rebirth. The mind creates the body, and colonialism creates the ego. As Pākehā, my ancestors know all about that one. Let me tell you a story about my whakapapa. Irish unionist and Trinity College professor Edward, whose life's work was studying Shakespeare, preferred to think of himself as an Englishman. His daughter Hester was an Irish spiritualist who once fell into a hypnotic sleep when Yeats put his hand on her shoulder. Hester was hired by the late Oscar Wilde's family to see if she might bring him back from the dead. Upon this Wilde request, Hester took her spirit guide Johannes to the theatre to see *The Importance of Being Earnest* with special guest. Oscar hated the performance and relayed a new play to Hester via Ouija board and automatic writing. No author acts alone, as evidenced by this absurd *ménage à trois*.

II. collective longing

Sometimes I wonder whether I'll ever have my own long moment of suffering in public with Oscar Wilde. To be honest, this current moment has gone on for some time now, and the arm's length at which I hold *The Picture of Dorian Gray* is close enough to a mirror for me. Potawatomi scientist Robin Wall Kimmerer in her book, *Braiding Sweetgrass*, writes about how fungal networks connect. In May, two weeks after I lectured on Kimmerer's mycorrhizal research, my aunty called from Waiuku to share the very same idea, which she had heard from her esteemed acquaintance Neil deGrasse Tyson.

Kimmerer says that every forest contains networks of fungal strands that drink nutrients from the soil, trading them with trees in exchange for energy. Fungal networks are basically the TradeMe of the forest. They connect neighbour to neighbour, sharing nutrients so that everyone gets to flourish together. Forests generate their own powerful universes by striking a balance between collective wins and collective woes. 'Through unity, survival. All flourishing is mutual.'

Tucked between the pages of the February *Metro* and twelve packets of Maggi onion soup mix, I read about the kauri in the ricked back of the Waitākere ranges. Tāne Mahuta, who is the father of all fungal kingdoms, is a vast culmination of collective forest energy. Did you know? 'It's not science until a white man said it first.' That's an old Pākehā proverb, but I framed it as a bon mot.

> *mauri*
> *1. (noun) life principle, life force, vital essence, special nature, a material symbol of a life principle, source of emotions—the essential quality and vitality of a being or entity. Also used for a physical object, individual, ecosystem or social group in which this essence is located.*

Nā, he mauri tō ngā pakake, he mauri tō ngā tāngata, he mauri tō ngā tuna, he mauri tō ngā manu, he mauri tō ngā ika, nā reira i mate ai ēnei mea katoa i te mākutu; ki te mākututia e te Māori ēnei mea, ka mate, ngaro tonu atu; ahakoa nui ēnei mea, ki te mākututia ka ngaro.

Years before the Waitākere rāhui, I tramped over those mycorrhizal networks with some mining engineer I'd brought home from Brisbane. Sometimes I wonder whether he rues the day he kissed a writer in the dark. Probably not. In my version, the engineer quietly continued eating Nando's on his parents' Norman Park porch between his fly-in-fly-out day job detonating Aboriginal heritage sites. He spent Christmas with us in Tāmaki Makaurau, and we argued our way from Waiheke through the Waitākeres via Piha's glittering sands.

Hone Tuwhare reckons Papatūānuku loves a good back massage, but the mining engineer was a bad masseuse. Most extractivists are. Like Locke and Gauguin, they think ownership is constituted by sticking one's dick into something and unloading a bacterial colony of disease. Sartre saw the world in the same series of holes and slimes. He, too, misread *Lordship and Bondage*, and upon seeing his own slime in the knotty roots of a chestnut became nauseously afraid of continental Papatūānuku.

At first, my ancestor Edward wasn't so fond of women. He thought about them the same way all the other Kants did back in the day. But whether it was love at first sight, or internalised misogyny, two separate women still married him, on two separate occasions. First he married Mary Clerke. She lends her last name to one of the moon's craters, and bore Hester, who became a golden dawn. Then he married Elizabeth Dickinson West, a poet who pre-empted Sartre's nausea.

Calmly to see the utter littleness
Of all within the individual soul,
And merge our restless care for our own lot
In a deep faith that in the large success
And grand sure tendings of the human whole,
Failure and loss of one life matters not.

Lorde is her mother's child, and we are all the daughters of many. It is possible to know things before you are born. Hera Lindsay Bird thinks it's

'almost sweet/ this collective longing for an imaginary past/ if they weren't
so obviously made by kids in sweatshops'. *God, I bet she's sick of flight puns
in poetry reviews.* But the ethic she writes about is not endemic to Smith and
Caughey's. The functional fantasy of the West is a giant zoology of continental
department stores, erected on stolen land and carved from the ivory tusks of
the elephant in the room.

If I construct this narrative as sudden, it's because it's not. We know. We
have always known. The settler colonial disease plagues us worse than those
'in these trying times' Covid emails—even *knowing* the pain of the Oxford
comma. In ~~Aotearoa~~ New Zealand, the Pākehā identity is predicated on a 'yeah,
nah' negation of itself; the largest and most preoccupied Palagi circlejerk this
side of Melbourne.

In 1769 the infamous murderer James Cook arrived in Aotearoa along
the coast of Te Kurī a Pāoa, bringing a whole host of infections and leaving a
settler colonial legacy of war, which points its bloody lasers into the undusted
corners of Paritai Drive. This is why 'post-colonialism' is a lie. It masks the
settler's original intentions; a genocide intermitting parabolically between the
cry for assimilation and the hushed, white-blanket tone of colonial murder.
In the tradition of Tasman and Cook, this country is plagued by John Key-
style commodity fetishism, David-Seymourian false consciousness, and the
meritocratic, half-gallon quarter-acre pavlova pretext of paradise. *Mein Kampf,
mein Führer: Sie ist gerichtet!*

III. for believing you were god

I confess, I went to Ihumātao for two reasons: to pay my respects and to
appease my white guilt. At least I've got one up on Jacinda. *And so, the negation
begins.* South Auckland is my physical birthplace. Audre Lorde wrote, 'when
we view living in the european [sic] mode only as a problem to be solved, we
rely solely upon our ideas to make us free, for these were what the white fathers
told us were precious'. I relied on the white fathers and, idolising Sartre, went
where no Labour prime minister had gone before. Praying for anonymity, I
set off in my parents' Mazda and a hospice shop Swanndri; settler, unsettled,
setting the scene for my obscene transgression like a rogue Eminem lyric (but
without the Italian noodles).

I think this is probably what bad faith feels like. In the final few hours of a Friday afternoon I watched myself through the settler colonial keyhole, desperate to prove I was not one of *those* Pākehā. But negation is always self-contained, and whiteness is always doubly unaware of itself. *Are we allowed to write like this?* In talking about whiteness, I'm also talking around whiteness. There aren't enough words in the English language to write about whiteness: first, because it is deliberately written out of our grasp, and second, because we will never tire of coke-bloating on about ourselves. We do not want to see the elephant in the room. That thing has taken up way more space than is necessary in our quarter-acre zoo. It's about time we let it out.

*

Edward rose again—this time, as one of Churchill's commandos. His modus operandi was to scare the living shit out of the Nazis. Above the equator he made fifty parachute jumps. He wrote in his diary that 'he felt he had run all over the country and climbed all of the mountains'. In Greece he was taken as a prisoner of war but made his escape by pretending he had to pee and flinging his belt into the face of his captor. For three months Edward survived alone in the mountains. When he returned he told his four children that he had shot a large German sergeant with a machine gun. It was the first time he had killed a man. His children told me about their Uncle George, remembering his pipe and moustache and his little boxes of Ricies and Weet-Bix. They think it unusual that he was a bachelor, and have declared him a spy. Below the equator, in Taihape and Papakura, Edward tilled the bed of the vege garden with the springs of an old mattress. Both he and his wife were marked by the narrative of war; every time the local fire siren wailed, longing for closure, she felt afraid.

*

The only thing millennials love more than a quiet 'fuck you' is a clever 'fuck you'. Audre Lorde replied to the tradition of Sartre as he sat, quivering at the roots of a chestnut tree: 'For each of us as women, there is a dark place within, where hidden and growing our true spirit rises, "Beautiful and tough as chestnut/ stanchions against [y]our nightmare of weakness" and of impotence.' I believe this is what Chlöe Swarbrick also meant when she retorted: 'Okay, boomer.'

If there's one thing I learned at *Men of Steel,* it's that Imperial man is afraid of his own body. He waltzes it around like a limp balloon, believing it his job as coloniser, as mind, to define and conquer. This is why the word 'boomer' bothers him so much. He is afraid of his ego popping—*no*—he is afraid of the half-assed whistle his latex body will make as it gives way to gravity and folds itself recklessly into his chaps. The whole process takes approximately twenty-two seconds—*and you wouldn't believe the uranium stench.*

The coloniser's winter is beginning to thaw at a rate rivalling Franz Josef Glacier. The world is becoming alien to him and, with it, the dominion of things he believes were created exclusively to bend to his will. Like Don Juan, the Pākehā believes he must repeat his stale rhetoric. He believes this again and again until one day, dishevelled and on an exclusive diet of beef and freshwater crayfish, Mike Hosking discovers that the nation is laughing back at him.

*

I wish I never believed we were god. Oscar Wilde believed that we could, 'by converting private property into public wealth, and substituting co-operation for competition … restore society to its proper condition of a thoroughly healthy organism, and insure the material well-being of each member of the community'. *As above, so below.* I have converted myself into public wealth so many times that my entire being is made of linen spun from mermaid dollars.

But I'm slowly learning to understand that the Western conception of public wealth is still the Western conception of private property.

I'm slowly learning that the West's historical fantasy is a projection I've been slinging around with me.

I'm slowly learning, after a long moment of suffering in silence, that *creation is a team sport.*

REFERENCES

We must not be deluded … Aimé Césaire, 'Culture and Colonization', *Social Text* 103, no. 2 (2010), p. 132.

a highly functional fantasy … Édouard Glissant, *Caribbean Discourse: Selected essays* (Charlottesville: University Press of Virginia, 1989), p. 64.

In 1979 two guys … S.J. Gould & R.C. Lewontin, 'The Spandrels of San Marco and the Panglossian Paradigm: A critique of the adaptationist programme', *Proceedings of the Royal Society of London. Series B: Biological Sciences (1934–1990)*, 205, no. 1161 (1979).

His daughter Hester … Helen Sword, *Ghostwriting Modernism* (Ithaca, London: Cornell University Press, 2018), p. 105.

Upon this Wilde request … Jeffrey Kahan, *Shakespiritualism: Shakespeare and the occult, 1850–1950* (New York: Palgrave Macmillan, 2013), p. 89.

every forest contains networks … Robin Wall Kimmerer, *Braiding Sweetgrass: Indigenous wisdom, scientific knowledge and the teachings of plants* (Minneapolis: Milkweed Editions, 2013), p. 20.

Through unity, survival … ibid, p. 20.

the kauri in the ricked back … Hone Tuwhare, *Small Holes in the Silence: Collected works*, ed. Herewini Muru, Waihoroi Shortland & Patu Hohepa (Auckland: Penguin, 2016), p. 178.

Tāne Mahuta … Bob Harvey, 'Death of the gods: The woeful response to kauri dieback disease', *Metro Magazine*, 21 Feb. 2019.

Mauri … John C Moorfield, 'Mauri', in *Te Aka Online Māori Dictionary*, ed. John C. Moorfield: https://maoridictionary.co.nz

Calmly to see … Elizabeth Dickinson West, *Verses 1856–1884: A critical edition*, ed. Wayne K. Chapman (Clemson: Clemson University Digital Press, 2013), p. 13.

almost sweet/ this collective longing … Hera Lindsay Bird, 'The Friday Poem: Colorado Springs 1989', The Spinoff: https://thespinoff.co.nz/books/27-09-2019/the-friday-poem-colorado-springs-1989-by-hera-lindsay-bird/

for believing you were god … Tayi Tibble, 'Tohunga': https://lithub.com/tohunga-a-poem-by-tayi-tibble/

when we view living … Audre Lorde, *Sister, Outsider* (New York: Ten Speed Press, 1984), p. 36.

For each of us as women … Ibid, p. 36.

by converting private property … Oscar Wilde, *The Soul of Man under Socialism* (Project Gutenberg, 1997), p. 6.

Laura Surynt

Feeling Around a Room in the Dark

When it rains in Auckland, the stairs leading down through the park's green to the art gallery slush and shimmer in the torrents of water. Auckland Art Gallery Toi o Tāmaki slopes down the hillside, and at the bottom the stairs open to a square covered by a canopy of kauri. This is the entrance one would usually arrive at, wowed by layers of glass and stone. Coming from the university, however, I always arrived from behind, snaking down the steps, a slow reveal. When it's not raining, boys use the stairs and the wide flat entrance for skateboarding, repeating the same tricks over and over.

The gallery's north atrium is cathedral-like, hushed and holy with views to the city, and from there the space is designed in such a way that visitors loop through, spiralling through time as the halls connect the newer building with the heritage spaces. A younger sibling to the north atrium, huge and flooded with families, is the south atrium. It looks away from the city and into the trees, but also at the service entrance with its cones and fluorescence. There are two benches, one at the top of the stairs and one at the bottom, shaped like beans— or drops or commas, a circle with a swoop for luck, a memory. The light is a luminous green, and busts of gods line the wall of window: Apollo, Artemis, Minerva. The sun only reaches them in high summer between the downpours. These gods and their light remind me of Kettle's Yard in Cambridge, on the other side of the world, where the sun tracks not to the north but to the south. The gods are there too.

In the dying half of the year, as the light begins to wane, there is a moment when the sun hits the Venetian mirror at the top of the stairs. The light bounces and refracts across the room and a beam of colour, a rainbow, rests on the face of Brâncuși's *Prometheus*. It's a cast of the original sculpted marble—there's also a bright bronze rendering in Brussels, but this one is only bright when the light is right. For the rest of the year Prometheus sits atop the glossy black piano as if

224

he's floating on water; Prometheus isolated on his rock of damnation perhaps. At first the sculpture is just a stone—so frequently seen at Kettle's Yard, where pebbles dot the mantle or swirl from white to grey to black—but when you move closer you can see the lines of a face forged into the surface. The lines arc across and out creating a nose and brow, and a rough ear faces up, listening maybe to the world around it; the other ear is pressed to the piano, listening, maybe. A Greek Māui, demigod Prometheus was the bearer of light, of fire, from the gods to humanity. He was eternally punished for this transgression. But here he rests, perhaps asleep, perhaps in pain, perhaps at peace with his sacrifice—for what is the cost of light, of fire, of hope?

*

Light allows the memory to shift and make sense. And isn't that all writing is? Memories, and my attempt at their formation, like the bean benches in the south atrium—drawing away from the circle, a drag (and it is a drag, most of the time) to create something solely from my own mind? The dawn plays tricks on us as the discarded pyjamas at the end of the bed take on uncertain form before becoming their mundane selves with the rising of the sun—something so familiar warps and changes in the early light. Memories do too.

Watching the sun is a bit like writing: waiting, and responding to what's illuminated. So much staring and stopping and spending time with myself until suddenly I find my mind fevered and full, thoughts spilling out at the worst times of the day—when there's a class full of students in front of me, or late at night in bed trying to type by the light of the laptop, or in the shower, stopped from ideas by paper's (pixels', really) incompatability with water. I'll see or say the same thing in repetition of the self, a subconscious self-plagiarising, and then, only then, suddenly realise and understand what I mean by it all.

Writing is a way of thinking, of feeling around a room in the dark. It's moving house and waking up in the middle of the night, fumbling down the stairs to the kitchen for a glass of water. And months later finding you know the way by heart—door, stairs, hallway, shelf, sink, tap—and wondering at what point you stopped needing the light on. Writing, in the words of Katherine Mansfield, is an attempt to 'lose my self in the soul of another'. It's learning to submit. It's yielding to homesickness. When I moved away from New Zealand I thought the coming adventures would form themselves into something tangible on the page, but instead I just wrote about home. I suppose it was an attempt at making those memories real, to stop them shifting with each recollection. Like Mansfield's desire for home, as she writes:

> Now—now I want to write recollections of my own country. Yes, I want to write about my own country till I simply exhaust my store. Not only because it is a 'sacred debt' that I pay to my country because my brother and I were born there, but also because in my thoughts I range with him over all the remembered places. I am never far away from them. I long to renew them in writing.

A friend, musing on her own imminent move from Auckland to London, wrote (in our years-long and faltering email thread, subject line SUMMER/ WINTER, titled for the seasons that push and pull between us and our hemispheres), 'It seems to me that your own absence has been a sharpening force and that you've seen things differently from afar.' In reply I typed,

> You are right … we can miss it together, and then see how we sway in and out of one another's spheres—surely there will be a time when we will both be in the same space at the same time and are looking in, not out (I have recently been thinking about looking in—an appreciation for the domestic, not of marriage or motherhood, but of corners of shadow and stairs and light and quiet and the spaces we make for ourselves).

Was that the moment of beginning—words unfurling out from there, and into this?

*

Like Toi o Tāmaki, Kettle's Yard is also a space of old and new. The original Victorian houses are connected by a bridge to an extension designed and built in the 1970s. Unlike the older part of the gallery, the extension is almost windowless. Instead, strips of skylight illuminate the rooms but block the sun, forming a perpetual twilight—it kind of glows at the height of summer, but winter's dim is dark and I rush through like the winter sun rushing across the sky. In primary school we learnt that Māui fished up the North Island and the South Island was his waka. We put on a play, dressed up in yellow and orange and red—rays of sun to be caught by Māui. Among his feats, his tricks, this was one of the greatest: the capture of Tamanuiterā, the sun. Māui slowed the sun's progress across the sky, lengthened the days, the light, the life.

*

When we moved to Cambridge we rented an attic flat; it was so fucking English, with sloped ceilings and disused fireplaces. To have arrived in autumn meant that in the emptiness I watched the light die and then come back, inch by inch. The creator of Kettle's Yard, Jim Ede, said that when one moves house each room should be left empty at first to see how it reacts with the light. I can just imagine him sitting in the empty rooms watching shadows as the seasons wax and wane. We didn't have art to fill the space—or antique furniture, or candlesticks, or sculptures—but the blank walls were enough. Then one spring evening we came home and found a door of light, dappled from the shifting trees, on the wall across from our bedroom's arched window. It went from white to gold to a red that faded into dusk. Spring's sunset surprised us.

That night I played recordings of birds on my phone as we lay in bed, windows thrown open in the heat. They echoed in the dark as he guessed: tūī? no, bellbird? no, kōkako?

How many kōkako are left? I googled. Hardly any, maybe a thousand? A few more?

The year after I was born only one breeding pair of North Island kōkako remained and attempts were being made to revive the population in the native bush behind our house. The bush that was wild and stretched for miles. The bush I would find at the end of the road—gravel ending in a wall of green. I walked, clambered, through the trees until I couldn't any more and had to wade upstream instead, pulling myself up by the rocks, slipping and tumbling into the icy water. I wanted to reach the waterfall, wondered if I could. But the river widened and the bush rose on all sides, the dark green of time—not like in England where, come spring, it's so green it's almost yellow. It's that glowing English green that takes my breath away when spring rolls around. I never quite expect it, that overwhelming green. In spring we cycle the streets and yell SO GREEN to each other at every corner. So fucking green. The bush wasn't that easy paddocked green, so I gave up and turned for home. But by then I was already within the boundaries of the kōkako revitalisation. They wouldn't— couldn't—survive in the easy green. Nothing does.

Ngā manu, our birds, are dying.

A pīwakawaka once flew into my bedroom. I woke up to the sound of its feathered frenzy before it landed on the edge of my desk. Years later I learned that a pīwakawaka indoors was an omen of death, for its laugh brought about the death of Māui on his quest for immortality. But Māui failed and was killed by Hine-nui-te-pō, the goddess of death. You can't fuck with the gods. Now I watch a kākāpō fuck a man's hand on Twitter as he collects sperm for artificial insemination. Scientists are attempting to prevent the mass extinction of New Zealand's indigenous biodiversity. Is this decolonisation? Undoing time? That pīwakawaka was an omen of death after all, I just didn't see it.

We had to move out of that attic flat, although we didn't want to, and so I spent the summer packing. To console myself I listened to 'Kākāpō Files', a podcast series documenting the biggest kākāpō breeding season to date. As the rooms emptied I filled myself with facts that spilled out to whoever I saw in the evenings: did you know that kākāpō live for decades/ almost one hundred years?/ the name means night parrot/ in order to protect them from predators, they are raised on offshore islands/ islands of sanctuary/ islands are sanctuary/ New Zealand used to be a sanctuary, before colonialism brought rabbits for fun, then stoats and weasels to control the rabbits, and with them, the death of our native birds/. But it isn't simply the stoats and the weasels, is it? It's the humans who cleared the native bush. It's that neon spring green—farmland—that replaced it.

As we settled into our new flat I felt unsettled by the move. And unsettled with the sentiments of settlement. Alongside the labours of Māui we were taught of the 'discovery' of New Zealand, the 'heroic' settlers who first arrived in New Zealand—it's time that's done this, allowed us to forget history and hope that too much time will forgive the transgressions. Some days I long for the southern hemisphere's bright white ocean light, for the light of home, but home? Home that's stolen islands, and the settler's unsettlement that comes with knowing I live on stolen land. Unsettlement seems to me synonymous with a sense of home. Maybe we need to unsettle to reverse the ravages of settlement. But how?

Maybe replace the gods with gods, language with language.

Return the land.

*

Writing is visiting the same gallery every day for a year and noticing when it changes, even if it doesn't. Writing is waiting for time to pass. I used to keep a daily diary, religiously, until I realised each day's recount was a half-hashed attempt to just get it done. Then I stopped writing for a while, save for Instagram captions and marking notes in the margins and DMs back and forth. It was too much to do anything else. How does one balance a vocation with the desire to write? Out of the habit, I took to reading what I'd already written a year (or two) ago. It was like reading the words of a stranger, surprising myself with phrases turned in a way that were unknown to me.

How do I write like that again—words that seem so easy and light, words that I had time for? These days my mind is a haze. It's not writers' block, it's a life that's so much off the page that the page itself blurs and warps, offering not comfort but exhaustion. The blank screen dims and shifts to black—a darkness parallel to the sunset that comes so soon after the dawn. It's not a hazy shade of winter or a certain slant of light—it's a weather app where the rising and setting of the sun sit side by side, no scrolling necessary. And the night scrolls into oblivion. It's a capitalist working week that prioritises the dark and evenings of exhaustion in the pitch black. It's looking up, and the sudden sunset has extinguished itself.

I want to watch the light coming back, and the words with it.

*

Teju Cole's essay 'Blind Spot' chronicles the loss and return of his eyesight. For a photographer and a writer, this loss is a moment of fear. It's also a moment of reflection as he makes the connection between his current state and his past writing: 'When we write fiction, we write within what we know. But we also write in the hope that what we have written will somehow outdistance us … through the spooky art of writing, to trick ourselves into divulging truths that we do not know we know.' His condition and subsequent essay led to the publication of *Blind Spot*, a book of photographs with accompanying prose as an exploration of light and looking. In describing his 'episode of blindness' he acknowledges, 'The photography changed after that. The looking changed.'

The photographs in *Blind Spot* map the world. There's only one from New Zealand: it's Auckland, just minutes from the art gallery—a frame of light and reflection and stairs. Unlike most of the other photos, which are each contained on one page, this one spills over the centre divide and towards the prose: 'Tane and his siblings conspire to push apart their mother, Papatuanuku, the earth, and father, Ranginui, the sky. In the space forced between the two is the light of the world. The light falls and flows between two eyelids.'

Blind Spot is a reminder to look and then look again. It's an exercise in taking words and images and rearranging them in order to rearrange time.

And that's what I do, lying in bed posting and scrolling on Instagram, organising my online self onto squares. It allows me to warp time—to layer moments of being, a shushed click almost forgotten, onto the present. I would perhaps have forgotten those moments, but isn't that what Instagram is for? To remember and construct and collect moments and thoughts in time to assist my increasingly incompetent memory?

I scroll through my feed and notice what I missed at the time: a leaf, a patch of light, an ankle at the edge. But more than that I notice time passing, and the tangibility of it. A few weeks ago I posted a photograph: mānuka and tī kōuka silhouetted against a peachy sky, the colours reflected in a rippled lake below, taken on a threshold when I was twenty-one, the door left ajar against autumn's chill. In that moment I longed to leave and didn't know how much I would want to return once I had. I was growing my hair out, only to chop it all off again (oh, that quick measure of time and its toll), and the room I returned to smelt of sap, a synaesthetic loop of time that hits when I think I'm laying low, beyond time. But I'm a time being, pushed and pulled by it all. And this is its measure.

In those little squares my summer's sphere can last just a little longer.

*

Our ozone is a realm of seven-minute burn time in the wide blue beckoning sky. As a kid I spent summers on the beach—white-hot golden sand and the blue-green of the gulf. We spent hours clambering around the tidal pools, lifting rocks to see the orangey-red crabs emerge or peeling starfish from the sides, feeling them suck our skin softly before putting them back again. My hair tangled like the seaweed (ha! Why was the beach embarrassed? my brother shouted. Because the sea weed!) but we were not embarrassed in our bare feet and chests. Skin to sky.

There was one pool that was big enough to swim in. Safe from the ocean's deep. We had to tread carefully to avoid the urchins and anemones, and then we floated out, arms and legs spread, as our own starfish—little bodies in the little pool. A huge rock loomed above us with a single tree at the top, roots holding it all together. Did the rock need the tree, or did the tree need the rock?

Each morning Mum slathered us with sticky sweet sunblock, a greasy layer that made it hard to hold on to the grass as we clambered down the cliff. Dusty clay clung to our hands and sand stuck to the round cheeks of our bums and gave us socks of grit. If we swam too soon the sunblock would lift and float into a hazy oil slick around us, purple and green and gold on the cool blue. A full dunk under, salt in our noses, washed it clean off.

And so I burnt, a red heat that radiated even in the night. White cotton sheets were too much. I kicked them off and lay in the heavy night, my hand on my stomach feeling the heat from the summer's stun. Even in the dark the sun shone through. But by morning I had browned while my siblings stayed red. I thought I was invincible. Only my shoulders peeled, and I relished pulling my skin off in swathes. By the end of summer I had brown tidelines marking the layers of my days. I never listened to Mum as she shook her head and continued to rub sunblock earnestly onto my back and neck every day. Don't forget your face! she shouted after me as I ran off, cheeks and nose open to the sun and sea.

*

Teju Cole says, 'when we sit down to make work we are made of all the things we have consumed. Our creative, artistic, musical, filmic diet goes towards our intellectual formation.' And maybe that's what this is: an attempt at threading together my obsessions, or, as Durga Chew-Bose says, of what turns you on and makes you want to make art.

*

After graduating, I wasn't in the city every day but in its periphery, looping in and out as the days turned. One Sunday morning I sat in the car and turned on the radio. I was greeted by the sound of birdsong before the news. The radio's birds were normal for me, swoops and bells and creaks echoing out of the car's shitty speakers—a sure contrast to the BBC's long, sharp bleeps to signal the hour and upcoming news (politics, nationalism, something royal). The news is nicer at the bottom of the world, or when it's not, at least its shock is softened by the sounds of the forest.

After driving through the rain I parked in the city and walked towards the gallery, this time from the front. I stood in that north atrium, my hot-pink umbrella dripping, before navigating the wide-open spaces to the upper floors. I came across a series of women, faces emerging from thick dark paint. One held a ruru in her palm, feathers haloed. The description on the wall read, 'A guardian and a teller of prophesies.' The artist was Star Gossage, and I took blurred photographs of each label, saving them to read later. I hovered before one in the corner—enamel on board, a spectral figure, a rising light—and the surrounding faces stared out in stillness as the rain poured beyond the walls of the gallery. These girls are gods, I thought.

REFERENCES

lose my self in the soul of another … *The Letters and Journals of Katherine Mansfield: A selection*, ed. C.K. Stead (London: Penguin Books, 1977), p. 214.

Now—now I want to write … Ibid., p. 65.

when one moves house … Kettle's Yard Guided House Tour, 26 July 2019.

I listened to 'Kākāpō Files' … www.rnz.co.nz/podcasts/kakapo-files.rss

When we write fiction … Teju Cole, *Known and Strange Things* (London: Faber & Faber, 2017), p. 383.

The photography changed after that … Teju Cole, *Blind Spot* (London: Faber & Faber, 2016), p. 208.

Tane and his siblings … Ibid., p. 10.

You know, when we sit down … Khalid Warsame, 'Teju Cole: "We Are Made of All the Things We Have Consumed"', *Literary Hub*, 4 April 2019: https://lithub.com/teju-cole-we-are-made-of-all-the-things-we-have-consumed/

what turns you on … Durga Chew-Bose, interview with Ella Yelich-O'Connor, Auckland Writers Festival, 19 May 2018.

A guardian and a teller of prophesies … Star Gossage, 'Fortrose Ruru', *Five Māori Painters*, Auckland Art Gallery Toi o Tāmaki, 2014.

Sarah Young

The Space to Feel

A woman is walking through the park behind my house, a phone held out before her, showing a view of the Port Hills to the person she is speaking to.

This is what we do now. Our spaces are smaller. To expand them we have to access the space of others, a mediated rather than direct experience.

Sometimes the world inside me feels smaller as well, the barriers that contain my self more rigid, my ability to feel reduced. Is this the after-effect of lockdown, or just a result of being so long in the city itself?

*

On a cold wet day, a month or so after lockdown, I looked out my window and saw a man walking across the park wearing a black hooded jacket, black office pants and a purple backpack. He turned and walked back the way he'd come. Then turned again. He walked back and forth on the same diagonal for at least twenty minutes, turning at exactly the same point each time, his head down, steps heavy and determined, back hunched and arms spread wide as if facing a strong wind.

I watched, mesmerised and confused. I wondered if he was stuck, if he needed someone to help him break this cycle or simply to find his way out of himself, out of the park; or if he was scared, if he needed reassurance, a helping hand to leave—

Or maybe he was atoning; or perhaps this was a ritual, counting his steps for luck or some other logic.

Would he understand me if I tried to help, would we speak the same language; did other voices compete—

Would he hurt me—

Was that a bad thing to think—

I felt guilty for watching him; I hid behind the curtain each time he turned to face my direction.

Then suddenly, he pivoted towards the exit and walked out. I felt relieved, which also made me feel worse.

Five minutes later the man was back. He turned abruptly onto the same diagonal, pulled up his hood and started walking back and forth again.

Maybe he was trying to make something come out. Release something. Something stuck.

I too had been stuck in my body at various times. I remembered an aunt walking away from my netball game when I was a teenager, unable to continue watching me, my clumsy body heavy with depression, incapable of making choices or moving freely on the court; so different to the girl who had won a netball scholarship only months earlier.

'You didn't even seem there,' she said later; 'That wasn't you, wasn't your body.'

It was hours of suicides in the gym at lunchtime, back and forth, that finally loosened me.

*

Finally, the man walked over to a tree on the perimeter. He dropped his backpack and lay down, staring at the sky as if exhausted, as if he had battled some relentless feeling to the ground. The grass would be muddy, wet. The wind was blowing the last of the yellow leaves off the tree.

I went back to my computer.

A few minutes later he was pacing again, hood up, backpack on. He had been there at least an hour, maybe more. I was sure it was some form of punishment. But dictated by whom or what?

*

Next morning I ran around the park, looking for the markers that had guided the man's turns. I found the white lines of the rugby pitch on the frosty grass. Somehow this felt worse. Had he felt trapped inside that rectangle, that enclosed shape? Was he walking harder, faster each time, attempting to push through the wall? Or did he have to cross it, say, fifty times in order to break free? Once he broke free, did he already know he had to go back and do it again, or did a pressure rebuild, seeking release? All of these possibilities felt familiar to me.

*

A few weeks earlier, freedom in the form of level two had arrived. Instead of running to restaurants or friends' houses, I drove to a cottage on a remote West Coast beach four hours away.

Two days later I was walking on the beach in the rain at dusk, collecting rocks, the bush-covered mountains swamped in mist behind me. I was happy, thinking about where to go next, what to study, I was—

I was crying.

The crying started, specifically, after I picked up a small arrow-shaped stone. It was a John stone, I told myself out loud, without knowing that I was about to say it. John was my late grandfather, a man I had been very close to. Some aspect of the colours—green, dark grey-blue and mustard—must have reminded me of something: his chess sets, a particular painting perhaps.

My mind glitched, would not allow—

Pause, consideration, or reflection—

The thoughts flew from my mind like the spray the wind ripped from the waves.

*

Some things are too big to be known. Things that cannot be named, that remain without parameters or measurement, threatening to engulf the body, the self. That beach was the only place large enough for me to feel; it was only there, alone, that I could cry, that I could let that feeling surge and break like the waves thundering before me.

It came back though. Each day I walked for hours, and each day I cried. I wanted to remain there alone. I did not want to return.

*

Everyone has a lockdown narrative. Mine went something like this:

I returned to Christchurch from London a few months prior.

Just before lockdown my mother attempted suicide, and I was told something about my grandfather that I did not want to know. I chose a state of cognitive dissonance instead, somehow both believing her and holding on to the memory of the man I believed would never do such a thing.

Two weeks into lockdown my friend slipped while running, fell over a cliff and died.

A couple of weeks later my new relationship ended. I moved back to my small flat. I busied myself with textbooks, I applied for a PhD.

My flatmate returned at level three, further compressing my space and me to a tiny rectangle with a single mattress on the floor.

*

It is only now I realise I still haven't really cried for that relationship; nor enough, probably, for my friend. I sobbed briefly at the kitchen table while watching the funeral online, the empty chapel containing only her coffin, her boyfriend and a few family members. My partner finished up a work call beside me, his face disturbed by my display of emotion, before telling me he had to go to the doctor, he had something in his eye. He had booked an appointment for the time I had told him, repeatedly, that the funeral was on.

*

A city requires you to hide emotion, to contain yourself as you are contained within it. When movement is restricted, when we are locked down, what else stops flowing? What else restricts within you? I felt increasingly compacted, forced inwards and compressed; my emotions fragmented, snippet-like; my brain short-circuiting on certain images, refusing to linger.

Sometimes we need bigger spaces to feel bigger things, to let them dissolve or dilute.

*

The moment on the Coast echoed a similar one on a hot day pre-lockdown. My partner and I were lying in a park when my aunt called to tell me about my mother's suicide attempt. I felt sick, but not shocked in the way I felt in the subsequent conversation about my grandfather—after that one I felt I had been pulverised, broken apart into tiny pieces that fell back together, rejoined but forever changed.

I told my partner, wiped a tear away. We drove to a crowded beach, went for a swim, didn't really talk about it again. Our relationship felt too new to bear the weight of that sort of news, news that made me feel tainted just for knowing it.

*

Three days later I walked home from work through the city, taking a shortcut across a rugby park. Alone for the first time, I sat in the middle of the empty field, put my head on my knees and sobbed.

Someone else entered the park. I got up quickly and left.

*

The man walking back and forth, head down, oblivious to anything except the white paint lines that demarcated his confinement—was he walking something out too? We never really know what people around us are trying to shed. 'Shed' is now a bad word: more than just dead skin cells, it implies infection, clusters, spread.

But we shed—and renew—other things too. Relationships, jobs, ideas, fashion, hair, blood, tissue, pain. Shedding and reinstating, tension and release, contraction and expansion, these seem the central rhythms of life.

*

On my lunchbreak I see purple chalk scrawled on the pavement in the inner city: *COVID kills your rights. What about Kiwi rights. All rights matter. I do not give my consent.*

I suddenly feel—angry. I want to wipe that voice away.

*

Space is always political; emotions too. What we are allowed to feel, circumscribed emotions, palatable to others, suitable for painless consumption. I remembered walking down a street in central London, tears pouring down my face after my mother rang to tell me what her husband had done to her. The only person to look me in the eye was a woman trying to hand me a Jesus pamphlet. There was no compassion, only what seemed to me at the time to be opportunism.

But our drinking culture, our obsession with sport and our levels of child and domestic abuse perhaps point to breach points, to circuitries of emotion that do manage to cross the boundaries of selves and spaces.

*

On a warm evening prior to lockdown, I left work and encountered an overweight man yelling at his pregnant partner outside Ballantynes department store. She sat on the edge of a planter box, staring at the ground, a growing crowd watching. Two Unicef volunteers—young girls in heavy makeup and bright blue jackets—were telling him to stop.

I knew that sort of yelling—the way it starts, the way it escalates, the way it seeks to destroy the silence in front of it, the way it does not back down and defends its own ground, particularly in front of others. I had heard it directed at my own mother.

I knew that being publicly saved—even just verbally defended—would mean being privately punished later. I knew that the woman knew it too. She pulled on her partner's T-shirt, still looking at the ground as he continued to yell.

'Come on,' she said, trying to walk away, ignoring the blue-jacket girls who told her not to go with him.

I knew that feeling too. That other people just don't get it. They don't know how to manage this man; you do.

Defensiveness, anger and shame filled the space, and me. I walked quickly away.

*

After lockdown my friend rented a tiny box of a building in a plumbing company's yard in Sydenham. Behind its bright yellow door she furnished the room with colourful prints, her own photographs, a rug, two wooden desks, plants, wooden chairs, lamps: a rich anomaly against the concrete, warehouses and empty retail spaces. We drank red wine to toast her new space as darkness fell. She recalled a Georgian saying: *Sweep the floor, put down a rug, paint the walls.* They could—had to—live anywhere.

She had been feeling low the past few weeks, and admitted she was escaping the anxiety and depression inside her own home. The men who worked next door had been coming over to chat and share their own photography. To her surprise, they did not make her feel weird, indulgent or frivolous. She asked if I thought she was too impulsive, though: she always did this, she said, always craved something new. Those were good qualities too, I said. Besides, I did the same.

'Maybe,' she said later, 'if you stopped moving, if you just stayed here—in one city—love might come more easily to you.'

*

My mother too still moves every few months, at least every year.

We seek new places to find new feeling, to wash away the old. But we can reclaim them too.

*

During lockdown my French ex-boyfriend called me for the first time in two years. He had texted earlier to say he wanted to walk through both our cities—Paris, Christchurch—using Google Maps, recording it on Teams for a documentary project.

I had not been back to Paris since we ended.

I said maybe, sometime; he told me I had to promise. When I did not immediately agree on a time, he called. He never called unless he was mad. I answered, heart racing, an anxious echo from the past. His words were slightly manic, full of nerves, his faltering English and unusual word choices more prominent.

'You will do it,' he said.

'Yes. Okay.'

'Good. Good. That's good.'

We were silent for a moment.

'When?'

'I don't know. What time do you get up?'

He laughed. 'Anywhere. 8am. 2pm yesterday. You still early?'

'Yes.'

'Maybe my night then yes.'

We had always existed in other timeframes, even when in the same time zone.

*

It was strange to see his face when it finally appeared. He wore a shirt, a beard; sat at a table in his tiny kitchen. I remembered it well. The black-and-white tiled floor, the mustard-coloured walls. Beautifully Parisian, terribly unhygienic. He was drinking red wine, I coffee.

We stared at each other, caught up slowly, compared lockdown experiences. I told him I had broken up with someone who lied about seeing his exes, that I often felt rejected, especially sexually.

He seemed surprised, then reflective.

'That was never a problem with us, was it? I never remember the one rejecting the other?'

'No,' I said. 'It wasn't.'

He found my eyes and I felt an old tug on the heart; the forgotten feeling of someone you banished long ago.

'You still look the same,' he said with surprise.

He did too.

'Slightly balder,' he admitted, holding the top of his head down to the screen.

He lit a cigarette and stared at me. I averted my eyes.

'Come on then,' I said. 'Walk.'

*

We started in Christchurch, but there was nothing to show him on my street but houses, a small cemetery, an empty park. Through his eyes the city looked like a small provincial town. I took him briefly to Lyttelton instead.

'That's enough,' I said, suddenly embarrassed.

I typed his street from memory, Rue des Pyrénées. We looked up at the turquoise wrought-iron balcony outside his apartment, and I remembered a balloon that landed there on the day I burnt my leg with hot coffee.

We went to Montmartre to visit the gallery we'd met in, noting the dates of the Google footage as we walked through the city in another time, before Covid; then to his old flat I'd only ever heard stories about, tales of rubbish hip-high, a hoarding I attributed to his father's early death. We went to our favourite Vietnamese restaurant near the bar where I had got drunk on rum and mewed loudly at anyone who looked at me; then to the canal we had sat beside when he told me about his father's mistress, a woman who had turned up at the door before and after his father died. We fought later when I asked if he would have an affair one day and he refused to say no because it was impossible to read the future. We went to the café we liked to write in, where he had left me after another fight about moving in together and his demands that I had to prove myself less jealous first.

I looked at the sink behind him and remembered the meals we shared—tomates farcies, blanquette de veau. I remembered too the time he tipped the breakfast I made on the floor, the way he tore my notebook apart for asking who a girl was in his photograph. The many times I questioned him, the numerous times I broke up with him only to return to wipe his tears and change my Eurostar ticket to have one more night together.

*

The contrast with my last relationship seemed stark, the closeness with that man in Lyttelton seemed less, that man whose house I showed my ex on Google because somehow I just navigated straight there, which should have been awkward but wasn't, although then I had to admit that yes, my jealousy had also been a contributing factor to the end of that relationship, 'but you know how I am,' I said with a forced smile that perhaps betrayed the shame I felt—

But he only smiled, and there was kindness in his silence.

'But you seem good,' he said a few beats later. 'Really good. Confident. Full of life.'

'Yes,' I said, 'I'm always better alone.'

We laughed, but there was sadness too as he tipped back his glass of red wine without taking his eyes from mine.

We had destroyed each other and our relationship but there was love there, had been; I was suddenly sure of it in the way he considered me: with a compassion and a deep knowing of me that others lacked, including myself.

*

We spoke for three hours, a sweet sort of belated goodbye, the final conversation we never had, mainly because I was too impatient to cut him off, just to feel nothing.

*

I knew he found it strange that I never cried, not during the worst of our fights, not when he smashed glasses or plates, not even when we broke up on my birthday, when he told me I pushed and pushed just like my mother, when he admitted we had to end it because he might hit me one day just to make me shut up.

It was only under an oak tree in London's Walthamstow Marshes early one wet morning, more than six months after we broke up that I finally cried, crumbling for a few heavy minutes until, with aching chest and restricted windpipe, I ran home soaked through.

*

My emotions are often foreign to me; put off for another day, a more suitable time when I have nothing else better to do. It seems that in order to feel I need space—and a storm. Something violent, an external force that will crack me open, that will draw me to the surface of myself, force—however gently—an abreaction.

And when I do finally feel, I am often overwhelmed. Emotionally drunk, as

I call it. Or, as another ex put it—like an engine that gets flooded and can't start again. I fight, or I run.

I am trying to learn how to regulate, how to find a safer and more moderate space in between.

*

I see us again now, clinging silently to each other on the metro to Gard du Nord each time he dropped me off, oblivious to anyone that looked our way, lost already in the pain of parting, the lead-up always worse than the separation itself.

*

I think of that call, of retrospective emotions, of movement. How Google Maps became a vehicle to access a softer, paler nostalgia, rather than to enter a space blocked or imbued with emotions; a vehicle to allow our conversation, our mutual remembering, a reconciliation and forgiveness of sorts.

*

Perhaps it is not just that I find it hard to feel in cities, but also that some things remain—even if only for a time—too big or too risky to name, for you don't know how you'll react, even who you might be, or what part of your story you might have lost.

I was reluctant to walk the streets while my ex filmed me, because I did not know how I would feel. The man walking across the park had to raise his hood, stare at the ground, pretend no one else was there. I could not let myself feel anything about my grandfather in front of people because I did not know how I might unravel, who I might become, or what I might transmit.

In the city we are always watched. CCTV, neighbours, strangers, workmates, Google mapping drones, our own laptops and phones, a person standing in their house watching you walk across a park.

As our world gets smaller, what will happen to our ability to feel, to know ourselves?

Perhaps it is in nature that the boundaries of the self more easily collapse. The elements get in. The elements tear things apart. Or maybe it is just that in open space, alone, it is harder to hide from yourself.

*

A few years ago I was running alone around the red zone by the Avon River when suddenly I was unable to breathe and was surprised to find myself sobbing, bent over with a rage I had not even known I felt after my mother returned to her husband again.

And if that space had not been available, had not been opened up by an earthquake, what then? Would I even know that powerful feeling resided in me, or that it had been masked by other feelings—and depression—instead? Rage seems a heavy thing not to know you hold; a growing pressure with future consequences, something that can knock you off guard at any time with its latent force, its sudden immediacy and power.

I cried too, a sudden surge of feeling, when I saw New Brighton beach at sunrise the day after lockdown ended, as I watched a seagull, spiralling upwards with a shell in its beak before dropping it onto the hard sand below, again and again until the shell cracked open to reveal the soft bits inside.

*

And what is the price of not being able to feel safely? A life of automation or disconnect, misalignment, of doing things—agreeing to or conceding things—without even really knowing why, of blindly wielding the potential to hurt others and ourselves?

That man in the park: where did he go, and with what feeling? What did he contain, or transmit? Was that pacing enough to relieve whatever pressure he felt, whatever compulsion—or did he explode somewhere else?

Must emotion be something we have to 'admit' or 'confess' to, something that must be walked out of us, back and forth across a field or a beach, a form of eradication, exhaustion as self-punishment? How do we make the world inside ourselves bigger, the pressure less?

*

I recently started dating someone new. We move slowly, we do not kiss until our fourth date when we visit Hinewai Reserve on Banks Peninsula, and he tells me about the gradual reclamation of gorse-infested farmland by native forest, a clean gentle annihilation, canopy growing over gorse, blocking out sunlight; like a bag over a flame. I wonder what would happen if a similar principle of minimal intervention was applied to a city; how would it grow? What would it snuff out?

What if I applied it too to relationships, opposing my impatience and my need to control and to run away when I cannot?

I am trying to be different. I am trying to feel slowly, less violently and extremely, and with more awareness; to wait until I am no longer flooded before I speak; to find, measure and share myself gently with words, feeling, touch. I am trying to find spaces where I can safely let down my borders, spaces this person can exist in too. I take myself regularly to the beach and to find open space and trees; I try not to let the pressure build. Vulnerability sometimes hurts, but I know it is more of a failure, and a risk, not to feel at all.

Wendy Parkins

Water Says Things So Clearly

Water says things so clearly—I thought of a line for a poem once, 'Saying it over with little words of water.'

—Robin Hyde, *A Home in this World*

There is a new urgency about saying things with water in New Zealand literature, reflecting a growing sense of our vulnerability as island-dwellers, two-thirds of whom live within five kilometres of the coast. Recent cli-fi novels have taken an apocalyptic future Aotearoa of rising oceans and depleted water resources as their setting, but I want to look back to Robin Hyde's novel *Wednesday's Children*, before going on to discuss Pip Adam's *The New Animals*, in order to consider what 'words of water' might have to say about inhabiting vulnerability in the present moment.

Eighty years separate the publication of *Wednesday's Children* (1937) from *The New Animals* (2017) but in some ways Hyde's novel foreshadowed *The New Animals* as an evocative exploration of a desire to 'find a new home' in the ocean. Both are novels that break free of the limitations of realism, where the littoral exceeds the literal, and each in its own way confronts transience and loss as unavoidable aspects of life. Hyde and Adam ask their readers to consider what it might mean to find a home in what is impermanent, and to live with an awareness of finitude.

Feminist philosopher Rosi Braidotti has argued that being mindful of our proximity to death influences not only the way we make sense of our individual lives but also our wider understanding of what makes a world worth living in. 'Making friends with the impersonal necessity of death,' Braidotti writes, 'is an ethical way of installing oneself in life as a transient, slightly wounded visitor.' In the vulnerable protagonists of *Wednesday's Children* and *The New Animals* we see examples of what Braidotti describes: the possibilities—and limits—of lives hospitable to hope, 'here and now, for as long as we can and as much as we can take.'

*

When Charles Brasch wrote of Robin Hyde, 'By choice you stood always on disputed ground/ At the utmost edge of life,' he may have glossed over the health issues and economic imperatives that determined so much of her short life. But Hyde's precarity—financial, psychological, creative—seemed to both draw her to, and find expression in, liminal spaces associated with water. Water returns again and again in Hyde's writing, and her attraction to baches and beach shacks provides one rather literal manifestation of inhabiting the edge.

In early 1937, for example, when Hyde was planning to leave the security of the Lodge at Avondale Mental Hospital, she wrote of her desire to find 'a little shack in sound of the sea', a place of shelter and solitude where she could write undisturbed at minimal cost. She eventually chose a 'stilt-legged Māori cabin' beside Whangaroa Harbour. Its permeability to the outside world was part of the cabin's appeal for Hyde, connecting her to the natural life of the harbour such as the night-time sounds of shrimps bubbling through the mangrove mud and the cries of terns. She would later describe this cabin as 'not a cell into which one can retreat, but a place from which one can advance'.

In Hyde's final and aptly named collection *Houses by the Sea* and other poems such as 'Sand', as well as in travel articles like 'The Flying-off Place' and 'Ways of the North', it is at the shoreline in particular that clarity and fragility meet. To live on the edge is to be left potentially exposed, lacking the security and permanence of a more substantial dwelling place and of everything that keeps us grounded—whether personal and familial relationships, national identity, or the continuities of time and nature. Nowhere in Hyde's writing is such edge-dwelling vulnerability more evident than in *Wednesday's Children*, where an island just off Auckland's coast, home to Wednesday Gilfillan, is the centre of the novel's world but where nothing is what it seems.

Hyde's novel opens on a rainy evening in central Auckland, the bitumen streets 'glistening wet and rough as shark-skin', the smell of salt in the air, and the proximity of the sea—'lying flat, black and restive' at the end of Queen Street—a tangible presence. It is a city of water, the occluded waterways returning like the repressed, and Wednesday, clad in a wet sealskin coat, traverses the slick city before rowing back to her island from the shore of Cockle Bay. The juxtaposition of recognisable settings in the novel—a downtown Auckland of lawcourts and newspaper offices, the impoverished backstreets of Freemans Bay and affluent villas of Remuera—emphasises the disparities and inequities of 1930s Auckland. At the same time, Wednesday's constant movement between these locations and her island continues to blur the binary between land and water—like that between fantasy and reality—which the novel establishes from the beginning. As Wednesday's brother Ronald says of her island, it 'seems to be only a matter of a few miles away, but we don't ask for particulars, and she doesn't volunteer them' (*WC*, p. 39).

While Wednesday is navigating the wet streets, Ronald and his wife are hosting a dinner for their daughter's English fiancé and his friend Hugo Bellister, where the substitution of toheroa for turtle soup is a source of shame to the hostess. When talk turns to Wednesday and her home, Ronald explains that the '[h]arbour and coast about Auckland's swarming with islands, you know' (*WC*. p. 39), an image that lends a protean air to these multiple islands, almost alive and unmoored, and exciting the imagination of Hugo, who 'could not get out of his head the picture of a little island with warm white sands and impudent blue wavelets' (*WC*, p. 42). This set-piece of the dinner party presents an affluent but insecure settler culture narrowly defined by its relationship with Britain, in stark contrast to Wednesday's island, which is rich in kai moana and native birdlife. The comparison is far from subtle but it suggests from the outset that, in a sense, all emotional investments in place are imaginary: a projection of desires or fears; a fantasy of how we might wish our lives to be; or an attempt to draw a boundary around ourselves and our community.

In *A Home in This World* Hyde idealised a place where '[o]ne wouldn't stand isolated on a little island of safety, cut off from the rest of humanity', but in *Wednesday's Children* the status of the island remains ambiguous throughout. It is described, variously, as a site of exile, a fantasy of inclusive community and a haven of plenitude. Wednesday calls her home there L'Entente Cordiale, a half-ironic name that acknowledges the range of ethnicities of the children she raises while also signalling an affiliation to a form of internationalism that Hyde herself advocated. The presence of Wednesday's housekeeper, Maritana, along with her 'Māori boy friends' (*WC*, p. 57), however, marks a problematic attempt to include indigeneity, as Michelle Elleray has persuasively argued. Like all the non-Anglo characters in the novel, Maritana is presented through ethnic caricature, underlining the limitations of Hyde's inclusivity despite her journalism in support of the campaign to preserve the Ōrākei kāinga in the mid-1930s.

The contested status of Wednesday's island is chiefly confined to its romance narrative, as Hugo's increasing fixation with the island—in contrast to '[g]reat blobs of continents, coloured a hearty pink to represent the outpoured blood of the British Empire, [which] left him cold' (*WC*, p. 101)—becomes conflated with his desire to possess Wednesday. Wednesday initially resists his advances, but it is perhaps inevitable that their romantic encounter takes place on the contact zone of the beach on 'the wrong side' of the island (*WC*, p. 262), the only place Wednesday will allow Hugo to come ashore.

Lovers in the warm sand on a moonlit night is the stuff of trite romance fiction but, in *Wednesday's Children*, it is just another unsustainable fantasy. After apparently accepting Hugo's proposal and dismissing him from the island, Wednesday looks out at the ocean which is 'like a shimmering bridge of silver' connecting the island with the mainland, thinking of all the '[p]eople coming and going' in her life (*WC*, p. 271). The following day she sends Hugo a letter revealing the truth: the island does not belong to her but is rented from the harbour board for £10 a year, and the children whose arrival she had publicly announced in the birth notices were all invented. Wednesday has no children, no housekeeper and, ultimately, no island. 'I am going for my swim now,' her letter concludes (*WC*, p. 277), and she is never seen again. Hugo returns to the island accompanied by Ronald, and finds nothing but a deserted 'wooden shack, little more than a shed' (*WC*, p. 280), barely big enough for a single occupant.

Wednesday's fate and the island's fictional community might seem to epitomise a modern tragedy of disconnection, isolation, purposelessness. As the narrator observes, there are

thousands of Wednesdays, of older women, of disillusioned and disconnected males, of frightened young girls, [who] wander unhappily about the world, wondering whether to die on a mountain-top or in the middle of the ocean would cause their relatives the lesser inconvenience. (*WC*, p. 112)

Wednesday had chosen, first, ostracism from her family for the sake of non-existent illegitimate children, then death 'in the middle of the ocean' rather than a secure existence that conformity to social expectations would have provided—a rather bleak appraisal of the options that Hyde envisaged for women like herself 'caught in the hinge of a slowly opening door, between one age and another'.

The meanings of Wednesday's island, however, are not so easily reducible to a temporary refuge for the disillusioned, or the tragic story of a Woman Alone. The first-person poem with which the novel closes, presumably in Wednesday's voice, not only insists on the island's centrality to the novel but repositions it within another story entirely. 'The Poem for the Island' speaks of 'An island shore,/ Still as a dream within a dream' (WC, p. 287), but, with Wednesday's dream exposed, it also finally acknowledges the prior claim that existed on the (is)land, its most telling absence of all:

> And the paraha flowers were the people
> Native to this place,
> Here, where all else was nomad …
> And I in a white boat rocking,
> Rocking and dreaming, in an island place. (WC, p. 287)

Caught between the apparent stability of settler culture where she never felt at home and a shack on land that she did not possess, Wednesday is forever adrift, 'rocking and dreaming' between two unbridgeable islands. All along, Wednesday had been—in Braidotti's words—'a transient, slightly wounded visitor', whose residence on the island was at the expense of others. 'The Poem for the Island' reminds the reader that our islands, like our shores, are always scenes of encounter and competing claims, where one person's home is another's loss.

*

If *Wednesday's Children* connects an Auckland on the edge of the world with the wider currents of global geopolitics and Māori dispossession in the turbulent 1930s, *The New Animals* depicts an Anthropocene Auckland as an equally volatile environment in a state of flux. In an interview, Adam described how the experience of viewing the tidal Ōrākei Basin from the train inspired her depiction of the city as a space of 'change and fluidity and evolution', at the mercy of natural forces like weather and the tides as well as the brutal ephemeralities of global capitalism and colonial usurpation.

Like Hyde's Wednesday Gilfillan, Elodie in *The New Animals* leads a life of economic and emotional precarity and, in response to forces beyond their control, both Wednesday and Elodie seek an imagined community on an island but end in apparently watery deaths. One night Elodie, tired of living from hand to mouth on the fringes of the fickle fashion scene, walks across the city to the edge of Ōrākei Basin before plunging into the water: 'She wanted to live, but live aquatically … She needed to be *in* the water, *of* the water' (*NA*, p. 180, original emphasis). For the remainder of the novel, Elodie never returns to dry land.

Eco-theorist Stacey Alaimo has talked about 'the permeability of the human' in the context of climate change in a way that echoes Elodie's oceanic journey. 'As the material self cannot be disentangled from networks that are simultaneously economic, political, cultural, scientific, and substantial,' Alaimo writes,

> what was once the ostensibly bounded human subject finds herself in a swirling landscape of uncertainty where practices and actions that were once not even remotely ethical or political matters suddenly become so.

Elodie could be seen as a version of Alaimo's unmoored human subject, all at sea. Her fluid relationships in the ocean—with, among others, a dog, an octopus, whales and sharks—make it increasingly difficult to distinguish between coexistence and conflict, self and other. Further, the presence of human corpses in the ocean—bodies on a small fishing boat and multiple floating casualties from a plane crash—may serve as harbingers of a grim human future in an environment where we can only tread water for so long but they also raise larger questions of the place of the human in Elodie's struggle for survival. Is Elodie responsible solely for her own life? Does she have any obligation to the sea creatures she encounters, to the humans she has left behind? Do such distinctions cease to carry the same weight that they had on dry land, or do they take on a new significance?

After days in the ocean—although time, like so much else, is indeterminate in the latter part of the novel—Elodie begins to dissolve, quite literally. Her skin peels and cracks, the boundary between internal and external breaking down as she ingests salt water, raw shark flesh and small pieces of plastic floating on the water's surface. Even as she fights to stay alive, she becomes increasingly corpse-like. To Elodie, this is a process not of decomposition and disintegration but of transformation into a new creature—'she was sure if her skin opened up it would be better in the end' (*NA*, p. 194)—with a changed understanding of what it means to inhabit a body:

> *She'd been living so long in her head. Listening to everything it said, like it was the truth. But it wasn't the truth now. Her body was the truth. Her body and the sea.* (*NA*, p. 217)

By this stage, however, *The New Animals* is part magic realism, part black comedy, rendering any notion of truth a slippery one. Suffering from dehydration and exhaustion and convinced 'she could breathe the sea' (*NA*, p. 187), Elodie becomes increasingly delusional and begins to fantasise about establishing a utopia in the ocean.

In a curious parallel to the imaginary island home at the heart of *Wednesday's Children*, *The New Animals* concludes with an island that can never be inhabited, the Great Pacific Garbage Patch, a soupy collection of debris almost entirely comprised of microplastics. Elodie imagines establishing a beach-head there, so to speak, becoming 'the coloniser of this new land—[the] prime minister, developer, real estate agent', while awaiting the arrival of others 'pushed out of their homes by the sea' (*NA*, p. 212). The irony of the novel's closing—where the plastics that have contributed to the destruction of the planet form the basis of a new life, a new society even, in the ocean—shows the thin line between utopian desires for new forms of community and delusions of mastery, acquisition and dominion. Like Wednesday in her flawed, if imaginary, L'Entente Cordiale, Elodie cannot leave behind the terrestrial values of capitalism and colonisation no matter how far from land she drifts.

The ghost of Robinson Crusoe, another delusional island dweller, may haunt both novels, as perhaps do Prospero and the countless female suicides by water in the Western literary tradition, from Ophelia to Virginia Woolf. But the presumed deaths of Elodie and Wednesday are not simply another iteration of a cultural trope of feminine insanity and self-destruction. Even as they end with death, both *Wednesday's Children* and *The New Animals* assume the interconnection of life and life-forms across apparently intractable boundaries: land and water, human and animal, existence and mortality, past and future. In their exploration of change and transience, marked in powerful ways by movement across and within water, these novels distinguish between finitude and what we used to call a death wish, understood as a desire for stasis, a repudiation of change and the passage of time. As Christine Downing has argued, the paradox at the heart of the death wish 'shows itself in our longing to be immortal … in *our longing not to die*', as well as in our fears of vulnerability and our resistance to change, to movement, to life.

*

In an essay called 'Sea Stories', Robin Hyde offered a scathing critique of Joseph Conrad's tales of men's attempts to master the ocean. 'Why doesn't somebody really write a story about the sea?' she asked, continuing:

> *it is foolish to treat the sea as an enemy … If one looks at the sea long enough, it is quite impossible to dislike or fear it, because these and all other emotions are simply swallowed up in the green depths. The sea is the beginning and the end—that is all. If every ship was to be swept away from it, and every island as silent as it was before light, it would still be the biggest story in the world.*

While life on these islands has always depended on the sea in myriad ways—from kai moana to migration, trade and empire—there has never been a time in planetary history when it would be more true to say the sea is *the biggest story in the world*. As the former commissioner for the environment, Dr Jan Wright, has said: 'It is certain the sea is rising and will continue to do so for centuries to come.' And yet even in the literature of climate change we can find a perpetuation of the language of aggression and hostility that Hyde critiqued in Conrad's masculine maritime. Neville Peat's *The Invading Sea*, for instance, frames its analysis of coastal hazards and climate change in martial terms: 'frontlines' and 'battlegrounds', a coastline 'under attack'. But who, or what, is the enemy? And what would victory look like?

In *Eating the Ocean*, Elspeth Probyn outlines what she calls 'a paradoxical human desire to both make meaning of and be caught in the mystery of the oceans', seeing 'the possibility of the oceanic and the oceanic as possibility' as a source of 'inspiration for new forms of being', but only if we can let go of the fantasy of mastery. Both *Wednesday's Children* and *The New Animals* explore this oceanic realm of mystery, possibility and inspiration and, in the process, expose the futility of fantasies of domination and control that would justify survival at any cost. If we can only think of water in terms of defeat or triumph, financial gain or loss, we will always refuse to contemplate what it might mean to make our home in vulnerability, to make our peace with the precious but precarious world that is the only home we will ever know.

The quotation from Robin Hyde with which this essay began, about '[s]aying it over with little words of water'—a line she never did put to use in a poem— also reminds us of the vast disparities of scale that water evokes. Hyde's 'little' words of water connote a harmless, soothing quality, a world away from the sea as a site of conflict where the maritime is relentlessly monetised and militarised. But I do not want to close by resorting to a stagnant gender binary of water— mighty oceans versus babbling brooks, for instance—any more than I want to romanticise disaster or reaffirm a Romantic myth of extinction, 'to cease upon the midnight with no pain'.

Change, as psychoanalyst Adam Phillips has said, 'is always there waiting to be moralised (as loss, progress, purpose, waste); it is the fact about which, out of which, we weave our fictions'. The challenge we face now is how to write about transience and destruction—or, in other words, time and bodily life—'without the refuge of optimism, the confidence of nihilism, or the omniscience of the tragic view'. It is the challenge of acknowledging that '[t]here was no island … There was nowhere to stand. It was a mess. This was her new home' (*NA*, pp. 219–20).

REFERENCES

Water says things so clearly … Robin Hyde, *A Home in This World* (Auckland: Longman Paul, 1984), p. 4.

two-thirds of us live … Neville Peat, *The Invading Sea: Coastal hazards and climate change in Aotearoa New Zealand* (Wellington: Cuba Press, 2018), p. 15.

Recent cli-fi novels … See, for example, Tim Jones, *Where We Land* (Wellington: Cuba Press, 2019); Jeff Murray, *Melt* (Mary Egan Publishing, 2019); and Chris Else, *Waterline* (Quentin Wilson Publishing, 2019).

find a new home … Pip Adam, *The New Animals* (Wellington: Victoria University Press, 2017), p. 180. All subsequent references are to this edition.

Making friends with the impersonal necessity … Rosi Braidotti, *The Posthuman* (Cambridge: Polity Press, 2013), p. 132.

here and now, for as long as we can … Ibid.

By choice you stood always … Charles Brasch, 'In Memory of Robin Hyde 1906–1939', *Collected Poems*, ed. Alan Roddick (Auckland: Oxford University Press, 1984), p. 35.

a little shack in sound of the sea … Derek Challis & Gloria Rawlinson, *The Book of Iris: A life of Robin Hyde* (Auckland: Auckland University Press, 2002), p. 395.

the night-time sounds of shrimps … Hyde, 'Ways of the North', *New Zealand Railways Magazine*, 1 Sept. 1937, pp. 19–20.

not a cell into which one can retreat … Hyde, *A Home in This World*, p. 10.

glistening wet and rough as shark-skin … Hyde, *Wednesday's Children* (Auckland: New Women's Press, 1989), pp. 14, 15. All subsequent references are to this edition.

One wouldn't stand isolated … Hyde, *A Home in This World*, p. 4.

a problematic attempt to include indigeneity … Michelle Elleray, 'Turning the Tables: Domesticity and nationalism in *Wednesday's Children*', in *Lighted Windows: Critical essays on Robin Hyde*, ed. Mary Edmond-Paul (Dunedin: University of Otago Press, 2008), p. 37.

her journalism in support of the campaign … Hyde, 'Naboth's Vineyard at Orakei', *Observer*, 17 Oct. 1935.

caught in the hinge … Hyde, *A Home in This World*, p. 28.

change and fluidity and evolution … Wellington Author Interview: Pip Adam: www.wcl.govt.nz/blog/index.php/2017/11/03/wellington-author-interview-pip-adam/

As the material self cannot be disentangled … Stacey Alaimo, *Exposed: Environmental politics and pleasures in posthuman times* (Minneapolis: University of Minnesota Press, 2016), p. 112.

shows itself in our longing … Christine Downing, 'Sigmund Freud's Mythology of Soul: The body as dwelling place of soul', *Depth Pyschology: Meditations in the field,* eds. Dennis Patrick Slattery & Lionel Corbett (Einsiedeln: Daimon Verlag, 2004), p. 71 (emphasis added).

Why doesn't somebody really write … Hyde, 'Sea Stories', *The Sun*, 9 Dec. 1927, rep. in *Disputed Ground: Robin Hyde, journalist*, eds. Gillian Boddy & Jacqueline Matthews (Wellington: Victoria University Press, 1991), p. 214.

It is certain the sea is rising …cited in Peat, *The Invading Sea*, p. 19.

frames its analysis of coastal hazards … Ibid., p. 44.

a paradoxical human desire … Elspeth Probyn, *Eating the Ocean* (Durham: Duke University Press, 2016), p. 38.

is always there waiting … Adam Phillips, *Darwin's Worms* (London: Faber & Faber, 1999), p. 130.

without the refuge of optimism … Ibid., p. 127.

About the Selecting Editor

Emma Neale has published six novels and six poetry collections, and edited several anthologies. She is a former Robert Burns fellow (2012) and has received numerous awards and grants for her writing including the Janet Frame/NZSA Memorial Prize for Literature (2008) and the University of Otago/Sir James Wallace Pah Residency (2014). She was the Philip and Diane Beatson/NZSA Writing Fellow in 2015. Emma received the 2011 Kathleen Grattan Award for her poetry collection *The Truth Garden*, and was a finalist for the Acorn Foundation Fiction Prize at the Ockham New Zealand Book Awards 2017 for her novel *Billy Bird*, which was also longlisted in the International Dublin Literary Awards 2018. She holds a PhD in New Zealand Literature from University College London (UK). *To the Occupant*, her latest collection of poems, was published in 2019, and in 2020 Emma received the Lauris Edmond Memorial Award for Distinguished Contribution to New Zealand Poetry. From 2018–21 Emma was the editor of *Landfall* journal.

Contributor Biographies

Sarah Jane Barnett is a writer and editor. Her poetry, essays, interviews and reviews have been published widely in Aotearoa. Her debut poetry collection *A Man Runs into a Woman* (Hue+Cry, 2012) was a finalist in the 2013 New Zealand Post Book Awards. Her essays explore the multifaceted theme of modern womanhood.

Anna Kate Blair is a writer from Whangārei. Her essays and short stories have appeared in publications including *Landfall, The Lifted Brow, Meanjin, Litro, Archer* and *Reckoning*. She has won prizes including the Warren Trust Award for Architectural Writing, the Wyndham Short Story Prize and the AAWP Creative Nonfiction Prize. She holds a PhD in History of Art and Architecture from the University of Cambridge.

Tobias Buck studied creative writing under Gregory O'Brien at Victoria University of Wellington. He completed a Master's in Literature at the University of Edinburgh. He has worked in digital publishing in London and, alongside owner Tilly Lloyd, project-managed the redesign of Unity Books Wellington. In 2014 Tobias won the Katherine Mansfield Prize for 'Islands in the Stream', and in 2020 was highly commended for his short story 'Hecuba' in the Sargeson Prize short story competition. 'Exit. Stage Left' was published in *Landfall 238*.

Shelley Burne-Field lives in Hawke's Bay. She has always worked in 'helping jobs' such as social services, local government, prisons, healthcare, community and youth development. Her stories find a home at events like union rallies, addiction centres, schools—anywhere where hard but hopeful tales may touch someone's life for good. In 2020 Shelley wrote her first novel—a bilingual middle-grade adventure—as part of the Master's of Creative Writing at the University of Auckland. Her essay appeared as 'The Grind of Racism' at *E-Tangata* (18 October 2020).

Una Cruickshank is an essayist from Pōneke Wellington and a recent graduate of the IIML Creative Writing Programme. She works at an audio-visual archive and is writing a book of historical essays about the intersection of luxury and filth.

Elese Dowden is a Pākehā writer and philosopher from Tāmaki Makaurau. She currently lives in Naarm/ Melbourne, where she's writing a manuscript and companion novella on settler colonialism, poetics and mythology. Elese is also the founder of the Australasian Post-Humanities.

Emily Duncan is a Dunedin-based writer, dramaturg and director, and held the 2019 University of Otago Robert Burns Fellowship. She is the co-founder of Prospect Park Productions, home of Ōtepoti Theatre Lab and Ōtepoti Writers Lab. Emily holds a PhD in Theatre from Otago and trained at the Strasberg Institute in New York City. Her plays have been published in the anthologies *Here/Now* (Playmarket, 2015) and *101 New Zealand Monologues for Youth* (Playmarket, 2019).

Joan Fleming is the author of two collections of poetry, *The Same as Yes* and *Failed Love Poems* (Victoria University Press, 2011 and 2015), and the pamphlets *Two Dreams in Which Things Are Taken* (Duets, 2010) and *Some People's Favourites* (Desperate Literature). Recent nonfiction has been published in *Meanjin*, *Westerley* and *The Pantograph Punch*. She is the winner of the Harri Jones Memorial Prize from the Hunter Writers Centre and the Biggs Poetry Prize, among other honours. She holds a PhD in Ethnopoetics from Monash University, and her dystopian verse novel is forthcoming from Cordite Books. 'Write First, Apologise Later' first appeared in the *Pantographic Punch* on 15 January 2020.

Tim Grgec was the 2018 recipient of the Biggs Family Prize for poetry. Having failed to achieve his childhood dream of playing for the Black Caps, he now has delusions of becoming a great writer. His first book of poetry, *All Tito's Children*, is forthcoming from Victoria University Press.

Sarah Harpur Ruigrok has been writing and performing comedy for over ten years. She has toured locally and internationally and won loads of awards along the way. But Sarah has always yearned for a career that can be pursued in pyjamas, so in 2017 she completed her Master's in Scriptwriting at Victoria University. She currently writes for animated children's television and lives on the Kāpiti Coast with her husband, her son and an annoying dog. 'Dead Dads Club' appeared in *Landfall 239*.

Siobhan Harvey is a displaced author of six books, including the poetry collections *Ghosts* (Otago University Press, 2021), and *Cloudboy* (Otago University Press, 2014), which was winner of the 2013 Kathleen Grattan Poetry Award. Her creative nonfiction has recently been published in *Asia Literary Review*, *Griffith Review* and the anthology *Feminine Divine: Voices of power and invisibility* (Cyren, 2019). She was awarded the 2020 NZSA Peter & Dianne Beatson Fellowship, the 2019 Kathleen Grattan Prize for a Sequence of Poems, and the 2019 Robert Burns

Poetry Competition. This essay also appears in *Ghosts*.

Ingrid Horrocks is Associate Professor in Creative Writing at Massey University, Wellington. Her publications include a travel book, a scholarly work on the history of women wanderers with Cambridge University Press, and two collections of poetry. She co-edited *Extraordinary Anywhere: Essays on place from Aotearoa New Zealand* (Victoria University Press, 2016). This essay is a reworked version of the original submitted for the Landfall Essay Competition. It appears in a longer form in Ingrid's new nonfiction book, *Where We Swim* (Victoria University Press, 2021).

John Horrocks was born in Auckland and now lives at Days Bay. In the late 1970s and early 1980s he worked as a researcher and campaigner for Friends of the Earth, and he continues to write on subjects related to environmental health, as well as reviews, essays, poetry and articles on New Zealand writers. He has a PhD in English from Victoria University. His most recent work is *Dark Empire* (Steele Roberts, 2020), a crime novel set in Wellington.

Anna Knox is a graduate of the UEA Creative Writing Programme. She writes essays and reviews and is working on a novel. She has lived in the US, Finland, the UK and Saudi Arabia, and now resides in Wellington with her partner and children.

Himali McInnes works in a busy Auckland medical practice and a prison. She writes essays, short stories, flash fiction and articles. She has been published locally and overseas, and has won or been shortlisted in a number of competitions. She is currently writing a book of non-fiction medical stories, due for publication in 2021 by Harper Collins. She is also a NZSA mentorship recipient for 2020, and is crafting a book of short stories with her mentor's wise help. Himali is obsessed with books and dogs.

A.M. McKinnon was educated in Christchurch and overseas and lives in Wellington. He has studied writing under Diane Comer and Anna Jaquiery through courses at Victoria University. 'Canterbury Gothic' was published in *Landfall 240*. His family memoir *Come Back to Mona Vale* is forthcoming from Otago University Press.

Mikaela Nyman is a writer and editor of poetry, fiction and non-fiction. Her first novel, *Sado* (Victoria University Press), was published in 2020. Her first poetry collection, *När vändkrets läggs mot vändkrets* (in Swedish, 2019), was nominated for the Nordic Council Literature Prize 2020. Most recently she has been project coordinator and co-editor of *Sista Stanap Strong!: A*

Vanuatu women's anthology (Victoria University Press, 2021).

Wendy Parkins is the author of *Every morning, so far, I'm alive: A memoir* (Otago University Press, 2019). She has taught at universities in New Zealand, Australia and the UK and has published widely in the field of Victorian literature. She lives near Tomarata, north of Auckland, and is completing her first novel.

Nina Mingya Powles is a poet and zinemaker from Wellington. Her debut poetry collection, *Magnolia 木蘭*, was shortlisted for the Forward Prize for Best First Collection in 2020. She is the founding editor of Bitter Melon, a small press that publishes limited-edition poetry books by Asian writers. 'Tender Gardens' first appeared in *Landfall 238*; this revised version is an excerpt from Nina's essay collection *Small Bodies of Water* (Canongate Books, 2021).

Derek Schulz was recipient of the Caselberg International Poetry Prize in 2018 and runner-up in 2019. He is currently assembling a 'New and Selected' introduction to his poetry, and is revising a book-length work of fiction.

Jillian Sullivan lives in the Ida Valley, Central Otago. Her thirteen books include creative non-fiction, novels, short stories and poetry. Once the drummer in a women's indie pop band, she is now a grandmother, earth plasterer and environmentalist. Her awards include the Juncture Memoir Award in America, and the Kathleen Grattan Prize for a Sequence of Poems. Her latest book is a collection of essays, *Map for the Heart: Ida Valley essays* (Otago University Press, 2020), which includes this essay.

Laura Surynt was born and raised in Tāmaki Makaurau and is author of the pamphlet *Speech Therapy*, published by Takeaway Press (2020). Her work also appears in *Ache Magazine*, *Sweet Mammalian* and *Oscen*. She teaches and writes in London.

Tan Tuck Ming is an essayist, poet and an MFA candidate at the University of Iowa. Born in Singapore and raised in Wellington, his current work examines the shifting structure of the family, especially in the context of welfare and immigration. His work is published or forthcoming in *The Pantograph Punch*, *Glass: A journal of poetry* and *A Clear Dawn*, an upcoming anthology of Asian writers in New Zealand. 'My Grandmother Glitches the Machine' was first published in *The Rumpus*.

Matt Vance is a New Zealand-based writer, lecturer and sailor who specialises in quirky tales from the South Pacific, Southern Ocean and Antarctica. His stories and photographs have appeared in the *NZ Listener*, *Smith Journal* and *Wilderness Magazine*. Matt has an immodest enthusiasm for his family, an old yacht named *Whitney Rose* and a motley collection of eccentric friends.

Sarah Young completed a Master's in Creative Writing in 2013–14 at the University of East Anglia, where she was recipient of the UEA Booker Prize Foundation Scholarship. She has been shortlisted for the Sozopol Fiction Seminar Fellowship in Bulgaria, and longlisted for the Bath Short Story Award and the BBC National Short Story Award. She has worked as a journalist in Dubai, Indonesia and New Zealand, and has recently returned to New Zealand.